Builders of Indian Anthropology

Books by the same author

- Anthropological Research Methodology: Theory and Practice
- Anthropology of Complex Society
- Bio-Cultural Evolution
- Communicational Anthropology
- Developmental Anthropology
- Indian Anthropology
- Indian Tribal Culture
- History of Anthropological Thought
- Indian Prehistoric Archaeological Anthropology
- Medical Anthropology: A Text Book
- Neo Anthropological Theory
- Social-Cultural Anthropology
- चिकित्सात्मक मानवशास्त्र (Medical Anthropology)
- संप्रेषणात्मक मानवशास्त्र (Communicational Anthropology)
- जटिल समाज का मानवशास्त्र (Anthropology of Complex Society)
- भारतीय मानवशास्त्र (Indian Anthropology)
- भारतीय प्रागैतिहासिक पुरातात्विक मानवशास्त्र
- मानवशास्त्रीय अनुसंधान: विधि एवं तकनीक
- मानवशास्त्रीय सिद्धांत: शास्त्रीय एवं आधुनिक (Anthropological Theory Classical and Modern)
- भारतीय जनजातीय संस्कृति (Indian Tribal Culture)
- जैविक सांस्कृतिक उद्विकास (Bio-Cultural Evolution)

About the Author

Gaya Pandey (b. 1954) is a retired Professor of Anthropology, Ranchi University, Ranchi. During his whole academic career, he has to his credit 30 books and 40 articles. Books are on different papers which are taught in different universities of India in undergraduate and postgraduate departments of Anthropology. The books are in both Hindi and English medium. Articles have been published in different journals of repute. He actively participated in more than two dozen national and international seminars held in India. Nine Ph.D. scholars have been awarded Ph.D. degree under his supervision by the University of Ranchi.

Builders of Indian Anthropology

Gaya Pandey

CONCEPT PUBLISHING COMPANY Pvt. Ltd.
NEW DELHI-110059

ISBN: 978-93-5594-537-2 (HB)
ISBN: 978-93-5594-538-9 (PB)

First Published 2022

Published and Printed by

Since 1974

Concept Publishing Company Pvt. Ltd.
A/15-16, Commercial Block, Mohan Garden
New Delhi-110059 (India)
T : +91-11-41101460
E: publishing@conceptpub.com, W: www.conceptpub.com

Cataloging in Publication Data–Courtesy: D.K. Agencies (P) Ltd. <docinfo@dkagencies.com>

Pandey, Gaya, 1954- author
Builders of Indian Anthropology / Gaya Pandey
pages cm
Includes bibliographical references and index.
ISBN 9789355945372 (HB)
ISBN 9789355945389 (PB)

1. Anthropology--India--History. 2. Anthropologists--India. 3. Anthropologists. I. Title.

LCC GN17.3.I4P36 2022 | DDC 301.0954 23

I dedicate this book to young generation of anthropologists of the country upon whose shoulders the responsibility is to carry forward the rich heritage of Indian Anthropology established by our forefathers who are now no more but their works are still with us for guide in future.

Preface

The book "Builders of Indian Anthropology" is an attempt to present the profiles and contributions of those Indian and foreign anthropologists who laid the foundation of Indian anthropology in our country by their researches, teachings and studies. They made Indian anthropology to travel from formulatory to critical or analytical phase through constructive phase. And now we have full-fledged Departments of Anthropology in almost all states of our country where Indian anthropology is taught as a paper along with other papers of the subject Anthropology.

This book could achieve its success with the help of a number of persons, scholars and research scholars at different levels of writing. Hence, this is my pious and moral duty to express thanks and gratefulness in their name individually and collectively.

First of all, I extend my sincere gratitude to all my gurus and colleagues whose articles, papers, books and suggestions have proved to be beneficial for me in completion of this book.

I am thankful to all teachers, research scholars and staff of the Department of Anthropology, Ranchi University, Ranchi, who encouraged me time to time to complete this book.

I am thankful to my family members—wife Shrimati Indu Devi, Daughters—Sudha, Suman, Sarita, Anu, son Shekhar, grandson Kushagra and Harshita for their full cooperation in completion of this book in post-retirement period.

I am thankful to Shri Ashok Kumar Mittal Ji and his team Concept Publishing Company Pvt. Ltd., New Delhi for printing my hand written manuscript with meticulous care.

Gayaneshwari
Ranchi

Gaya Pandey

Contents

Preface vii

I. Indian Builders of Indian Anthropology 1

1. L.K. Ananta Krishna Iyer (1861-1937) **1**
Books, *3*
Papers, *4*

2. L.A. Krishna Iyer **4**
Contribution of L.A. Krishna Iyer, *5*
Contribution of L.K. Balaratna, *6*

3. S.C. Roy (1871-1942) **6**
Books, *10*
Papers, *11*
Major Contributions in Anthropology, *13*
Contribution on Tribal Studies, *14*
Contribution on the Study of Physical Anthropology, *17*
Contribution on the Study of Prehistoric Archaeology, *18*
Contribution on Anthropology of Castes, *21*
Contribution on the Study of Folklore, *22*
Contribution on Applied Anthropology and Tribal Policy, *24*

4. B.S. Guha (1894-1961) **26**
Publications, *30*

5. K.P. Chattopadhyay (1897-1963) **31**
Publications, *34*
Books, *38*

6. N.K. Bose (1901-1972) **39**
Publications, *41*
Books in Bengali Language, *41*
Impact of Franz Boas, *42*
Influence of A.L. Kroeker, *42*
Impact of Diffusionism, *42*
Influence of Sigmond Freud, *43*
Influence of Karl Marx, *43*

Influence of Malinowski, *43*
Bose as a Social Worker, *44*
Impact of Silpis (Architect) of Orissa, *45*
Role as Director in Anthropological Survey of India, *46*
Contribution on Caste Study, *46*
Study of Culture Zones and Pattern of Unity, *48*
Contribution on Civilisation at a Phase of Confidence, *49*
Contribution on Problem of National Integration and Modernisation, *50*
Contribution on Gandhism, *50*
Contribution on Prehistoric Archaeology, *51*
Contribution on Research Methodology, *51*

7. D.N. Majumdar (1903-1960).. 52
Contribution through Research Papers, *54*
Books, *65*
Contribution in Cultural Anthropology, *65*
Contribution on Village Study, *67*
Contribution in Applied and Action Anthropology, *69*
Contribution on City Study, *69*
Contribution on Physical Anthropology, *71*

8. Iravati Karve (1905-1970).. 72
Publications of Research Papers, *73*
Books, *78*

9. A. Aiyappan (1905-1988).. 78
Books, *79*
Papers, *80*

10. M.N. Srinivas (1916-1999) 81
Publication of Papers, *83*
Publication of Books, *85*
Concept of Sanskritisation, *86*
Brahminical Model of Sanskritisation, *87*
Kshatriya Model of Sanskritisation, *88*
Vaishya Model of Sanskritisation, *89*
Desanskritisation, *89*
Westernisation, *90*
Westernisation, Urbanisation and Industrialisation, *92*
Westernisation and Modernisation, *93*
Secularisation, *94*
Concept of Dominant Caste, *95*

Concept of Spread, *97*
Concept of Vertical and Horizontal Caste Solidarity, *98*
Contribution on Village Study, *99*

11. S.C. Dube (1922-1996) **100**
Publication of Books, *101*
Contributions to Books and Journals, *102*
Contribution on Tribal Study, *103*
Contribution on Village Study, *104*
Contribution on Family Planning, *106*
Contribution in Political Anthropology, *106*
Contribution on Modernisation, *107*

12. Sachchidananda (1925-2015) **108**
Publications, *109*
Contribution on Tribal Studies, *110*
Contribution on Village Study, *111*
Contribution on Agricultural Anthropology, *111*
Contribution on Political Anthropology, *112*
Contribution on Scheduled Castes Study, *112*
Contribution on Women Study, *113*
Contribution on Industrialisation and Social Disorganisation, *113*

14. Lalita Prasad Vidyarthi (1931-1985) **113**
Publication of Books, *116*
Edited Books, *117*
Contribution on Sacred Complex Study, *118*
Contribution on Nature-Man-Spirit Complex, *122*
Contribution on Tribal Studies, *127*
Contribution on the Phases of Growth of Indian Anthropology, *128*
Contribution on Urban and Anthropological Researches, *132*
Contribution on Political Anthropology, *135*
Contribution on Psychological Anthropology, *135*
Contribution of Folklore, *136*
Contribution on Scheduled Caste Study, *137*
Contribution on Applied and Action Anthropology, *137*
Contribution on Restudy, *138*

15. R.K. Mukherjee (1919-) **139**
Publications, *139*

16. G.S. Ghurye (1893-1983) **143**
Publications, *143*
Contribution on Scheduled Tribes, *144*

Contribution on Village Study, *145*
Contribution on Caste Study, *146*

17. Surjit Chandra Sinha (1926-) **147**
Publications, *148*

18. B.K. Roy Burman (1922-2012) **148**
Publications, *148*
Contribution on Geographical Distribution of Tribes, *149*
Contribution on Cultural Classification of Tribes, *149*
Concept of Bridge and Buffer, *150*

19. R.D. Singh **150**

20. R.S. Khare **151**

21. Gauranga Chattopadhyay **152**

22. K.S. Mathur **153**

23. B.R. Chauhan **154**

24. Yogesh Atal **155**

25. Y.V. Lakshmana Rao **156**

26. H.S. Dhillon **157**

27. K. Ishwaran **158**

28. K.N. Dikshit **159**

29. H.D. Sankalia **160**

30. Narmadeshwar Prasad **160**
Contributions, *160*

31. Kumar Suresh Singh (1935-2006) **162**
Academic Contribution, *163*
People of India: A Unique Research Project, *167*
Other Academic Contributions, *168*
Books authored, *172*
People of India Series: Authored/Co-Authored, *172*
Edited Series People of India, *173*
Articles in Edited Books, *175*
Articles in Journals, *180*
Book Reviewed in Journals, *184*
Books Edited, *187*
Awards & Distinction, *188*

Conclusion, *188*
References, *189*

32. Rann Singh Mann (1936-2013).. 189

II. Foreign Builders of Indian Anthropology..............192

33. Sir William Jones.. 192

34. Jones Princep 193

35. Alexander Cunningham.. 193

36. Sir John Marshal... 194

37. Sir Martimer Wheeler.. 196

38. H.H. Risley 197

39. J.H. Hutton.. 198
Publications, *200*

40. Verrier Elwin (1902-)... 200
Publications, *202*

41. C. Von Furer Haimendorf (1909-1995)......................... 203
Publications, *203*

42. A.C. Mayer.. 204

43. Oscar Lewis... 206
Contribution on Culture of Poverty, *208*
Concept of Rural Cosmopolitanism, *209*

44. McKim Marriott.. 209
Concept of Universalisation and Parochialisation, *210*
Contribution on Caste Ranking, *211*

45. David C. Mandelbaum.. 212
Publications, *212*

46. Morris E. Opler 213
Reserach Journals, *214*

47. Herald A. Gould.. 220
Publications, *220*

48. Milton Singer 222
Publications, *223*

Contribution on Cultural Role of City, *223*
Contribution on the Study of Madras City, *224*
Contribution on Traditional India : Structure and Changes, *224*
Contribution on Modernisation of Great Tradition, *225*

49. A.R. Beals 225

50. W. McCormack 227
Publications, *228*

51. E.B. Harper 228

52. T. Scarlett Epstein 229
Publications, *229*

53. Geital P. Steed 231

54. E. Kathleen Gough 231
Publications, *232*

55. F.G. Bailey 233
Publications, *234*

56. W.H. Wiser 236
Publications, *237*

57. G.M. Carstairs 239

58. Henry Orenstein 241
Research Papers, *242*

59. Louis Dumont 242

60. Paul G. Herbert 244

61. DeTerra and T.D. Patterson 245

62. Joan Mencher 245

63. Dagfinn Silvert Sen 246

64. Andre Beteille 247
Publications, *247*

65. Brenda F. Beck 249

66. Celestin Bougle 250

67. Thomas O. Beidelmen 251

Bibliography 253

Index 270

I

Indian Builders of Indian Anthropology

L.K. ANANTA KRISHNA IYER (1861-1937)

Dewan Bahadur L.K. Ananta Krishna Iyer was born in 1861 in a village named Laksminarayanapuram in the Palghat district of Kerala state. It was formerly a part of Madras state. He passed his matriculation examination from Palghat High School in 1878. Then he proceeded to Calicut for his undergraduate studies at Kerala Vidyasala. He passed his B.A. examination in 1883 from Christian College in Madras.

He was able to obtain an employment as a clerk in the Land Settlement Office, Wayanad when he was of 23 years of age under Castle Stuari. But he decided to enter into teaching profession. He joined the Victoria College at Palghat. He experienced his life as a teacher very stimulating and for the sake of confirmation he went to Madras for his L.T. degree. He received his L.T. degree but became depressed due to sudden death of his wife. He was so shocked that he decided to accept the post of Headmaster of a school run by a local Christian Mission at Changanachery. He felt this job very tiresome. So he resigned from this post and joined Maharaja College, Ernakulam as Science Assistant. In Maharaja College, Ernakulam, the foundation of his subsequent career was laid. He was examiner of Madras University to examine answer books of matriculation candidates.

Ananta Krishna Iyer was specially interested in the study of the development of human society. He was able to gather considerable amount of experience since he had entered the service. As he was in close contact with numerous people, he was able to develop the close and critical observation of the people and their manners. This kind of deep observation generated in him his interest towards anthropological studies.

In 1902, Ananta Krishna Iyer was successful in getting the order of the Government for a systematic ethnographic survey of the state. This marked the beginning of an epoch in his life. This new assignment was in addition to his teaching work at Ernakulam College. The results of investigations were published in the form of monograph from time to time for each tribe and caste.

In the year 1908, the first volume on "Kochin Tribes and Castes" was published. The publication of this volume earned great appreciation from the eminent foreign anthropologists. The second volume on "Tribes and Castes" was published in between 1909-12.

Ananta Krishna Iyer was elected as president of the section of Ethnology, now known as section of Anthropology and Archaeology when Indian Science Congress first met at Calcutta in 1914.

He was appointed as the Deputy Inspector of Schools by Albion Banerjee, the then Diwan of Kochin. In 1914, he was appointed as curator in state museum and superintendent of Zoological Gardens of Trichur.

Ananta Krishna Iyer was offered the post of a lecturer in Anthropology in Calcutta University in May 1920. He was also in charge of the Department of Anthropology, Calcutta University from 1920 to 1933 after which he retired from the service of the university.

On the invitation of the University of Madras in February 1916, Ananta Krishna Iyer had delivered a series of lectures on Ethnology in India. These lectures were first of their kind for Indian universities. The subject was covered under 9 lectures which were delivered between February 14 to 19 and February 21 to 23.

Within the few months of his joining in Calcutta University, his work in Cochin was recognised by the Indian Government and he was awarded by the title of Rao Bahadur in the King's Birthday Honour. He was the first to receive this title in Kochin. His final work for Cochin state, the "Anthropology of the Syrian Christians" was published in 1924. In the following year Special Readership lectures delivered by him were published in the book form under the title, "Lectures on Ethnography" by Calcutta University.

After his retirement from University of Calcutta in 1933, a programme of lectures was arranged for him by some of his friends in England and Europe. Accepting the invitation of friends of England and Europe, he left Bombay on April 23, 1934. At Florescence, he delivered lecture on Primitive Culture in Southern India at the Institute of Anthropology on 16th May, 1934. The Vice-President of the institute conferred on him honorary membership of the Institute and the Rector of the University honoured him with the award of Special University Medal. He also delivered several lectures on the Ethnography of India in Paris, Vienna, Berlin, Cambridge and attended International Congress of Anthropological and Ethnological Sciences in London in 1934. In the International Congress he presented paper, "Agricultural Basis of Religion in South India". He breathed his last on 25th February, 1937 in Madras. His contribution in the form of some books and papers are as follows:

Books

1909 : *The Cochin Tribes and Castes*. Vol. 1, Madras : Published for the Government of Cochin by Higginbotham & Company, London, Luzac and Co.

1912 : *The Cochin Tribes and Castes.* Vol. 2, London : Higginbotham and Co.

1925 : *Lectures on Ethnography.* Calcutta : Calcutta University.

1926 : *The Anthropology of Syrian Christian.* Ernakulam : Cochin Government Press.

1928 : *The Mysore Tribes and Castes.* Vol. 2, Mysore : Mysore University Press.

1930: *The Mysore Tribes and Castes.* Vol. 3, Mysore : Mysore University Press.

1931: *Mysore Tribes and Castes.* Vol. 4, Mysore : Mysore University Press.

1935 : *Mysore Tribes and Castes,* Vol. 1, Mysore : Mysore University Press.

Papers

1910 : "Peringala Vettuvans". *Quarterly Journal of Mystic Society,* Vol. 1, pp. 146-51.

1914 : "A Comparative Study of the Marriage Customs of Cochin Castes". *Journal of Asiatic Society of Bengal,* Vol. 10, pp. 295-315.

1915 : "Prehistoric Monuments of Cochin State". Paper presented at Ethnography Section, Indian Science Congress, 2nd Session, Madras.

1922 : "The Mala Aryans or Kannikars of Travencore Forest". *Man In India*, Vol. 2, pp. 55-61.

1927 : "Devdasis in South India : Their Traditional Origin and Development". *Man In India,* Vol. 7, pp. 47-52.

1929 : "South Indian Christian". *Man In India,* Vol. 9, pp. 7-46.

1929 : "Kadu Kurubas". *Man In India,* Vol. 9, pp. 223-229.

1929 : "The Kahars of Mysore". *Man In India*, Vol. 9, pp 171-72.

1930 : "The Musalmans of Mysore". *Madras Christian College Magazine,* pp. 94-103.

1932 : "Nayar Polyandry", *Man,* Vol. 32, No. 320.

L.A. KRISHNA IYER

L.A. Krishna Iyer was illustrious son of Ananta Krishna Iyer. He was formerly Head of the Department of Anthropology, Madras University. He was assigned ethnographic survey of primitive tribes and low castes of Travencore in 1933. He firstly concentrated his study on the hill tribes. The hill tribes were dying out fastly or they were assimilating themselves into castes of the plains. He published his first volume in 1937. In this volume, he brought to light an ethnographic account of seven hill tribes like Kannikar, Malakuraban, Malapantharam, Malapalaya, Malavetan, Malarayan, and Mansan. The second volume was published in 1939 and the third volume was published in 1941. These volumes were related to tribes and castes of Travancore and also dealt with serelogical studies and anthropometric studies of those communities.

L.K. Balaratnam, the son of L.A. Krishna Iyer maintained the tradition of his father L.A. Krishna and grandfather L.K. Ananta Krishna Iyer by undertaking anthropological researches and publishing and editing a couple of books. He was a trained anthropologist from Madras University, Department of Anthropology.

Contribution of L.A. Krishna Iyer

1924 : "Marriage Customs Among the Muthuvans of Travancore". *Man in India,* Vol. 4.

1934 : "The Religion of Primitive Tribes of Travancore". *Quarterly Journal of Mystic Society,* Bangalore.

1937 : *The Travancore Tribes and Castes.* Vol. 1. Trivandrum : Government Press.

1939 : *The Travancore Tribes and Castes.* Vol. 2. Trivandrum : Government Press.

1941 : *The Travancore Tribes and Castes.* Vol. 3. Trivandrum : Government Press.

1944 : "Matriarchy in Kerala". *Man In India.* Vol. 24, No. 1.

1948 : *The Coorgs Tribes and Castes.* (with L.K. Balaratnam). Trivandrum : Government Press.

1961 : *Kerala and Her People.* Palghat : Educational Supplied Depot.

1961 : "Taboos Among Primitive Tribes of Travancore". *Quarterly Journal of Asiatic Society of Bengal.* Silver Jubilee Special Number, Vol. 28.

Contribution of L.K. Balaratna

1958 : *Society in India*. Madras : Social Science Association.

1963 : *Anthropology on the March*. Madras : The Book Centre, 1/155 Mount.

S.C. ROY (1871-1942)

Rai Bahadur Sarat Chandra Roy popularly known as S.C. Roy was adorned with many great titles by Indian and foreign anthropologists. He was given title as a father of Indian ethnology, first Indian ethnographer and first Indian anthropologist. These great titles for S.C. Roy clearly reveal his contribution in the development of Indian anthropology. S.C. Roy was born on 4th November, 1871 in a well known and prestigious Kayastha family in a village named Karapara of Khulna district, now in Bangladesh. One of his ancestors, Parmanand Roy was one of the 12 big landlords of the East Bangladesh. His family was closely related to Raja Basant Roy, a big landlord of the area. His father Purnachandra Roy was a member of Bengal Judicial Service. Sarat Chandra Roy moved with his father where ever he was posted. When his father was posted at Purulia, S.C. Roy came in contact with tribal people for the first time. When S.C. Roy was only 14 years old, his father died in 1885. For the next few years his life spent in adversity due to litigation of family property. However, S.C. Roy continued his study at Calcutta (now Kolkata) under the guardianship of his maternal uncle. He passed his matriculation examination in 1888 and graduated with Hons. in English in 1892 from General Assembly Institute, now known as Scottish Church College, Kolkata. He passed his M.A. examination in English from the same college and took his Law degree in 1895 from the Ripon College, Kolkata. He worked as Headmaster of Mymen Singh High School. He was later invited to work as Principal of GEL Mission High School, Ranchi. It was during his sojourn at Ranchi that he was ultimately drawn towards the sad plight of the tribals. He left the profession of teaching to set up a practice as a lawyer. He became pleader in the district court of 24 Pargana at Alipur, Kolkata in 1897. But from the following year, he settled at Ranchi in 1888 and successfully built up a considerable practice and made a good name for himself in the Bar of Judical Commissioner's Court.

While practising Law at Ranchi, he was moved by the oppression and hardship of aboriginal tribes of Chotanagpur Division at the hands of outsiders and veritable denial of justice to these people due to the appalling apathy and ignorance of the administrative and Judicial Commissioner's Court. As a lawyer he used to visit the interior areas of Chotanagpur on commission from courts. He was distressed by the way tribals were treated in the Court of Law. He observed that Courts of Law could not provide them justice because their cases were not pursued with sympathy by the lawyers dealing with them. This could not be done as a lawyer had no knowledge of tribal languages. He, therefore, made it a point to investigate tribal culture in depth and to master their language. He devoted himself wholeheartedly over the study of language, modes, manner and customs of Munda which resulted in publication of his first monograph on Munda under the title, "Munda and Their Country" (1912). This book is first monograph written on an Indian tribe by an Indian scholar. That is why he is known as the father of Indian Ethology, first Indian ethnographer and first Indian anthropologist. The missionaries had done some spade work in the line, but it was Rai Bahadur S.C. Roy who pioneered the scientific investigation into tribal and agrarian history of Mundas and other aboriginal people. The publication of the book had attracted the attention of Sir Edward Gait, the then Lieutenant Governor of Bihar. He saw and read this book and gave financial assistance to Roy to undertake the further researches on Oraon, an another major tribe of Chotanagpur. His book on Oraon under the title, "*Oraon of Chotanagpur*" was published in 1915 from Ranchi. In this way, he was launched as an anthropologist and in course of time produced a number of monographs on Tribes of Chotanagpur. For example, *The Birhor : Little Known Jungle Tribe of Chotanagpur* (1925), *Oraon Religion and Custom* (1928), *Hill Bhuiya of Orissa* (1935) and *Kharia*—two volumes in 1937. In this way, he presented himself as a pioneer of ethnological studies in India. He attained a worldwide fame as an authority on aboriginals of India and especially of Chotanagpur. Professor J.H. Hutton in his presidential address read at the annual meeting of Indian Anthropological Society at Kolkata on 5 January, 1938 described S.C. Roy as the "Father of Indian Ethnology".

Since S.C. Roy was devoted to Indological Researches, he took keen interest in Bihar and Orissa Research Society. This society was started in January 1915. S.C. Roy became General Secretary of this Society. Anthropology and folklore were included in the scope of research in this Society. Roy was made in charge of Anthropology and Folklore Section. Sir Edward Gait and Mahamahopadhyay Har Prasad Shastri were members of the Society. He regularly contributed to the Journal of Bihar, Orissa Research Society and also enriched the Anthropology and Prehistoric Gallery of Patna Museum with his personal collection.

His deep concern for the poor and the downtrodden tribals of Chotanagpur and devoted labour for their upliftment led the election of Sarat Chandra Roy as a member of Bihar Legislative Council for several terms between 1921 to 1937. He was also elected as a member of Provincial Committee that sat with Simon Commission in 1928. He also served as a member of Indian Franchise Committee headed by Lord Lothian. His interest in anthropological studies began to take most of his time and he gave up legal practice in 1933. From then till his death, he devoted himself to his own researches and to editing to *Man In India,* the first anthropological Journal in country which he founded in 1921.

S.C. Roy was also deeply interested in social work. He served Ranchi District Board as a Vice Chairman for many years. He was the President of the Governing Body of the Bengali Boy's School and also of Bengali Girl's School at Ranchi. At the same time, he was President of Harijan Sevak Samiti, Anti-Drink Society, Oraon-Munda Shiskha Sabha and Brahmacharya Sangh. These wide ranging works kept him extremely busy. One wonders how he could combine his professional work as a lawyer and scholarly interest as an anthropologist along with huge burden of social work

In fullness of time, the services of S.C. Roy in the field of Anthropology and in that of social service received due recognition. He was awarded Kaiser-i-Hind silver medal in 1913 and title of Rai Bahadur in 1919, besides two certificates of honour and two gold medals. In 1920, he was elected as an honorary member of Folklore Society of London. He was the only Indian to be honoured with this distinction. In the same year, he was elected President of the Anthropological Section in Indian Science Congress. In two successive years, 1932 and 1933, he was elected President of Anthropology and Folklore Section of the All India Oriental Congress. Later, he was elected as a member of the Council of the International Congress of Ethnological Sciences. He was a foundation fellow of the National Institute of Sciences in India and also of Patna University. In 1941, on the occasion of his 70th birthday, the Indian Science Congress decided to present him with the commemorative volume, "Essays in Anthropology" written in his honour by some of eminent anthropologists of the day. Unfortunately, this volume was published one week after his death. The list of contributors of this volume show high esteem in which S.C. Roy was held by his colleagues at home and abroad.

Sarat Chandra Roy breathed his last in the morning of Buddha Purnima, 30th April, 1942, after a prolonged illness of several months. His death was widely mourned not only at Ranchi, but by the anthropologists of India and abroad. The famous scientific Journal *Nature* in its editorial observed, "The dry light of pure science and disinterested research was kept aflame (in India) by a small band of devoted enthusiasts among whom the veteran anthropologist Sarat Chandra Roy will ever be held in honour."

Although Anthropology was more a labour of love than profession for Sarat Chandra Roy, but his devotion to the subject was unbounded and he left no stone unturned to stress its importance and usefulness in quarters where it mattered most. He was the first person to deliver a University Readership Lecture in Anthropology in Patna University in 1920 on the topic, "The Principles and the Methods of Physical Anthropology". This was a year before the first full-fledged Department of Anthropology was established at Calcutta University through the efforts of Sir Asutosh Mukherjee. He used to deliver special lecture at this newly established Department of Anthropology at Calcutta from time to time. He used to ethuse its members to make the Department of Anthropology, Calcutta University, Calcutta as an excellent centre of anthropological researches in the country. In different presidential addresses he delivered to Indian Science Congress, Oriental Conference and other learned bodies, he dwelt upon the current status of researches in different branches of Anthropology. In this way, he raised the status of the subject Anthropology at National Scientific gathering. He also demanded opening of Anthropology in different universities in different states of the country. In order to promote Anthropological researches, he started a research journal named *Man In India* in 1921. This journal attracted contributions from scholars at home and abroad. Besides original papers, this journal carried book reviews, notes and queries and also notices of anthropological interest in current Indian literature. Its publication is continuing even now.

S.C. Roy was a source of inspiration and a tower of strength to many budding anthropologists.

D.N. Majumdar and N.K. Bose received active encouragement and guidance from him in their early years. It was at his best that S.S. Sarkar studied Maler of Rajmahal hills in 1935. He also encouraged Charu Lal, an advocate like him at Dumka to undertake researches on Santhal of Mayurbhanj in Orissa. His research was later published as monograph. In this way, Roy not only helped train and guide professional anthropologists, but built up and nourished a vigorous tradition of anthropological research in anthropology. The contributions of S.C. Roy (Sarat Chandra Roy) in the form of books and papers are as follows:

Books

1912 : *The Mundas and Their Country*, Kolkata : City Book Agency.

1915 : *The Oraons of Chotanagpur*, Kolkata: Brahmo Mission Press.

1920 : *The Principles and Methods of Physical Anthropology*, Patna : Patna University.

1925 : *The Birhors : A Little Known Jungle Tribes of Chotanagpur.* Ranchi : *Man In India* Office.

1928 : *Oraon Religion and Custom*. Kolkata : The Industry Press (Ranchi) : *Man In India* Office).

1935 : *The Hill Bhuiyas of Orissa.* Ranchi : *Man In India* Office.

1937 : *The Kharias* (with R.C. Roy). Two Volumes, Ranchi : *Man In India* Office.

Papers

1914 : "Magic and Witchcraft on the Chotanagpur Plateau". *Journal of Assam Research Society*, 44 : 324-350.

1915 : "Orientation of Grave Stone and Houses in Chotanagpur". *Journal of Bihar and Orissa Research Society*, 1:2, 270-80.

1915 : "A Note on Some Remains of Ancient Asuras in the Ranchi District". *Journal of Bihar and Orissa Research Society,* 1:2, 229-53.

1915 : "The Artificial Moulding of Physical Features in India". *Journal of Bihar and Orissa Research Society,* 1:1, 27-30.

1915 : "The Corn Spirit and Tree Spirit in Chotanagpur". *Journal of Bihar and Orissa Research Society,* 1:1, 47-52.

1916 : "The Divine Myths of Mundas". *Journal of Bihar and Orissa Research Society,* 2:2, 201-14.

1916 : "A Lepcha Funeral". *Journal of Bihar and Orissa Research Society,* 2:4, 475-480.

1916 : "Note on Some Prehistoric Stone Implements". *Journal of Bihar and Orissa Research Society,* 2:1, 61-77.

1916 : "Find of Ancient Bronze Articles in Ranchi District". *Journal of Bihar and Orissa Research Society.* 2:4, 485-87.

1917 : "Note on Totemism Among Asura". *Journal of Bihar and Orissa Research Society,* 3:4, 567-71.

1919 : "Obituary of Dr. Andrew Campbell, D.D.". *Journal of Bihar and Orissa Research Society,* 5:4, 411-12.

1920 : "The Distribution and Nature of Asura Sites in Chotanagpur". *Journal of Bihar and Orissa Research Society,* 6, 393-423.

1920 : "The Pahiras of Chotanagpur". *Journal of Bihar and Orissa Research Society,* 6, 527-39.

1921 : "Kinship and Marriage Organisation of Pahiras". *Journal of Bihar and Orissa Research Society,* 7 : 1, 25-32.

1921 : "Ethnographical Investigation in Official Records". *Journal of Bihar and Orissa Research Society,* 7 : 4, 1-34.

1921 : "Kinship Organisation of Mangers of Sikkim". *Journal of Bihar and Orissa Research Society,* 7 : 2&3, 81-91.

1921 : "President Address : Anthropology, 8th Indian Science Congress", *Man In India,* 1:1, 118-39.

1922 : "A Pahira Folktale About the Creation of Man". *Man in India,* 2 : 4, 270-72.

1923 : "Exorcism in Chotanagpur". *Journal of Bihar and Orissa Research Society,* 9-1, 118-39.

1924 : "The Black Bhils of Jaisamand Lake in Rajputana". *Journal of Bihar and Orissa Research Society,* 10 : 1&2, 97-113.

1925 : "Totemism and Religion". *Journal of Bihar and Orissa Research Society,* 11:2, 162-76.

1926 : "The Asura Ancient and Modern". *Journal of Bihar and Orissa Research Society,* 12:1, 147-52.

1927 : "The Bull Roarer in India". *Journal of Bihar and Orissa Research Society,* 13:1, 54-61.

1927 : "A Report of Anthropological Work in 1928-29". *Journal of Bihar and Orissa Research Society,* 13 : 3&4, 291-95.

1928 : "Primitive Religion in Chotanagpur". *Journal of Bihar and Orissa Research Society,* 14:1, 65-74.

1929 : "Glimpses into Primitive Gleanings from An Anthropologist's Note Book". *Journal of Bihar and Orissa Research Society,* 15:122, 204-223.

1929 : "Report of Anthropological Work 1928-29". *Journal of Bihar and Orissa Research* Society, 15 : 3&4, 573-82.

1930 : "Hindu Exogamy by S.V. Karandikar : A Review". *Journal of Bihar and Orissa Research Society,* 16 : 3&4, 428-30.

1930 : "Munda Magyar Maori by F.A. Uxbound : A Review". *Journal of Bihar and Orissa Research Society,* 16 : 3&4, 428-30.

1930 : "Report of Anthropological Work 1929-1930". *Journal of Bihar and Orissa Research Society,* 16 : 3&4, 428-30.

1931 : "The Effect on the Aboriginals of Chotanagpur of their Contact with Western Civilization". *Journal of Bihar and Orissa Research Society,* 17 : 4, 358-94.

1932 : "Chotanagpur : The Ghutiyas and Bhuiyas". *Journal of Bihar and Orissa Research Society,* 18 : 1, 51-78.

1932 : "The Study of Folklore and Tradition in India". *Journal of Bihar and Orissa Research Society,* 18 : 3&4, 534-81.

1933 : "Presidential Address : Anthropological Section". All India Oriental Conference.

1933 : "Anthropology of Bihar and Orissa". *Indian Science Congress and Hand Book,* Patna.

1935 : "Report of Anthropological Work 1932-33 & 1933-34 (The Korwa) and 1934-35". *Journal of Bihar and Orissa Research Society.*

1935 : "Ethnological Investigation in Official Records". *Journal of Bihar and Orissa Research Society,* 21:4, 231-50.

1936 : "A Note on Korku Memorial Tablet". *Man In India,* 16:172-78.

1937 : "Study of Anthropology from the Indian Viewpoint". *Journal of Banaras Hindu University,* 2:2, 32-40.

1938 : "The Importance of Anthropological Study in India". *New Review,* 7, 136-50.

1939 : "The Aboriginals and Depressed Class in India". *New Review,* 10, 105-30.

Major Contributions in Anthropology

The Major Contribution of S.C. Roy in Anthropology can be discussed under the following headings:

- Contribution on Tribal Studies
- Contribution on Physical Anthropology
- Contribution on Prehistoric Archaeology
- Contribution on Study of Castes
- Contribution on Folklore Study
- Contribution on Applied Anthropology and Tribal Policy

Now let us discuss about each types of anthropological contribution of S.C. Roy one by one.

Contribution on Tribal Studies

As referred to earlier, the sad plight and miserable condition of tribals of Chotanagpur attracted S.C. Roy, an eminent lawyer by profession to undertake studies on tribal beliefs, customs, traditions, lifeways, habits, behaviour and culture. He was first attracted towards the study of Munda, a major tribe of Chotanagpur. He wrote few articles about their culture in journals. But finally, he published a monograph on Munda under the title, "The Mundas and Their Country" in 1912. It was the time when most of anthropologists even in West were engaged in evolutionary and diffusional studies. They were of view that anthropology is a branch of history dealing with tribals. This history was partly valid and partly conjectural. Its reconstruction was based scanty evidence drawn from myth, legends and folklore. Roy believed that the knowledge of history of a tribe would help us appreciate its culture better. It is thus, no surprise that Roy's monograph on Mundas contains five chapters on history and only one chapter on ethnography. In the earlier chapters, Roy tried to trace the origin of tribe from clues drawn from folklore, linguistics and prehistoric evidences. He then proceeded to reconstruct the long history of the tribe from the time of Vedas to the beginning of Christian era. It is only in early medieval and modern period that some historical evidences on tribe are available. In modern period, he brings the narrative down to Birsa revolt. In the chapter of the modern history of Munda, he traced in detail the various socio-economic movements that took place in Munda during 19th century. The section of ethnography deals with physical appearance, dress, ornaments, weapons, material culture, description of tribal village, detail of agriculture operations and processes, social organisations, political organisations, religion, festivals, superstitions and art. The book gives a short and generalised account of Munda life and culture. He also gave some details about Mundari language, folktales, proverbs, songs and others. But the book does not deal with regional variations and differences of customs and practices of Munda.

In his another Monograph, "*The Oraons of Chotanagpur*" (1915), Roy deals with Oraon, another major tribe of Chotanagpur. In this book he dealt with history and migration of Oraon tribe in only one chapter, while rest of the chapters were devoted to ethnographic description of Oraon life and culture. The informations and materials collected on Oraon tribe was so voluminous that the bulk of data on religion and customs were left to be dealt within an another volume under the title of "*Oraon Religion and Custom*" (1928). Roy threw light on social organisation of Oraon community. He was the first scholar to draw attention towards the existence of Dhamkuria or youth dormitory in Oraon community. He detailed its functions and explained its role in social and economic life of Oraon. He also gave a detailed description of the village organisation, village Panchayat and Parhaa Panchayat. In the study of cultural change among Oraon, the greatest difficulty Roy faced was in regard to regional variation. It is, therefore, difficult to treat Sarat Chandra Roy's first book on Oraon as a benchmark data for future comparison. Since pioneers have to work under limitation and as at that time and anthropology had not developed sophistication, precision or objectivity as now, the book was ranked among the very best monograph of an Indian tribe. Sir James Frazer, a British evolutionist anthropologist congratulated Roy for collecting so rich anthropological data, information and materials and setting forth facts carefully distinguished them from the inferences which Roy drew from them. A.C. Haddon, an another British anthropologist wrote introduction to his first book on Oraon tried to relate some of Roy's findings to the current thinking in British ethnography.

The second book on Oraon (1928) is devoted to description of religious and magical beliefs, life cycle of socio-religious rites and ceremonies, feast and festivals and the magical practices of the Oraon. This is first monograph in India which is completely devoted to a study of one particular aspect of Indian culture. Roy does not deal only with description of rituals but shows as to how some of these feasts and festivals intensify the feelings of social solidarity in the village. Towards the end of the book, we find a detailed description of various nativistic and reform movements among the Oraon. All this reflects the impact of Hinduism. Not only have the origins of Tanabhagat movement been traced, but some of their important hymns have been translated into English in this book. Roy came to the conclusion that these puritanical movements among Oraon were not just religious in nature, but had the strong social and economical undertones. The movement offered them as escape from the general dissatisfaction with their current economic condition and social status. He believes that movement was more or less based on Oraon's traditional way of thought and belief. Roy, however, did not elaborate the political implications of the Tanabhagat movement and he also underplayed very important role played by Oraons National Non-Cooperation Movement in 1921 as well as in national freedom in the year that followed.

S.C. Roy did not confine his attention to the study of larger tribes alone. One of his monographs is on Birhor (1925), a small tribe which only numbered 2000 in his time. The study of this nomadic tribe took more than fifteen years. In the study of Birhor, he had taken help of a young and intelligent Birhor who acted as primary informant and guided Roy to the Uthalu Tanda (temporary settlement) spread throughout Chotanagpur. The arrangement of data follows the traditional pattern of a tribal monograph. He succeeded in giving a description of Birhor life from which 'nomadism' emerged as a style of life. He made an occasional distinction between the pattern of living of settled (Jaghie) and normadic (Uthalu) Birhors. At the end of the book he appended sixteen folktales and gave details of games, proverbs, riddles and other means of recreation of the Birhor.

His other book was "Hill Bhuiya of Orissa" (1935). In this study, his son Ramesh Chandra Roy, a trained anthropologist helped him in the collection and analysis of anthropometric data. This book gives a comparative description of plain and hill Bhuiyas. Roy did not mention the name of the village from where data were gathered. But he took care to describe the local and regional variations in culture of Bhuiyas.

The last monograph "Kharia" was published in two volumes in 1937. Roy wrote this monograph in collaboration with his son

Ramesh Chandra Roy who was also a trained anthropologist. He helped Roy in collection and analysis of anthropometric data. The Kharias live in south-west corner of the Ranchi district. Researches on Kharias were carried out in 12 years. It was possible for Roy to give a comparative picture of all three divisions of Kharia : Dhudh Kharia, Dhelki Kharia and Hill Kharia. Roy held that the three sections of the tribe represent the three successive layers in the development of primitive culture. Since the bulk of this tribe has been converted to Christianity, it was possible for Roy to take help of some educated informants. He was helped in his mission by Christian Missionaries, too. The monograph was published in two volumes and may be ranked among all published books of Roy as the most scientific and elaborate. In this monograph, Roy did not attempt to reconstruct the history of the Kharia. He took into consideration the history of migration as well as the origins of the tribe as revealed by myth. Roy described the social, economic, political and religious life of the community. Anthropometric measurements taken from each section of the tribe were also analysed and presented systematically.

Besides monographs, Roy also contributed a number of research papers on some aspects of life and the culture of other tribes and communities both in and out of Bihar. He wrote on totemism among the Asur, the Ho of Singhbhum, and Pahira of Chotanagpur. He also published articles on the Lepcha funeral, kinship among people of Sikkim, Khashi kinship terms, Khond human sacrifice, Korku memorial tablets, the Black Bhils of Jaisamand lake in Rajputana and on the people of Burm.

Contribution on the Study of Physical Anthropology

Although Sarat Chandra Roy was essentially a cultural anthropologist, he did not neglect other branches of anthropology, like physical anthropology, prehistoric archaeology and folklore. In fact, his Patna University lectures were exclusively devoted to the physical anthropology. In these, he dealt with at length the scope, divisions, methods of physical anthropology, man's place in nature, the antiquity of man, characteristics of fossil man, human evolution, the background of general theory of evolution, controversies regarding the first home of man, racial migration, and finally the classification of human races, racial taxonomies, and others.

In his various tribal monographs, he tried to give, as far as possible, details about physical characteristics. For example, in his monograph "Munda and their Country" (1912 : 209), he observed head inclined to be long (Dolicocephalic), nose was thick and broad, and sometimes depressed at the root, the lip was thick, facial angle comparatively low, face wide and fleshy, feature irregular, figure squat, limbs sturdy and well formed and the stature rather short.

Roy also took care to mention the anthropometric measurement of one hundred Munda from the specimens provided by Sir Herbert Risley in his book, "*Tribes and Castes of Bengal*" (1895). He gave details about length, breadth, as well as cephallic index, nasal index, nasomalar index, frontozygomatic index, verticocephalic index, verticobimalar index, vertico frontal index, vertico bizygomatic index, facial angle, nasal height, nasal breadth and minimum frontal breadth. He also wrote about their skin colour and breadth.

In his last two monographs, "Hill Bhuiyas of Orissa" (1935) and "Kharia" (1937), he did not depend upon any earlier reference but used his own resources to get the measurement done. In taking physical measurement, he was helped by his son Ramesh Chandra Roy, a trained anthropologist. P.C. Mahalanobis, who was at that time at Presidency College, Kolkata assigned him in the analysis of anthropometric data and the statistical calculations in the form of an appendix in his book on Kharia. The measurements were taken from hundred individuals of each section of Kharia—Dudhkharia, Delkikharia and Hill Kharia.

Contribution on the Study of Prehistoric Archaeology

S.C. Roy was of the opinion that a number of problems of Indian ethnology could be solved by an exploration of prehistoric evidences. He was the third person to study prehistoric sites in Ranchi district. The first two were Valentine Ball and WHP Driver. Ball discovered a beautifully made stoneaxe at the foot near the village Baruadih in Tamar, while Driver found a few small stone arrowheads at Ranchi. Both of these were briefly described in archaeological report. S.C. Roy's attention was drawn towards a triangular stone axehead presented to him by one of his clients in 1914. Then he started collecting stone implements. In a couple of years, his collection went up to a hundred. In all, about 46 prehistoric sites were reported by him. Most of them were located in Ranchi district. In Jardag, he found a palaeolithic implement. Later some flakes, scrapers, knives, and burins were collected from site near Chakradharpur. They were found mostly between gravel and alluvial deposit at approximately 18 ft below the existing soil level along the banks of Binjai and Sanjai rivers. The polished stone implements were made of gneiss, schist, slate, quartzite, basalt etc. Most of the celts were polished over the whole surface. Some were chipped and not ground except on the edge and a small number of them were merely chipped into shape and not ground even at the edge.

S.C. Roy's main contribution in the field of prehistoric archaeology is digging up of Asura site. The traditions about the Ancient Asura are still widespread in Ranchi district. Implements and ornaments of copper, bronze and iron dug up are variably attributed to these Munda inhabitants of Chotanagpur. He made exploratory investigation and found here and there villages containing remains of very ancient brick buildings, stone temples, sculptures, cinetary urns, huge slabs, column of sculptural stones, large tank, mostly silted up, which were locally attributed to an ancient people called the Asura. Roy discovered the stone implements, stone sculptures, stone beads, potsherds, copper implements, ornaments, bronze tools, iron implements from the Asura sites. His contention was that Asura belonged to same age as that of Indus Valley Civilization. On many points he found the two areas resembling to a surprising degree. In Asura culture of Chotanagpur, Roy finds an earlier stage of :

- Organisation of society into cities.
- The continued but sparing use of stone, side by side with

copper and bronze for manufacturing of weapons, tools and vessels.

- Invention of potter's wheel and production of improved kind of pottery with its help.
- Invention of wheeled vehicles, construction of buildings with kiln and sunburn bricks.
- Use of maces of stone.
- Fashioning of ornaments out of faince, shell and stone.

The absence of some features like pictographs, artifacts of gold and silver, and human figure in different forms in these finds does not preclude the possibility of these finds in unexplored and partially explored track of Chotanagpur. The sites discovered by Sarat Chandra Roy afforded evidences of Chalcolithic Culture in Ranchi district. Although relics of palaeolithic culture is not well marked in Chotanagpur, there appeared to be abundance of relics of Neolithic period particularly in Northern and North-Eastern part of Ranchi district, and from the association of some stone object with reputed sites of Asuras. The presence of stone and copper tools bear evidences of a period of transition from Neolithic age to Copper age. The presence of iron tools in Asura sites indicates another phase of prehistoric development, i.e. iron age. Roy also came across a number of Asura burial sites locally known as Asurkhulty. The excavations of Asura burial sites revealed the existence of earthen jars which were placed one above the other up to maximum four at a time. Placed in Jars were copper ornaments and beads together with the bones of the dead. The Asura civilisation in Chotanagpur, according to Roy, continued at least up to Kushana period as indicated by the existence of three Kushana gold coins in the excavated finds.

The Asura problem has been above of contention between archaeologists and anthropologists. While Sarat Chandra Roy believed that Asura sites discovered by him could be connected with the ancient civilised people called Asura, but archaeologists do not agree. They do not see any connection between Asura sites in Chotanagpur and the Asura Tribes which was supposed to have preceded the Munda in south-Eastern part of Ranchi district. Asura tribes living in Netarhat plateau were known for their iron smelting. Roy felt that these Asura Tribes living in Netarhat Plateau were known for their iron smelting. Roy felt that these tribes were the same people who were the creators of civilization as appeared in excavation of Asura sites.

Contribution on Anthropology of Castes

S.C. Roy was of opinion that our ancient scared texts, like Vedas, Puranas, Samhitas, Dharmshastras, Upanishads and Griha Sutra and great epics *Ramayana* and *Mahabharata* held a rich treasure house of data for Social Anthropology. The Puranas attempt to present a crude picture of origin of man and of gradual development of society and culture from very early time. The Puranas and Dharma Shastras form the store house of social customs, usages, rites, and ceremonies, ethics, politics and law. They furnish picture of contemporary Indian society with its ideals and different types and levels of culture. According to Roy, Puranas combine in them history, cultural anthropology and ethics. The Samhitas and Griha Sutras describe the various social regulations and customs prevalent in various localities and communities in India. By arranging, classifying and correlating them, contemporaneous Hindu society governed by a system of socio-religious and religio-legal rules suited to different levels of culture in the land can be delineated. Of the eight kinds of Hindu marriages enumerated in Samhitas, we find many of them prevalent in tribal areas. Among eight types of Hindu marriages, the first four were considered good, while others were tolerated but not recommended.

The Puranic literature has been styled as Itihasa, Purana or history and tradition. The tradition is in itself an important subject matter for anthropologists and as such it could not be neglected by them. Since history in Roy's days dealt with activities of kings, dynasties and courts, he believed that it could not reveal a complete picture of the life of society. The style of daily life of men and women organised in society, their economic and social aspirations and activities form the real life of the community which anthropologists seek to understand. This could easily be accomplished by the study of Puranas and Samhitas. It is for this reason that Roy recommended the anthropologists to study the ancient text. According to him, anthropology is not a study of quaint and exotic manners and customs of the primitive tribes. Anthropology is not only a study of primitive man but the study of mankind. The broad subject matter of anthropology is a study of entire life of mankind. The only reason behind the study of primitive people by anthropologists is that primitive society exhibits the ground plan upon which the more complex structure, which we call civilization, is built up.

According to Roy, in India, the task of anthropologist must be the study of complex civilizations. It is in this context that he made a detailed study of caste, race and religion in India. He tried to explore the origin of caste system and for this reason he included in his study not only ancient Hindu literatures, but a vast amount of ethnographic data on caste and tribes of India. He began with a critique of different theories of caste system in India propounded by different scholars. This was followed by an assessment of contribution of various ethnic elements to the evolution of Indian culture with special reference to caste system. The caste system is unique feature of Indian society. But certain elements of Caste System may be seen outside the Indian subcontinent. The complexity of caste system is a peculiarly Indian phenomena. The constant interaction between people belonging to diverse ethnic elements and cultural area must have had a bearing on making of the caste system in India. S.C. Roy took care to make fine distinction between different areas in India with regard to the rigidity of caste system and the way it affected the life of the people.

Contribution on the Study of Folklore

In his presidential address to the Anthropological Section of 6th Oriental Congress held in 1930 at Patna, Roy made a strong plea for the study of folklore by anthropologists. It is not difficult to observe, record and study the traditional customs, rites, beliefs, stories and myths. Such customs, rites, beliefs, may belong either to individuals, families, clans or other groups. They may stand on a lower intellectual level and are often inconsistent with orthodox or officially recognised customs, beliefs and rituals of people wherever they occur. The term folklore is not only restricted to traditional customs, rites and beliefs of the past lingering among backward people in complex civilization. But now, it is extended to include folk arts, folk abuse, folk proverbs, folk riddles, idioms and others of both people of Civilized Civilization and Primitive Civilizations. According to Roy, folklores throw a flash of light on the early intellectual evolution of human society. That is why Roy regarded folklore as prehistory of human mind.

Roy held that Indian students work in most advantageous position to collect and study folklore, although many folkloric traditions have already disappeared due to various reasons. He emphasized upon the need to collect and preserve folkloric traditions because they were our heritage of the past handed down from generation to generation. According to him, in the study of folkloric traditions in India, a systematic collection of folkloric traditions could be done on the basis of districts, *talukas*, cultural regions and smaller territorial segments. He held that the study of folkloric traditions should include songs, *geets, bhajans*, ballads, myths, tales, stories, proverbs, riddles, rites, plays, magic, *totka,* folk recreation and folk abuse.

To know exclusively about the origin of any one item of folklore, students will have to make a deep analysis and distributional study of such folkloric items by plotting it out on a map, determining its focal centre and tracing its diffusion to marginal area. Roy did not refuse the possibility of independent origin of a custom of different places. He, however, adviced the students to study different items in the context of the culture complex in which they figure. The search for tracing the origin of folklore custom was termed by Roy as tracing the genealogy of folklore. To engage in this task, the students must not acquire only full knowledge of culture, mentality and past history of the people whose folklore they study but equip themselves in knowledge of life and culture of neighbouring communities with whom they have been in contact. The folklorist must draw upon the resources of comparative ethnology, social psychology, prehistory, philosophy as well as literature.

Contribution on Applied Anthropology and Tribal Policy

S.C. Roy was a highly respected public man known for his deep scholarship and sympathy for tribal life and culture. As such Government sought his advice whenever it faced any administrative problem in dealing with tribals. A few such cases may be sited in which Roy assumed the role of trouble shooter. He showed how timely intervention by anthropologists can lead to ending a condition of stress and strain in the society.

During the days of non-cooperation movement in 1921, a police officer came across a notice circulated in the name of Raja of some Munda Parha (intervillage council). In this notice, British officer smelt a plot to subvert the British Government in Chotanagpur and established Munda Raj. Deputy Commissioner felt concern at this and called Sarat Chandra Roy for consultation. Roy consulted the Mundas and found that it was just for a meeting of Parha in which there was nothing wrong. He advised not to send police officer to observe the proceedings of the meeting. Since authorities were still worried, Roy was sent to attend this meeting along with some policemen in a plain dress. In this meeting, Munda ventilated a number of agrarian grievances and discussed their educational and other needs. Roy made a promise to represent their troubles to authorities and secure such redress as much as possible. In this way, through the proper handling of the situation, a violent situation was prevented.

In the Chotanagpur area, during intertribal dancing meet, known as *Jatra*, each village carries a flag of its own. No village can use the strands of the other village. Once a Railway Bridge was being constructed over a river near Lohardaga. The bridge repeatedly gave way. It was believed that this was happening because supernatural spirits of two villages on either sides were displeased with the idea of bridge construction. When contractor repaired old dilapidated temple of the Hindu village located on one side of river and offered a new flag to Oraon village located on another side of river, the bridge was constructed successfully. The new flag contained the replica of a railway train. The another village also made the same kind of flag for itself and this led to trouble at *Jatra* held at Bhasko. At this time, Sub-divisional Magistrate thought of consulting Roy. Roy knew the belief of Oraon that emblem of the flag endowed the village with an extraordinary power. Therefore, he got a large flag made with the symbol of an aeroplane on it. The people of other village became to accept it easily because aeroplane was superior to the railway train.

In his various speeches, addresses and memoranda, Roy made a strong plea for giving anthropological training not only to administrative and judicial officers, but to forest and excise officers also who were posted in the tribal areas. He thought that such training would not only improve the quality of judicial and excise work, but also help the cause of science through observation and investigation of aboriginal customs that might be recorded in field by such trained officers. He strongly felt that anthropology would be applied to solve certain problems of national life. He felt that study of races, customs, religions and manners of one another might help in natural unity and knitting even more closely the bonds of unity between them and, thus, help in banishing much of the commercial animosity, which is bane of Indian national life at present time.

Throughout his public life and also as a member of Bihar and Orissa Legislative Council for more than fifteen years, S.C. Roy was solicitous of welfare of tribal people of Chotanagpur. He was cautious and conservationist in matters relating to the political advance of the tribals.

In 1935, the Bihar Legislative Council passed a resolution recommending to the Government to take step to see that no part of Chotanagpur is made excluded or partly excluded area. The resolution was strongly opposed by the Government which declared that such a move was not desirable. Four reasons were advanced for the Government's views:

- The tribals had not attained the same standard of civilization as other minority communities, nor were the tribals equal in the wealth and position.
- They were extremely backward in literacy and education.
- They were not strongly organised politically.
- It was necessary to include tribal areas in excluded or partly excluded category.

S.C. Roy rebutted all the four points enumerated above and added that the immediate need of tribal people was to promulgate a well considered tenancy law, and also a law against us was, greater employment to tribal people in public services, promotion of education and culture, gradual step leading to temperance among them and posting of qualified and sympathetic officers conversant with their language and customs. Their interest could be safeguarded by the Governor under his special responsibility for minority communities. Therefore, it was not necessary to include Chotanagpur in excluded and partially excluded categories.

S.C. Roy saw that when it comes to the question of poverty or social inequality, there is little difference between now advanced sections of population treated rural cultivators, artisans and tribals. He held that the problem of development of the peasant and handicraft workers is just the same, whether a person speaks a tribal language or one belongs to Indo-Aryan or Dravidian language family. It is the problem of poverty, lack of education, worst sanitary conditions and belief in superstitions which needs to be solved immediately. These problems need to be removed without making any distinction between tribal and non-tribal communities.

B.S. GUHA (1894-1961)

Birja Shankar Guha was originally a student of Philosophy. He received his master degree in Philosophy in 1915 from the University of Calcutta. From the very beginning he was interested in Natural History, Antiquarianism and Primitive Tribes. Guha belonged to a well known family of Indian Civil Service officers. He was greatly influenced by the efforts of British officers to conduct the ethnographic Survey of India. He came in contact with Prof. R.B. Dixon who helped him in making the decision to switch over anthropology and also to come to Harvard for professional training as graduate assistant at Harvard University in Peabody Museum. He received his M.A. degree in Anthropology in 1922 and Ph.D. degree in 1924.

While at Harvard, he studied Physical Anthropology, Cultural Anthropology, Criminal Anthropology, race mixture and applied Physical Anthropology, Prehistoric European Archaeology, European Ethnography and Ethnography of Africa with Professor E.A. Hooton, American Archaeology, American Ethnography of Oceania, Ethnography of Asia, primitive arts and industries and general ethnology with Prof. R.B. Dixon and Primitive Sociology with Prof. A.M. Tozer. His doctoral thesis in Anthropology was on, "Racial Basis of Caste System in India".

When he returned to India on completion of his studies in United States (1920-24), Anthropology was just introduced as an academic discipline in one of universities in the country. He was invited to join as a faculty in the Department of Anthropology, Calcutta University. He joined Calcutta University in 1925. In 1927, Government of India created for the first time a post of anthropologist in its rank in the Zoological Survey of India and offered it to Guha and he accepted it. This post became the nucleus of the growth of Anthropology in India. Guha relentlessly worked for expanding the anthropology section of Zoological Survey, but for about ten years there was no result. In 1936, with the cooperation of British administrators interested in ethnology of India and a handful of Indian anthropologists interested in customs and practices of primitive people, he established the Indian Anthropological Institute at Kolkata. In 1938, he helped in organising National Institute of Sciences of India and was its founding fellow and Treasurer during 1938-42. He was elected as a fellow of Royal Asiatic Society of Bengal in 1939 and served as its Honorary Secretary for three years (1939-42). He presided over the anthropology section of joint session of Indian Science Congress and British Association for the advancement of science held at Kolkata in 1938 and in the same year he served as the Vice President of the section of Physical Anthropology and racial Biology, International Congress of Anthropology, Copenhagen, Denmark.

In 1943, Guha was awarded Anandale Memorial Medal for his distinguished contribution to Anthropology of Asia by Royal Asiatic Society of Bengal. Guha succeeded in removing Anthropology from the folds of zoology and created a separate organisation named "Anthropological Survey of India" at Kolkata in 1946. Since its inception, he served as its Director and Anthropological Adviser to the Government of India until his superannuation in 1954. In 1955-56, he organised a training centre for the social education organizers (extension officers) for the India's Community Development Programme working in Tribal Areas on the invitation of Government of India. In 1956-1959, he became Director of Bihar Tribal Welfare Research Institute at Ranchi. He recognised Bihar Tribal Research Institute as a centre of interdisciplinary research. He emphasised upon the need of social-culture, physical, Prehistoric and Linguistic anthropological research in Tribal Research Institute at Ranchi. He also stressed upon the need of historical, social, psychological, linguistic and bio-statistical and statistical study at Tribal Welfare Research Institute at Ranchi. At the time of his death, he was working for the Ministry of Education, Government of India on the reconstruction of pre-historic skulls from north-western India.

In his early years in Anthropology, Guha was greatly excited with fieldwork and visited many tribal communities in inaccessible regions of India. Before he came to Harvard, he had visited several tribes of Assam and Bengal. In the United States his first research assignment was to carry out investigations among the Utes and the Navajoj of Colorado and New Mexico in 1921 as a special research officer of Smithonian Institution, Washington DC.

As an anthropologist at Zoological Survey of India, he went on an expedition for the abolition of human sacrifice in Naga hills near the Burmese border in 1926-27. In 1931, he carried out a Comprehensive Racial Survey of India, which took him to all parts of country. He took an expedition to Chittral in north-west Balochistan (now in Pakistan) to solve the problem of linguistic affinity of tribes of Central India and Brahuls of North-West frontier of India. For several years, he worked among the polyandrous Khasas of Cis Himalayan region. Fieldwork took him several times to the north-east frontiers of India and to the Andaman islands, where he established a sub-station of Anthropological Survey of India (1952). His love for variety did not allow him to maintain interest in our field or in one problem for long. He always championed fieldwork. He often used to say in professional meetings in India that Indian anthropologists had first to collect complete ethnological data from all tribes of India and only then could it go in for theory. He believed strongly in the method of Natural History and had a positive dislike for any theoretical work based on insufficient data.

The significant contribution that Guha made to Indian anthropology was in his persistent effort to retain it as a holistic discipline. He looked anthropology as a united science of ethnology, ethnography, physical anthropology, prehistory, and linguistics with close relation with other sciences including psychology and biometrics. This viewpoint on anthropology was in a way opposed to that of some Indian anthropologists who were trained in sociologically oriented schools and who tended to compartmentalise the scope of Anthropology. Although this led to a division in small groups of professional anthropologists in India, but Guha went ahead with his own views. The two largest Research Organisations in India—the Anthropological Survey of India and Indian Museum, Kolkata of which he was founder Director and Bihar Tribal Welfare Research Institute, bear testimony in this regard. These reflect his ingenious skill as an organiser.

Guha divided the Bihar Tribal Research Institute, Ranchi into six sections, which are as follows:

- Cultural Anthropology
- Physical Anthropology and Human Biology

- Linguistics
- History
- Social Psycology
- Biometric and Statistics

He wanted to place each section under an experienced and competent individual assisted by a group of research assistants. He coordinated each section as a director. He built an excellent library and a rich museum. He projected for an equally fine division on primitive arts and photography. Although the Department of Anthropology, Kolkata where he spent most of his active life, bears the same design with richer collections. He took great interest in Tribal Research Institute at Ranchi. With the University of Ranchi having an excellent Department of Anthropology, Government of India and Tribal Research Institute Ranchi. Guha planned to make Ranchi the centre for anthropological research and teaching in India.

He invited and attracted many scholars from Europe, United States and Japan to Ranchi, but circumstances unfortunately cut short his plan.

Publications

1924 : "The Racial Basis of Caste System in India". Ph.D. Thesis Harvard University.

1928 : "Some Anthropological Problems in India". *Modern Review,* 44 : 134-41.

1931 : "Report of Human Relics Recovered by the Naga". *Anthropological Bulletin of Zoological Survey of India.* No-1CC (with P.C. Basu).

1932 : "A Note on Somatic Characters of Brahmanas and Other Groups of Kannada People". *Census of India,* 1931: Vol-25, Mysore : Bangalore Part-1.

1935 : "The Racial Affinity of People of India". *Census of India,* 1931, Vol-1, Part-III-B, Shimla.

1936-37 : "New Light on the Indus Valley Civilization". *Science and Culture,* Vol- 2, 49-50.

1937 : "Progress of Anthropology in India During the Past 25 Years". Kolkata : Baptist Mission Press.

1937: "An Outline of Racial Ethnology in India". In *Outline of Field Sciences in India* (ed.), by S.L. Hora, Kolkata.

1938 : "Racial Compositions of Hindukush Tribes". Presidential Address, Section of Anthropology, 25th Indian Science Congress, Kolkata.

1939 : "The Aboriginal Races of India". *Science and Culture*, 4 : 12, 677- 83.

1944 : "Racial Elements in Population". *Oxford Pamphlet on Indian Affairs.,* No. 2, Oxford University Press.

1951 : "The Indian Aborigines and Their Administration". *Journal of Asiatic Society, Science,* 17:1,19-44.

K.P. CHATTOPADHYAY (1897-1963)

Ksitish Prasad Chattopadhyay was born in Kolkata on 14th December, 1897. His childhood was spent partly in Kolkata and partly in some district towns and his mother's village in Bengal. His father Jamini Mohan was a metallurgist who had been trained in France. He came from a family well-known for its spirit of independence and fiery temperament. Jamini Mohan was the grandson and heir aparent of Radha Prasad Roy, son of Raja Ram Mohan Roy. But as he chose to marry Pandit Ishwar Chandra Vidyasagar's grand-daughter against the wishes of his maternal uncle, the second son of Radha Prasad Roy, Jamini Mohan Roy was disinherited. Without an income to fall back upon, Jamini Mohan tried to use his professional skill and earn his living. But due to his quick temper, Jamini Mohan lost jobs frequently. The family had to depend upon largely on his wife's careful management of their meagre resources to carry on. Thus, in very beginning of life K.P. Chattopadhyay learnt about the evils that haunt decadent feudal family. Therefore, he started labouring hard in study from school days. As he was very meritorious from beginning, he received scholarship at every stage of his education. He stood either at the top or near the top in various university examinations of Calcutta University. While he was studying in M.Sc. Physics at Calcutta University, he set out for U.K. to make preparation of I.C.S. At U.K., he met with Subhas Chandra Bose and M.N. Roy and became a close associate of them. Their association caused apathy towards I.C.S. He decided to give up preparation for I.C.S. and to work in Nuclear Physics under Sir J.J. Thomson. But he had to leave this work, too. Because his health started deteriorating due to lack of proper guard against radiation in those days. Now he returned towards Anthropology, a subject about he had studied while preparing for I.C.S. examination. He got admission in M.Sc. Anthropology at Cambridge University. Here, he got chance to study under W.H.R. Rivers, A.C. Haddon, and M.S. Bekitt. He got his M.Sc. degree in Anthropology from Cambridge University. After that he received the Anthony-Mikins Studentship. He wanted to utilise this grant for working among the Newars of Nepal. But British police found out his connection with the revolutionaries who were then staying at U.K. and the continent. The British police found that he was the chief organiser of Indian seamen living in the East End of London. As a result, he was never permitted to enter in Nepal. The Anthony-Mikins Scholarship was also withdrawn. Now, he found himself in stranded situation as he had no financial resources to stay at London to complete his Ph.D. work. His guide W.H.R. Rivers was offered a chair in Anthropology in Calcutta University. Rivers advised Kshitish to go back to Kolkata and complete his Ph.D. work in Calcutta University after his arrival. But unfortunately Rivers died at operation table during appendictomy. Kshitish, somehow managed loan and also earn some money by giving French and German lessons at Cambridge University and returned to India in 1923.

Coming back to Kolkata, he joined in the Department of Anthropology in Calcutta University as its Head with the rank of a senior lecturer. He got married to Manjushree, the eldest daughter of Surendra Nath Tagore, a great grandson of Prince Dwarkanath. K.P. did not continue at Calcutta University for a long. He and his wife both became disciples of Deshbandhu Chitraranjan Das. When Kolkata Corporation was captured by Indian National Congress, K.P. Chattopadhyay became its first Education Officer at the request of C.R. Das. He had to give up headship and lecturership jobs at Calcutta University in the Department of Anthropology. As a result, he had to face economic hardship, too. But he was able to establish some new schools in this vast organisation. He not only opened these schools, but also recruited intelligent and patriotic young men as a teacher in these schools. He used to arrange training programme for newly recruited teachers. The entire Education Department of Kolkata Corporation was a massive patriotic organisation in those days. Teachers used to teach efficiently. They were active politically, too. Subhas Chandra Bose was the then Mayor of Kolkata Corporation. On 26th January, 1930, a massive march was organised by Bose in which K.P. had participated actively with his all staff. K.P. moved always with Bose in his protection.

K.P. Chattopadhyay left Kolkata Corporation in 1937, when the Congress lost power. Now, he joined Calcutta University in the Department of Anthropology again in 1937 as its first Professor in Anthropology. He worked here till his retirement in March 1962. During this phase of his life, his intellectual activities were equally complemented by patriotic and nation building activities. He was an active Congressman till 1947 and worked for Congress Party wherever his services were required. He worked in relief operations during great famine of 1943. He organised People's Relief Committee, arbitrated between trade unions and management, organised anti-communal riots activities and Refugee Rehabilitation during 1946-48. After independence, he tirelessly fought to preserve the independence of common man through Civil Liberties Committee. He sat at the West Bengal State Legislature for two terms and tried to ensure the freedom of common man. Through his efforts Students Day Home was started at Kolkata. This was done to provide free reading facilities to poor graduating students.

Between 1934 to 1963, he was conferred many academic honours. He was elected as honorary fellow of Ecole Frances de extreme Oriente (Hanoi) and Vice-President of the Learned Society of Arts Prehistorique (Paris). He was also a member of Permanent Council of International Congress of Anthropology from 1934 when he represented India at its Vienna Session. In India, he was elected as a fellow of the National Institute of the Sciences. The Kolkata Pandit Samaj conferred upon him the title of 'Sarvabhauma'. The Kolkata Sanskrit College elected him as honorary fellow. He was also invited by many renowned academic institutions in India like Gokhale Institute of Economics and Politics. He also made academic trips to U.S.S.R., France and U.K. to attend seminar and deliver special lectures.

After retirement in 1962, he continued to work as a researcher under the retired Scientists Scheme of CSIR. He died on 31st May of 1963, while working on proofs of his last book: *Ancient Indian Culture : Contacts and Migration.* As an anthropologist, his main field-work was among Santhals and his chief interest was kinship and material culture. He had planned to publish two volumes on Santhal. He completed the last volume and gave it to Calcutta University Press for publication in 1962, but till date it had not been published. He had started organising data for his second volume, but could not complete it due to cerebral thrombosis which put an end to his dynamic life.

Some publications of K.P. Chattopadhyay are as follows:

1921 : "Some Malayalam Kinship Terms". *Man In India,* Vol.1, 53-55.

1922 : "Levirate and Kinship in India". *Man,* Vol. 22.

1923 : "An Essay on the History of Newar Culture". *Journal of Asiatic Society of Bengal,* Vol.19, 465-560.

1927 : "Social Organisations of Satkarnis and Sunga". *Journal of Asiatic Society of Bengal,* Vol. 23, 503.

1931 : "Contact of Peoples as Affecting Marriage Rules". *Proceedings of Indian Science Congress,* Kolkata, 18th Presidential Address.

1934 : "Indian Social Organisation". *Inst. Des. Sc. Anthropo., Pt., Ethnol.*

1934 : "The Munda Festival of Chotanagpur" (with N.K. Bose), *Journal of Asiatic Society of Bengal,* Vol. 30 : 151-61.

1935 : "History of Indian Social Organisation". *Journal of Asiatic Society of Bengal* : 1, Letters : 377-99.

1935 : "The Chadak Festival". *Journal of Asiatic Society of Bengal* : 1 Letters : 397-406.

1936 : "The Chadak Festival". *Journal of Asiatic Society of Bengal* : 2, 3rd series, 158.

1936 : "History of Indian Social Organisation". *Journal of Asiatic Society of Bengal* : 2,

3rd series, 163.

1938 : "Indian Oil Presser and Oil Extraction". *Journal of Indian Anthropological Institute,* 1: No. 1/2 : 41-61.

1938 : "Conflict and Social Behaviour". In *Essays in Anthropology*, B.S. Guha and others.

1939 : "Determination of Nation in the Living". *Proceedings of Indian Science Congress, Kolkata,* (26) 149.

1939 : "The Nation in the Living". *American Journal of Physical Anthropology*, Philadelphia, USA. Vol. 25, No. 2.

1939 : "Importance of Anthropological Studies in India". *Kolkata Review*; 67-70.

1939 : "A Case Study of Temporary Loss of Memory". *Indian Journal of Psychology* : 117-23.

1939 : "Origin of Ameridian Sugar Press". *Man,* Vol. 39, 139-41.

1939 : "Satkarni Succession and Marriage Rules". *Journal of Asiatic Society of Bengal;* Letters-5, Vol. 2, 317-39.

1939-40 : "Kinship in the Veda Period". *Journal of Indian Anthropological Institute,* Vol. 2, 115-21.

1940 : "The Santhal Tree Press and Plank Press". *Proceedings of Indian Science Congress* (27) : 188.

1941 : "The Korku-Munda". *Proceedings of Indian Science Congress* (28) : 215.

1941 : "Khasi Kinship and Social Organisation". *Kolkata University Anthropological Papers,* No. 6 : 1-39.

1941 : "Effects of Bride Price and Dowry on Marital Conditions Among Hindus of Bengal". *Modern Review* : 360-63.

1942 : "Application of Statistical Methods to Anthropological Research". *Sankhya,* Vol. 6, Pt. 1 : 99-104.

1942 : "Dharma Workship". *Journal of Asiatic Society of Bengal".* 3rd Series, 8 : 99-135.

1942 : "Kinship in Vedic Period". *Proceedings of Indian Science Congress,* p. 183.

1943 : "Bengal Coiled Basketry". *Journal of Asiatic Society of Bengal,* Vol. 9, 39-42.

1943 : "Korku Funeral Customs and Memorial Posts". *Journal of Asiatic Society of Bengal,* Vol. 9, 201-09.

1943-44 : "The Cultural Basis of Rules of Inheritance". *Science and Culture,* Vol. 9, 56-62.

1944 : "Santhal Migration". *Proceedings of Indian Science Congress*, 31 : 101.

1945 : "Famine and Destitution in Rural Bengal". *Science and Culture,* Vol. 11 : 228-39.

1945-46 : "Famine and Disintegration of Education in Rural Bengal" (with R.K. Mukherjee). *Science and Culture,* Vol. 11 : 20-26.

1946 : "Economic Condition of Korkus of Melghat Forest". *Journal of Asiatic Society of Bengal,* Vol. 12 : 19-30.

1946 : "Korku Marriage Customs and Some Changes". *Journal of Asiatic Society of Bengal,* Vol. 12 : 43-70.

1946 : "Our Education". *Modern Review,* 194-98.

1947 : "Report on the Santhals in Northern and Western Bengal". *Calcutta University Annual Paper*, No. 8 : 1-54.

1948 : "The Korku Village and House Type in Melghat". *Proceedings of Indian Science Congress,* 35:7.

1948 : "A Santhal Scissors Trap". *Proceedings of Indian Science Congress,* 35:67.

1948 : "A Preliminary Note on Comparability of Measurement". *Proceedings of Indian Science Congress,* 35:67.

1948 : "Santhal Economy in Bengal". *Proceedings of Indian Science Congress,* 35:67.

1948 : "Upajati Samasya in Bengal". *Janam O Bigvan.*

1949 : "Kashi Landownership and Sale". *Eastern Anthropologist,* Vol. 2, 133-37.

1949 : "Santhal Bird Net". *Proceedings of Indian Science Congress,* 36:173.

1949 : "Changes in Santhal Economy". *Man In India,* Vol. 29 : 71-75.

1949 : "A Short Note on Khasi Bone Disposal". *Proceedings of Indian Science Congress*, 36 : 174.
1949 : "The Korku Physical Type". *Proceedings of Indian Science Congress,* 36 : 174.
1950 : "The Tribal Problem and Its Solution". *Eastern Anthropologist,* Vol. 3 : 15-21.
1951 : "The Toe Peg Sandal in India". *Ethnos,* Vol. 16 : 131-33.
1951 : "The Conference for Tribal Welfare at Delhi". *Man In India,* Vol. 23, 167-69.
1952 : "The Cultural Contact and Changes in Rigvedic Society". *Proceedings of Indian Science Congress,* 39:46.
1952 : "Korku Physical Type and Racial Affinities". *Journal of Asiatic Society of Bengal,* Vol. 18 : 23-24.
1953 : "Tribal Education". *Man In India,* Vol. 33 : 1-18.
1954 : "A Short Note on Cultivation Among Tribal Folk in India". *Vanya Jati,* Vol. 2 : 110-112.
1954 : "Korku Dress and Ornament". *Proceedings of Indian Science Congress,* 42:330.
1955 : "A Trison Trap of Korku". *Vanya Jati,* Vol. 3 : 58-59.
1955 : "A Santhal Trap". *Journal of Asiatic Society of Bengal,* Vol. 21, 29-30.
1955 : "Santhal Riddles". *Journal of Asiatic Society of Bengal,* Vol. 21, 31-34.
1957 : "A Note on Polyandry". *Journal of Asiatic Society of Bengal,* Vol. 22, No. 2.
1957 : "How Korku Live", *Journal of Asiatic Society of Bengal,* Vol. 22, 99-138.
1957 : "Santhal Sibs—Their Traditional History and Observed Intermarriage Frequency". *Proceeding of National Institute of Science,* 2313, No. 1/2 : 35-41.
1958 : "The Bondo Oil Press and Its Links". *Journal of Asiatic Society of Bengal,* Vol. 24.
1958 : "Note on the Language of Commission". *Science and Culture,* Vol. 23, 325-29.
1959 : "Some Approaches to the Study of Social Change". *Kale Memorial Lecture,* Gokhale Institute of Politics and Economics, Pune.

1959 : "The Problem of Unity *versus* Group Isolation in India". *Modern Review,* 189-93.

1959 : "Art of Tribal Folk". *Journal of Anthropological Research Society,* Vol. 13 : 34-36.

1960 : "Some Changes in Khasi Culture". *Journal of Asiatic Society of Bengal,* Vol. 1 : 25-37.

1960 : "National Planning and Culture Change". *Modern Review,* 105-12.

1960 : "Social Cooperation, Freedom and Progress." *Modern Review,* 353-62.

1960 : "Changing Values and Social Pattern in Caste Society in West Bengal Village". Gokhale Institute and Congress of Cultural Freedom.

1961 : "A Study of Santhal Family Size." *Journal of National Institute of Science,* Silver Jubilee Volume.

1961 : "On Definition Mainly of Family Type". *In Sociology, Social Research and Social Problems in India* (ed.) by R.N. Saxena.

1962 : "City Survey : Method and Analysis of Data". *Journal of Social Research,* Vol. 5, 10-22.

1962 : "On Terms of Kinship and Social Relationship." In *Indian Anthropology* (ed.) by T.N. Madan and Gopala Sarana.

1962 : "Teaching of Science : Its Why and How". *Modern Review,* 308 -13.

1962 : "Pattern of Juvenile Delinquency in Kolkata". *International Journal of Comparative Sociology.*

1962 : "Class Relation in Bengal Village". Rabindra Nath Tagore Birth Centenary Celebration Conference Proceeding.

1963 : "Diffusion of a Religious Cult". In *Anthropology on March* (ed.) by Balaratnam, Madras.

1963 : "A Note on Race Characteristics through Special Sex Habit". *Bulletin of Cultural Research Institute,* West Bengal, Vol. 2, No. 1.

Books

1946 : *A Plan for Rehabilitation in Bengal.* Kolkata : 151.

1947 : *A Report on Santhals in Bengal.* Kolkata : 151.

1947 : *Municipal Labour in Kolkata.* Kolkata : Calcutta University.
1948 : *Our Education,* National Council of Education, Kolkata.
1952 : *Socio-economic Survey of Jute Labour.* Calcutta University.
1954: *Undergraduate Students in Kolkata : How they Live and Work.* Calcutta University.
1957 : *Study of Change in Traditional Culture.* Kolkata : Calcutta University.
1962 : *How Guardians Plan Education.* Kolkata : Calcutta University.
1965: *Ancient Indian Culture : Contact and Migration.* WBC Press, Sanskrit College.

N.K. BOSE (1901-1972)

Nirmal Kumar Bose was born in Kolkata on 22 January, 1901. He received his early education in Anglo-Sanskrit School, Patna, Sagar Datta Free High School, Kamarhati, 24 Parganas, Ranchi Zila School, Ranchi, and Puri Zila School, Puri. For his college education he went to Scottish Church College, Presidency College and University College of Science, Kolkata. He passed matriculation examination in 1917, Intermediate Science Examination in 1919, B.Sc. Geology (Hons.) in 1921, and M.Sc. Anthropology in 1925. He got first division in all the examinations.

He got appointment as Research Fellow in Anthropology at Calcutta University in 1929-30, but he could not join it due to Salt Satyagraha Movement to which he was closely and actively related. Again in 1937, he was invited by Shyama Prasad Mukherjee, the then Vice Chancellor, to join in Anthropology as Assistant Lecturer. He accepted this post and continued to work on this post till 1942. In 1942, he was arrested by the British and had to leave his post. He returned in 1945, and got appointment as Lecturer in Human Geography. He became reader in Geography in Science College, Kolkata.

Bose was invited as a visiting professor in the University of California, Berkley in the Department of South Asian Studies

(1958), University of Chicago, Department of Anthropology (1959). He was also invited at the University Wisconcin and Michigan to deliver lecture on Social and Cultural Change in India. On his return, he was appointed as a Director of Anthropological Survey of India in 1959. He served this post for a period of five years (1959-1964). During this period, he also worked as adviser to the Government of India on Tribal Affairs.

In post-retirement period, he was invited in study team for hill district of Assam under the chairmanship of Tarlok Singh in 1965. In 1966, he was invited by the administration of NEFA to report on educational problems. In 1965, he was again invited by USA to represent India at the Annual Conference of Association for Asian Studies in New York. He delivered lecture on Social and Political Changes in India and also on the Political Philosophy of Mahatma Gandhi in Columbia University, New York, University of California, Berkley, University of Michigan, Anna Arbor, Duke University North California, University of New York, and Harvard University, Washington.

In recognition of his excellent work in Anthropology, N.K. Bose was awarded Annandale Gold Medal of Asiatic Society of Bengal in 1948. He was elected as President of Anthropology and Archacology Section of Indian Science Congress in 1949. He was elected as Fellow of National Institute of Science of India in 1955. In course of his career, he became life member of a large number of professional organisations. He was also invited by a number of organisations to deliver special lectures.

Professor N.K. Bose, a devoted social worker, served in various capacities in many philanthropic organisations. He served as a volunteer in famine relief organisation by Sadharan Brahma Samaj in Bankura district in 1917, as an honorary Director in Goa Bagan Working Men's Institution in 1919 and as Chairman of Pali Seva Niketan. He organised Khadi Sangh in Bolpur in 1930. In 1940, he was invited by Mahatma Gandhi to act as his interpreter and secretary during his march in Bihar and Bengal. He received President's award of Padmashri in 1956.

Publications

1929 : *Cultural Anthropology.* Bombay : Asia Publishing House.
1932 : *Canons of Orissan Architecture.* Kolkata : Ramnanda Chatterjee.
1948 : *Excavations in Mayurbhanj.* Kolkata : Calcutta University.
1953 : *My Days with Gandhi.* Kolkata : Merit Publishers.
1957 : *Problems of National Integration.* Shimla : Indian Institute of Advanced Study.
1959 : *Modern Bengal.* Vidyodya Library, Kolkata.
1959, 1962 : *Studies in Gandhism.* Kolkata : Merit Publishers.
1963 : *Fifty Years of Science in India : Progress of Anthropology and Archaeology.*
1967 : *Culture and Society in India.* Bombay : Asia Publishing House.
1968 : *Selection from Gandhi. Bombay* : Navjiwan Publishing House.
1969 : *Problems of Nationalism.* Kolkata : Allied Publishers.

Books in Bengali Language

1926 : *Konarkar Bibran.* Kolkata : Viswa Bharati Granthalaya.
1949 : *Hindu Samaj Gadan.* Kolkata : Viswa Bharati Granthalaya.
1956 : *Navin O Prachin.* Kolkata : Bengali Publisher.
1954 : *Swaraj O Gandhivad.* Kolkata : B.S. IAP Co. Ltd.
1954 : *Parivarjakar Dacri.* (Book of Travellers). Kolkata.
1961 : *Bharatar Gram Jeevan* (Peasant Life in India). Kolkata : Vanijya Sahitya Parishad.
1967 : *Ganatantrer Sankat.* (Democracy in Danger). Kolkata : Merit Publishers.
1969 : *Gandhi Charit.* Kolkata : Merit Publishers.
1969 : *Gandhi Ki Chao.* Kolkata : Merit Publishers.

Besides above books in English and Bengali, Bose had contributed 700 articles in Journals of National and International repute. He was also editor of the Journal *Man In India,* since 1951.

Impact of Franz Boas

Bose was greatly influenced by Franz Boas, the founder of American Anthropology. He was influenced by the theories of cultural relativism and historical particularism propounded by Franz Boas. Boas had started researches with observation and then moved towards classifications and generalisations rather than starting with a deductive and hypothetical model like evoluationists. Bose supported Boasian formulation that language, race and culture are independent yet historically linked variables.

Influence of A.L. Kroeker

Bose was also influenced by A.L. Kroeker, an another American Anthropologist. He was influenced by the concept of super organic propounded by A.L. Kroeker. But he was also critical of super organic concept of Kroeker. According to Bose, it is true that majority of people play passive role, but they can behave in different ways too. Creative deviant individuals play a significant role in the creation of cultures. History is a witness of a good number of individuals creating changes in society and culture. Hence, the role of individuals in creation and diffusion of culture cannot be ignored.

Impact of Diffusionism

Bose was greatly influenced by the diffusional theory particularly trait distribution study of American Anthropologist Kroeker and Wissler. Following this approach, he had made a study of diffusion and distribution of Spring Festivals Culture Complex (1927), Elements of Temple Architecture (1949) and Basic Material traits in Rural India. His small book *Cultural Anthropology* had attracted the attention of A.L. Kroeker who had made review of this book in the *Journal of American Anthropologist* (1929). Later on, Kroeker and Klukhohn in their *Compendium of Culture : A Critical Review of Concepts and Definition* (1952) had taken as many as 10 citations from Bose's book *Cultural Anthropology* (1929).

Influence of Sigmund Freud

Bose was also influenced by Sigmond Freud to a great extent. However, he had not utilised Freudian theory in most of his writings. But he felt that Freudian concepts had stimulated in him a great deal of interest on the behaviour of individual under stressed condition. Freudian concept of sublimation had helped Bose to understand the apparently paradoxical behaviour of Mahatma Gandhi in the critical situation of Noakhali Pilgrimage in 1946-47.

Influence of Karl Marx

Bose was also influenced by the writings of Karl Marx which had brought revolutionary changes in society through capitalism. But he was critical of Marxism in the same manner as he had done with Kroebar's theory of Superorganicism. According to Bose, human behaviour is much more random, individualistic, and purposive than the theory of economic determinism (Bose, 1940). But he accepted Marxism, the critical significance of social organisation of production in the study of persistence and change in the caste system in India.

Influence of Malinowski

Bose was greatly influenced by the theory of functionalism propounded by Malinowski, a great British Anthropologist who introduced the participant observation technique in Anthropological research. In his book, *Cultural Anthropology* (1929), Bose had taken a functional approach in defining the nature of the culture as an adaptive device organised around what Bose figuratively called Soul of Culture. But he rejected the historicism of functionalist. He had taken a consistent position that the proper domain of Cultural Anthropology is a functional study of Culture Change. Thus, in his book one finds a clear expression of 'Adaptive Function of Culture' and 'Soul of Culture'.

Bose was of opinion that beneath the outer frame of culture, there lies a body of beliefs and sentiments which are responsible for particular manifestation of culture. Such a body of ideas and sentiments grows out of life's philosophy and is consequently conditioned by the needs and aspirations of each particular age. Historical development bring in a number of unresolved problems. If the cultural heritage of an age does not serve those needs, it is sure to undergo changes by those who inherit it. Thus, culture is a perpetually unstable equilibrium with the experience of men.

Bose opined that Hindu textual categories like *Satva*, *Raja*, *Tamas*, and *Dharma, Artha*, *Kama* and *Moksha* may be utilised in the classifications of culture. According to Bose, four distinct categories of behaviour may be identified in any culture. They are: *Vastu* (Material Objects), *Kriya* (Habitual Action), *Samhatic* (Social groupings) and *Tattava* (Knowledge). The last one *Taltava* may be again divided into two: *Vicharamulaka* (based on experiment) and *Vishwasamulaka* (based on faith).

Bose as a Social Worker

Although Bose was an intellectual and writer, he was also a great social worker. At the young age of 17 years, Bose participated in a famine relief operation in Bankura district organised by Sadharan Brahma Samaj in 1917. He used this opportunity to conduct a systematic survey of economic condition of a large number of rural families. This was his self-styled initiation to field study before he had any knowledge of disciplines of anthropology and sociology. In 1921, following the suggestion of C.F. Andrew, Bose and two of his associates organised the repatriation of indentured Indian labourers from Fiji. Here again his passion for religious survey of social facts found expression in conducting detailed census on social background of 1050 persons belonging to 450 families. This survey and census work provided plenty of information as to how Indian rural society placed numerous obstacles in the process of reabsorption and reabsorption of indentured labours who had migrated to other countries from India and wanted to come back their home.

In 1922, Bose had left Presidency College of Kolkata in response to the Non-Cooperation Movement under the leadership of Mahatma Gandhi. From then onwards Gandhiji's ideas and action programme were the major subjects of his intellectual interests. During 1930-1936 he was engaged in Gandhian village reconstruction programme of a slum in outskirt of Bolpur town. Many of his co-workers were untouchables belonging to Harijan, Mochi and Bauri castes. His interest in caste study had developed in course of working for Gandhian village reconstruction programme.

Impact of Silpis (Architect) of Orissa

Bose received his formal training in Anthropology as M.Sc. student in Calcutta University during 1923-24. He came to the discipline of Anthropology by an accident. In 1921, after obtaining his B.Sc. (Hons.) degree in Geology, he was preparing for his career as a Geologist. In Geology, his special interests were in Petrology and Palaeontology. When non-cooperation movement was launched, he decided to leave the Government Science College, Kolkata for ever. He left Kolkata and settled down at Puri. In Puri, he met with a master Silpi (Temple Architect) named Ram Maharana. He initiated Bose to the traditional canons of architecture. He edited an Oriya manuscript on *Shilpa Shastra* which was later published in 1932. Bose learnt from the field that a student of civilisation needed to collect and integrate informations from various sources like texts, material products, specialists and architecture and art. The elegance of ancient Orissan temples had fascinated Bose so much that he had started delivering lectures about these temples to the visitors of India and abroad. It was in this connection that he came in contact with Sir Ashutosh Mukherjee, the then Vice Chancellor of Calcutta University. He persuaded Bose to join the new Department of Anthropology as an M.Sc. student. He passed his M.Sc. examination in Anthropology with brilliant record. His M.Sc. dissertation was on Diffusional study of Spring Festival in India. Since 1923, Bose had published 37 books, 23 in English and 14 in Bengali. He had written more than 700 articles in different Journals of National and International repute. Of these half number belong to the domain of Anthropology proper and rest covered varied interests like politics, travelogues, art, architecture, literature, social work, Gandhian philosophy and Gandhian reconstruction of villages. His many articles have been written in

Bengali. As editor of the Journal *Man In India* since 1951, he had played a very constructive role in encouraging young scholars to publish the result of their research.

Role as Director in Anthropological Survey of India

As referred to earlier that Bose was Director of Anthropological Survey of India during the period 1959-1964. To encourage and highlight the work and researches of Anthropological Survey of India, Bose had divided the research programme of the survey in five phases which were as follows:

Phase I : Study of distribution of material traits all over India and mapping out the pattern of their distribution *vis-à-vis* linguistic areas.

Phase II : Study of few important craft techniques—Pottery, basketry, net making, rope making and other material crafts.

Phase III : Study of Social Organisation of Crafts and of Caste organisation in different regions of India.

Phase IV : The Study of Superstructure of Indian Society through the study of temples, *Mathas* and Kingships

Phase V : Study of the process of modernisation in castes, occupations, urbanisation, tribal movements, social movements and other movements in different parts of India.

Contribution on Caste Study

As referred to earlier, interest towards caste study appeared in the mind of Bose, when he was working in a slum of untouchables in Bolpur town for Gandhian reconstruction programme. On the basis of his experience and scientific outlook, he rejected the myth of divine origin, reincarnation, and notion of purity and pollution. In a series of brilliant articles : *Hindu Method of Tribal Absorption* (1941), *Caste in India* (1951), *Some Aspects of Caste in Bengal* (1958), Bose proposed that the root of persistence of caste system was embedded in economic and cultural security provided by non-competitive, hereditary, vocation based structure of Indian Civilisation as a whole. During 1942-1945, as a political prisoner under British Government, he gave a series of lectures to the fellow political prisoners on the Structure of Hindu Society. These lectures were the basis of his book written in Bengali entitled, "*Hindu Samajer Gadan*" (Structure of Hindu Society, 1949). This book was published few years before, when comparison of civilisation became a proper subject of study by American anthropologist Robert Redfield and his associates Milton Singer, McKim Marriott and others. In this book, Bose highlighted many dimensions of Indian Civilisation and social processes such as tribal enclaves and their absorbtion, the dual themes of self-sufficiency of village communities and their border links with kinship and kingship, fairs, pilgrimage centres, norms of sacred and secular life in ancient texts, social movement in Medieval period in relation to Islam, the impact of British rule, emerging economy of Indian Society, particularly of caste system. From the study of this book, it appears that anthropological study of Indian Civilization involved a combination of many perspectives such as analysis of classical and medieval texts, administrative records, land tenures, study of villages, individual caste associations, wider social network of kingships, fairs, pilgrimage centres and others. The main focus of this book was on the fate of *Varnajati* system at different phases of Indian history.

Bose observed that the historical situation in which *Varnajati* system of social order was established, would not be repeated in modern time. Because the population of India has increased many fold and land per capita decreased considerably. But some values and designs of traditional system were still relevant in modern time, too. Therefore, the traditional value system should not be ignored in the study of Indian Civilisation. Because, they are also in existence in new form. Although the inhabitants of India present diversified scenes on the basis of region, caste, religion, language, dress, food, occupation and material possession, but they share many traits, customs, beliefs, philosophy and others in common. These are handed down from generation to generation. The diversified groups are tied together through the system of *Jajmani* in which each individual caste serves other castes according to hereditary positions and occupations. Interregional and interethnic unity is maintained through festivals, specialists, fairs, and pilgrimage. In this way, Indian Civilisation presents unique example of unity in diversity.

Study of Culture Zones and Pattern of Unity

To the students of Indian society and history, the great cultural divisions of India were Aryan North *vis-à-vis,* Dravidian South. This has also been indicated by Iravati Karve in her extensive study of *Hindu Kinship Organisation in India* (1953). But as an observer of cultural facts and indefatigable traveller, Bose in his *Diary of Wonders* (1940) observed that the division of Indian population on the basis of language was not acceptable. He suggested cultural classifications on the basis of material traits and the technique of their production. For example, North-West continuous with West Central Asia and East continuous with Southern Asia. This proposition was later on elaborately worked out on the basis of extensive survey of distribution of material traits, forms and techniques of potters all over India. Bose's attempt was to show as to how different linguistic zones of India were showing similarity in their many material cultural traits. They shared common materials, forms and technique of pottery.

In his book, "*Peasant Life in India : A Study in Indian Unity and Diversity*", Bose proposed pyramidal imagery of Unity of Indian Civilisation. The structure of Indian unity could be compared with a pyramid. There is more differentiation at the material base of life and progressively less as one mounted to higher and higher.

In an another article, "Geographical Background of Indian Culture" (1950), Bose discussed as to how a kind of uniformity grew up between geographically and even ecologically distinguishable regions of India, through economic tradition of caste system. He also discussed about various traditional cultural media which provided a mechanism through which unifying thoughts and feelings of thinkers, artists, architects, saints of India were brought to the door of most distant communities and enabled them to share some common intellectual and emotional elements of civilization.

In his Jagdish Bose Memorial Lecture (1971), Bose stated that Indian civilization was in contrast to the civilisation of Europe. The civilisation of Europe was essentially based on repeated experience of war leading to the spirit of nationalism. The civilization of India, on the other hand developed a pattern of cultural pluralism under relatively peaceful conditions sheltered by geographical barriers along its frontiers. He was of the opinion that Indian civilisation encouraged diversity of culture, but in its economic organisation, it tried to weave all communities into a network of interdependence, but distinct entities.

Contribution on Civilisation at a Phase of Confidence

According to N.K. Bose, the creative potentiality of traditional structure of Indian Civilisation cannot be assessed properly, if observations are limited only to Medieval and Modern phases of Civilisation. Indian Civilisation should be studied in phases of expansion and confidence. In his article written in Bengali entitled, "Temple of Konarka", Bose referred expensive and confidence phase of Indian Civilisation in a vivid manner. According to him, Konarka temple was built in a glorious period of Odisan history. The King Narsingh Deo of Ganga dynasty had just defeated the Sultan of Gaura with the support of his powerful army. The state was prosperous and the people were infused with passionate mood to enjoy life and assert independence. Architects were brought and they tried to give shape of confidence and livelihood in their work. The sculptures are full of light. The mind of sculptors and architects were not laden with any false shame. Even today, the temple of Konarka presents picture of a bygone confidence of past.

Bose tried to capture the expressive modern thrust of Indian Civilisation through a number of critical character sketches of few outstanding personality. In his book written in Bengali, "*Navin-O-Prachin*", Bose wrote about Gandhi's Satyagraha and search of truth, Tagore's creative pursuits and paintings, Jamini Roy's view on Art and Ram Kinkar Baij's painting. Although Bose was a student of Indian Civilisation but he did not attempt to distinguish the concept of civilization from the concept of culture. He had thrown some general hints about characteristics of a civilisation.

In case of encounter of East and West in Bengal, Bose was of the opinion that the civilisation of Bengal could not be defined in terms of spatial and temporal continuity of tradition. According to him, in the venture of cultural recognition, Bengali culture was always in the process of becoming, instead of merely being. This tradition of becoming something is the characteristic of any civilisation. In this way, study of civilisation is essentially a study of inner moods, i.e. matters of mind responding to the changing life experiences of a people.

Contribution on Problem of National Integration and Modernisation

Bose had delivered a series of lecturers on the problem of National Integration at Indian Institute of Advanced Study, Shimla in 1966. The main theme of these lectures was the development of post-independence of sub-nationalist movement. He was of the opinion that main causes of emergence of sub-nationalist movements were unequal social, economic, political, and regional developments. Under such circumstances, the rise of middle class took place. Middle class created boundaries around narrow parochial lines in order to consolidate their sectorial advantage.

Bose took a constant plea against a communal basis for administrative categorisation of backwardness. His suggestion was that modern India should set her primary task and dispersal of political powers irrespective of caste and communities. Being the Commissioner for Scheduled Castes and Scheduled Tribes during 1967-1969, he emphasized upon the same points in his various reports.

Contribution on Gandhism

Bose was greatly influenced by the ideologies of Mahatma Gandhi. Right from Non-Cooperation Movement in 1921, he was an ardent student of Gandhian philosophy and ideology. He was influenced by Gandhiji's experiments on truth with ordinary people. Instead of depending upon middle class intelligentsia to spearhead political movement, Gandhiji focused upon common people to bring social change. His intellectual involvement with Gandhism was through three phases :

- Classification of whole range of Gandhian ideologies in cluster of themes.
- Critical analysis of Gandhian and economic action plan.
- Explanation of political ideas of Gandhi.

Bose had published a number of books on Gandhian ideology and philosophy. For example, *Selection from Gandhi* (1934, 1952 and 1968), *My Days with Gandhi* (1953), *Gandhi Charit* (1969), and *Gandhi Ki Chao* (1969).

Contribution on Prehistoric Archaeology

Bose had carried out pioneering field research in Palaeolithic archaeology of Mayurbhanj in collaboration with Dharni Sen. The work was designed to establish stratigraphic sequence between different types of tools recovered by excavation. Hitherto different types of tools in Peninsular India was used almost as index fossils, without talking the stratigraphic context in consideration. He was completely against this practice. He attempted to establish purely on the bases of stratigraphy and tectonic movements, a regional scale which might be used later on for dating a nearby area, instead of using the pluvial and glacial cycle sequences established in far away places like Narmada Valley and Soan Valley. His another attempt was to correlate the finding of prehistory with contemporary ethnographic informations on ancient crafts like pottery and casting of non-ferrous metals.

Contribution on Research Methodology

Bose was influenced to a great extent by American School of Diffusionism as appears from the study of his book, "*Cultural Anthropology*" (1926). In the study of distribution of temple elements and architecture, he attempted to date the temple by combining the distributional techniques with epigraphical information. One of his major conclusion was that different elements of architecture travelled at different rates in space. As a director of Anthropological Survey of India, he encouraged researches for collecting informations on distribution of selected traits from all over India and some major ancient craft techniques.

D.N. MAJUMDAR (1903-1960)

Dhirendra Nath Majumdar was born on June 3 of 1903 at Patna. He was the second son of his parents Mrs. Kusum Kumari and Mr. Rebati Mohan Majumdar. Mr. Rebati Mohan Majumdar was a Zamindar of Kushumathy Estate (Dacca, Bangladesh). Kushum Kumari had come to his brother Mr. Jagdish Chandra Dutta, who was a Magistrate in Patna at that time. At Patna, she delivered her second child who was named as Dhirendra Nath Majumdar.

Majumdar was educated at Dacca Government College, University College, Kolkata, Cambridge University, London, and Dalton Laboratory, London. He passed his matriculation and intermediate science examinations with first division from Dacca Government College. He was admitted to Faculty of Arts of University College, Kolkata for graduate study. He graduated from University College with distinction in Bachelor's examination in 1922. In 1924, he received his M.Sc. degree in Anthropology from Kolkata University and topped the list among all first class candidates. In the same year, he made his first trip to Chotanagpur. Here, he was initiated into an anthropological fieldwork by veteran ethnographer Sarat Chandra Roy, the father of Indian ethnology, first Indian ethnographer and first Indian anthropologist. In 1926, he was awarded by much coveted Premchand Roychand Scholarship of Kolkata University in his recognition of already done researches. The study enabled him to continue his researches 'On Ho tribe of Kolhan (Chaibasa)'. In 1929, he was awarded by the Mount Gold Medal from Calcutta University.

In 1928, Majumdar was appointed as a lecturer in Primitive Economics in the Department of Economics and Sociology at the University of Lucknow. After a period of five years, he went to Cambridge in 1933 to study Social Anthropology with Professor T.C. Hadon and Physical Anthropology with Professor G.M. Morant. While at London, he also got a chance to attend Malinowski's Seminar at London School of Economics. Here he was greatly influenced by Malinowski's theory of functionalism. He received his Ph.D. degree from Cambridge University in 1935. He was elected as a fellow of Royal Anthropological Institute of Great Britain and Ireland in 1936. While at Cambridge he also delivered a series of lectures on Indian Culture. After receiving his doctoral degree, he visited to Vienna, where he delivered a series of lectures on Tribal Culture in India.

Majumdar returned to India in 1936 and joined his old post at Lucknow University. In 1936, he presided over the Anthropology and Archaeology Section of Indian Science Congress held at Lahore. In 1941, he was elected as a fellow of National Institute of Sciences. He was also elected as a fellow of American Association of Physical Anthropology. He was awarded a Research Medal by Gujarat Research Society, Bombay in 1950 and Anandale Gold Medal by Asiatic Society of Bengal in 1958, for his contribution to Asian Anthropology.

Majumdar was invited by a number of national and international organisations to deliver the lectures and undertake *ad hoc* researches. He delivered Rathodkar Memorial Researchship Lecture at Nagpur University in 1946. He was visiting Professor of Cornell University, U.S.A. (1952-53), and School of Oriental and African Studies (1957-58). He attended a number of International Anthropological Congresses organised by Wenner Green Foundation in New York (1952), World Conference on Population held in Rome (1954) and International Sociological Conference in Paris (1954).

In 1945, he founded the Ethnographic and Folk Culture Society. He started the publication of a quarterly Journal, *Eastern Anthropologist* in 1947. He was member of number of national bodies like the Research Programme Committee of Planning Commission (1955-60), Member of Central Advisory Board for Anthropology (1958), Indian Council of Medical Research (1958). He also presided over a number of National Conferences such as Indian Sociological Conference and Convention of Indian Anthropologists.

In 1946, the University of Lucknow had promoted him to the post of Reader in Department of Economics and Sociology and Professor of Anthropology in the same institution in 1950. In 1951, the University of Lucknow created a separate Department of Anthropology, the third university in India to do so. The first was Calcutta University in 1920 and second was Delhi University in 1947. Thus, in 1950, he was made Professor of Anthropology in Lucknow University.

Majumdar collaborated with Morris E. Opler of Cornell University in project on village studies near Lucknow in 1953. This was followed by another village study near Delhi. An ambitious City Survey of Kanpur was undertaken by him in collaboration of Dr. N.S. Reddy former Head, Department of Anthropology, Madras University. This project was financed by the Research Programme Committee and final report came out a few weeks before his death. A third major project on process and problems of Physical Growth among children in U.P., financed by Indian Council of Medical Research was in progress at the time of his death.

On April 1, 1960 he took over as Dean, Faculty of Arts at the University of Lucknow. Two months later on May 31, 1960 he breathed his last.

Contribution through Research Papers

1923 : "The Custom of Burning Effigies of Straw on the Last Day of Bengali Month". *Man In India,* 3 : 3&4, 202-05.

1923 : "Notes on Kali Nauch in the District of Dacca". *Man In India,* 3 : 3&4, 202-05.

1923 : "Customs and Taboos Observed by an East Bengal Women from Pregnancy to Children". *Man In India,* 3 : 3&4, 232-42.

1924 : "Physical Characteristics of the Hos of Kolhan". *Man in India,* Vol. 5 : 83-114.

1924 : "The Traditional Origin of Hos : With a Brief Description of Chief Bongas (Gods of Hos)". *Journal and Proceedings of Asiatic Society of Bengal,* Vol. 20, 193-98.

1924 : "Some Characteristics of Kolarian Songs". *Journal and Proceedings of Asiatic Society of Bengal,* Vol. 20, 181-92.

1924 : "On the Terminology of Relationships of the Hos of Kolhan". *Journal and Proceedings of Asiatic Society of Bengal,* Vol. 20, 199-204.

1924 : "A Few Remarks on Sema Naga Kinship Terms". *Man In India*, Vol. 4, 193-208.

1925 : "Some Ethnographic Notes on Hos of Kolhan". *Man In India,* Vol. 5, 183-89.

1925 : "Some Outdoor and Sedentary Games of the Hos of Kolhan". *Man In India,* Vol. 5, 190-98.

1925 : "Hargari and Its Origin". *Man In India,* Vol. 5, 199-204.

1925 : "Religion of the Kols". *12th Proceeding of Indian Science Congress,* 12 : 265.

1925 : "The Physical Characteristics of the Kols". *12th Proceeding of Indian Science Congress,* 12:266.

1926 : "The Polias, Babupolias, Polias aur Rajvanshi : An Instance of Conversion of Tribes into Castes in Bengal". *13th Proceeding of Indian Science Congress,* 13 : 326.

1926 : "The Kinship Terms of the Polias, Babupolias and Rajvanshis". *Abstract of Proceeding of 13th Indian Science Congress,* 13 : 326.

1926 : "A Few Types of Dramatic and Sedentary Games of the Hos of Kolhan". *Abstract of Proceeding of 13th Indian Science Congress,* 13:326.

1926 : "Marriage Customs of the Hos of Kolhan". *(Abstract) Proceeding of 13th Indian Science Congress,* 13 : 327.

1926 : "The Belief about Disease, Death and After". *(Abstract) Proceeding of 13th Indian Science Congress,* 13 : 327.

1926 : "Ethnographic Notes about Ideas of Eclipses, Ex-communication, Adoption, Rainmaking, Hoarfrosts, Hail-Stones, Dream and Earthquakes of the Hos". *Abstract of the Proceeding of 13th Indian Science Congress,* 13 : 327.

1926 : "Ho Life in Ho Riddles". *Abstract of Proceeding of 13th Indian Science Congress,* 13:327.

1926 : "Pseudo-Rajput : The Polias, Palias, Babupolias or Rajvanshi of North Bengal : An Instance of Formation of Tribes in Castes". *Man In India,* Vol. 6, 155-73.

1926 : "The Bigonial Breadth of Some Hos of Kolhan". *Journal and Proceeding of Asiatic Society of Bengal,* Vol. 22, 347-49.

1927 : "A Few Types of Ho Songs". *Journal and Proceeding of Asiatic Society of Bengal,* Vol. 23, 27-36.

1927 : "Death and Connected Ceremonies Among the Hos of Kolhan". *Journal and Proceeding of Asiatic Society of Bengal,* Vol. 23, 37-44.

1927 : "Some of the Worship Festivals of the Hos of Kolhan". *Journal and Proceeding of Asiatic Society of Bengal,* Vol. 23, 277-85.

1928 : "Some Norms of Ho Culture". *Abstract of Proceeding of 15th Indian Science Congress,* 15-317.

1928 : "The Cult of the Dead Among the Hos". *Abstract of Proceeding of the 15th Indian Science Congress,* p., 318.

1929 : "Race and Adaptability". *Journal and Proceeding of Asiatic Society of Bengal,* Vol. 25, 149-56.

1929 : "Maternity and Couvade in Primitive Society". *Man In India,* Vol. 9, 66-71.

1929 : "The Korwas of United Province". *Man In India,* Vol. 9, 237-50.

1929 : "The Sex and Sex Control in Primitive Society". *Man In India,* Vol. 10, 104-15.

1930 : "The Social Organisation Among the Korwas". *Man In India,* Vol. 10, 104-15.

1930 : "The Economic Background of Social Institutions in Primitive Society". *Man In India,* Vol. 10, 160-6.

1930 : "Totemism and Origin of Clans". *Journal of America Oriental Society,* Vol. 50, 221-232.

1930 : "The Korwa and their Country". *Abstract of Proceeding of 17th Indian Science Congress,* 17 : 395.

1930 : "The Cycle of Life Among the Korwas". *Abstract of Proceeding of 17th Indian Science Congress,* 17 : 396.

1931 : "The Clash and Fusion of Cultures in Dudhi Pargana of Mirzapur District, U.P.". *Man In India,* Vol. 11, 54-55.

1931 : " The Darlung Kukis of the Lushai Hill". *Man In India,* Vol. 11, 55-56.

1931 : "The Position of Women in Ho Society". *Man In India,* Vol. 11, 56.

1931 : "Sorcery and Divination of Primitive Society". *Man In India,* Vol. 11, 65-67.

1931 : "The Economic Life of the Hos". *Man In India,* Vol. 11, 57.

1931 : "Economic Background of Social Institutions". *Abstract of Proceeding of 18th Indian Science Congress,* 18 : 414.

1931 : "Economic Life in Primitive Society". *Abstract of Proceeding of 18th Indian Science Congress,* 18 : 15.

1931 : "Forms and Functions of Primitive Religion". *Abstract of Proceeding of 18th Indian Science Congress,* 18 : 415.

1931 : "Marriage and Marital Life Among Rawaltas" (with S.D. Bahuguna). *Abstract of Proceeding of 18th Indian Science Congress,* 18 : 415.

1931 : "Religious Life Among Rowaltas" (with S.D. Bahuguna). *Abstract of Proceeding of 18th Indian Science Congress,* 18 : 416.

1931 : "Festivals Among the Rawaltas" (with S.D. Bahagnua). *Abstract of Proceeding of 18th Indian Science Congress,* 18 : 416.

1932 : "Marital Problem : A Reorientation". *Man In India*, Vol. 12, 161-74.

1932 : "The Cycle of Life Among the Korwas". *Man in India,* Vol. 12, 255-75.

1933 : "Disease, Death and Divination Among Certain Primitive Societies in India". *Man In India,* Vol. 13, 115-49.

1936 : "The Decline of Primitive Tribes in India". *The Journal of United Provinces Historical Society,* April 1936.

1936 : "A Plea for Better Treatment of Aboriginal Population in India". *Kolkata Review,* October : 67-75.

1936 : "Food and Feeding in Austric Tribes". *Abstract of Proceeding of Indian Science Congress,* 23 : 395.

1936 : "The Spirit of Bongaism". *Abstract of Proceeding of Indian Science Congress,* 23 : 397.

1937 : "Comparative Anthropometry of a Group of Saoras of Both Sexes". *Man In India,* Vol. 17 : 17.

1937 : "Some Aspects of Economic Life of the Bhokasas and Tharus of Nainital Tarai". *Journal of Anthropological Society,* Bombay, Jubilee Vol. : 133-135.

1937 : "The Cultural Pattern of Tharus". *Abstract of Proceeding of Indian Science Congress,* 24 : 335.

1937 : "The Material Culture of Rawaltas of Rawain" (with S.D. Bahuguna). *Abstract of Proceeding of Indian Science Congress,* 24 : 338.

1938 : "Racial Admixture in United Provinces". *Man In India,* Vol. 18, 9-18.

1938 : "Modern Trends in Social Anthropology". *Kolkata Review,* February 162-76.

1938 : "The Marriage and Nishpat Customs of Rishis". *Man In India,* Vol. 18 : 59.

1938 : "The Tribal Population and Christianity". *Modern Review,* May.

1938 : "Race and Language in India". *Nature,* Vol. 141 : 1019.

1938 : "The Relationships of Austric Speaking Tribes of India with Special Reference to the Measurement of Hos and Saoras". *Proceeding of Indian Academy of Sciences,* Vol. 7, 1-21.

1939 : "The Murias of Narayanpur, Bastar State" (with Kumar Indrajit Singh). *Man In India,* Vol. 19 : 68.

1939 : "Sex and Marriage in Doon District". *Kolkata Review,* March, 309-18.

1939 : "The Tribal Culture and Acculturation". Presidential Address, Section of Anthropology and Archaeology, 26th Indian Science Congress, 26:19 also in *Man In India,* Vol. 19, 99-173.

1939 : "Primitive Society and Its Discomfort". *Proceeding of Second Population and Family Conference.*

1940 : "The Cultural Pattern of a Polyandrous People of Jaunsar Bawar in Dehradun District". *Journal of United Province Historical Society,* Vol. 13, 35-50.

1940 : "Blood Groups and their Distribution in Certain Castes of United Provinces". *Science and Culture,* Vol. 5, 519-22.

1940 : "Bongaism". In *Essays in Anthropology* presented in Rai Bahadur Sarat Chandra Roy, J.P. Mills, D.N. Majumdar *et. al* (eds.), Lucknow, Maxwell and Company.

1940 : "Some Aspects of Life of the Khasas of Cis Himalayan Region". *Journal and Proceedings of Asiatic Society of Bengal,* Vol. 6, 1-44.

1941 : "Bacial Affiliation of the Gonds of Central Provinces". *Journal and Proceedings of Asiatic Society of Bengal,* Vol. 7, 35-56.

1941: "Blood Groups of Criminal Tribes". *Science and Culture,* Vol. 7, 334.

1941 : "Blood Groups of Criminal Tribes". *Man In India,* Vol. 22, 239-44.

1942 : "Blood Groups of the Doms". *Man In India,* Vol. 22, 239-44.

1942 : "The Tharus and Their Blood Groups". *Journal of the Royal Asiatic Society of Bengal,* Vol. 8, 25-38.

1942 : "Anthropometric Measurements of the Bhils". *Journal of Gujarat Research Society,* Vol. 4, 220-37.

1943 : "Blood Groups of Tribes and Castes of U.P. with Special Reference to the Korwas". *Journal of the Royal Asiatic Society of Bengal,* Vol. 11, 81-94.

1944 : "Racial Affiliation of Bhils of Gujarat". *Journal of Gujarat Research Society,* Vol. 6, 172-86.

1944 : "Review of Verrier Elwin's Book, 'Maria Murder and Suicide'." *Man In India,* Vol. 22, 88-94.

1944 : "What is Frazerism". *Man In India,* Vol. 24, 172-86.

1946 : "The Malaise of Culture in Snowballs of Garwal". (Folk Culture Series) (ed.) by D.N. Majumdar, Lucknow : Universal Publishers.

1946 : "Biometric Analysis of Anthropological Measurements on Castes and Tribes of United Province". (with P.C. Mahalanobis and C.R. Rao), *Proceedings of Indian Science Congress,* 23:138.

1947 : "Anthropology During the War". *Journal of American Anthropologist,* Vol. 49, 159-64.

1947 : "United Provinces—A Cultural Mosaic". In S.C. Dube's book Field Songs of Chhattisgarh, Lucknow : Universal Publishers.

1947 : "Racial Problems in Asia". Indian Council of World Affairs.

1947 : "Progress of Anthropology in India (1911-1946) : A Brief Review". Jointly published by Indian Science Congress Association and the Council of Scientific and Industrial Research, p. 31.

1947 : "Blood Group Distribution to United Provinces". (with Kunwar Kishan) *Eastern Anthropologist,* Vol. 1, 69-70.

1947 : "Some Folk Tales of Kolhan". In S.C. Dube's *Field Songs of Chhattisgarh,* Lucknow : The Universal Publishers Ltd.

1947 : "A Report on Serological Survey of United Provinces". 1941 Census, *Eastern Anthropologist,* Vol. 1, 8-15.

1947 : "The Criminal Tribes of Northern India". *Journal of Eastern Anthropologist,* Vol. 1, 33-40.

1947 : "Review of W.G. Archer's. 'The Vertical Man'." *Eastern Anthropologist,* Vol. 1, 66-68.

1947 : "Review of W.V. Grigson's, 'Challenges of Backwardness'." *Eastern Anthropologist,* 69-70.

1948 : "Rh Frequency in People of Lucknow". *Heredity,* Vol. 2, 399-40.

1948 : "Blood Groups in Gujarat Population". (with K. Kishan), *Gujarat Journal of Research Society,* Vol. 10, 161.

1948 : "Review of Verrier Elwin's book 'Muria and their Gothul'." *Eastern Anthropologist,* Vol. 142-47.

1948 : "Review of Marriage Magazine". *Eastern Anthropologist,* Vol. 1, 33-40.

1948 : "Review of Furer-Haimendorf's book 'The Reddis of the Bison Hills'." *Eastern Anthropologist,* Vol. 1, 48-49.

1948 : "Review of Swami Akhilananda's 'Hindu Psychology'." *Eastern Anthropologist,* Vol. 1, 49-50.

1948 : "Review of Mrs. Iravati Karve's 'Anthropometric Measurements of Marathas'." *Eastern Anthropologist,* Vol. 1, 50-51.

1949 : "Serological Status of Castes and Tribes of Cultural Gujarat". (with Kunwar Kishan), *Eastern Anthropologist,* Vol. 2, 92-97.

1949 : "Report of Racial Serological and Health Survey of Gujarat". Part II, *Anthropometric Status of Tribes and Castes of Gujarat* (with A.K. Sen), *Journal of Gujarat Research Society,* Vol. 11, 118.

1949 : "Anthropometric Survey of United Provinces : A Statistical Study". (with Mahalanobis and C.R. Rao), *Sankhya,* Vol. 9, 89-304.

1949 : "The Racial Basis of Indian Social Structure". *Journal of Eastern Anthropologist,* Vol. 2, 145-52.

1949 : "Review of C. Von Furer-Haimendorf's 'The Raj Gond of Adilabad'." *Eastern Anthropologist.* Vol. 2, 171-73.

1949 : "Racial Element in Gujarat". *Journal of Gujarat Research Society,* Vol. 11, 188.

1949 : "Anthropometry and Crime". *Man In India,* Vol. 29, 46-58.

1949 : "Growth Trends in Aboriginal Boys of Kolhan". *Eastern Anthropologist,* Vol. 2, 201-04.

1949 : "Changing Canvas of Tribal Life". *Eastern Anthropologist,* Vol. 3, 40-47.

1949 : "Hamari Sanskriti Ka Vikas". (Hindi) *Parechya Manure Vigyanik,* Vol. 1, 21-35.

1949 : "The Social Economy of the Bhotiyas". In K.S. Pangtey's *Lonely Furrows of the Border Land,* Lucknow : Universal Publishers.

1949 : "Racial Status of Nuniya, Nunera, Gota, Agaria, Shorgar, Kharkar, and Similar Castes of Etah, Mainpuri and Farrukhabad, U.P. ". *Eastern Anthropologist,* Vol. 3, 101-19.

1950 : "Review of C. Klukhohn and Henry A. Murray's (eds.) 'Personality in Nature, Society and Culture'." *Eastern Anthropologist,* Vol. 3, 113-14.

1950 : "ABO Blood Among the Garos of Eastern Pakistan". *Man In India,* Vol. 30, 32-25.

1950-51 : "The Sankha Bank of Dacca". *Eastern Anthropologist,* Vol. 4, 98-103.

1950-51 : "Review of A.V. Thakkar's 'Tribes of India'." *Eastern Anthropologist,* Vol. 4, 116-17.

1950-51 : "Review of Stephan Fuchs, 'The Children of Hari'." *Eastern Anthropologist,* Vol. 4, 112:15.

1951 : "The Tribal Rehabilitation in India". *International Social Science Bulletin,* Vol. 3, 802-13.

1951 : "Review of Cora Du-Bois The People of Alor : A Social Psychological Study of an Eastern Indian Island". *Eastern Anthropologist,* Vol. 4, 189-91.

1951 : "Manav Riti Vigyan Tatha Jana Sanskriti Samiti Uttar Pradesh". *Prachya Manav Vaigyanik,* Vol. 2, 1-3.

1951: "Adim Jatiya Jivan Men Prayog". *Prachya Manav Vaigyanik,* Vol. 2, 72-93.

1951-52 : "ABO Blood in India" (with S. Bahadur), *Eastern Anthropologist*, Vol. 5, 101-22.

1952 : "Review of Laura Thomson's 'Culture In Crisis : A Study of the Hoki Indians'." *Eastern Anthropologist,* Vol. 6, 90-92.

1952 : "Adivasi Jivan Ki Chunauti". *Aaj-Kal,* Vol. 8, 15-18.

1953 : "Children in Polyandrous Society". *Eastern Anthropologist,* Vol. 6, 177-89.

1953 : "On Acculturation". *An Appraisal of Anthropology Today,* SolTax *et. al.* (eds.), Chicago : Chicago University Press, 125-26.

1953 : "On National Character". *An Appraisal of Anthropology Today,* SolTax *et. al.* (eds.), Chicago : Chicago University Press, 139.

1953 : "On Prestige and Food". *An Appraisal of Anthropology Today,* SolTax *et. al.* (eds.), Chicago : Chicago University Press, 146.

1953 : "On Anthropology and Medicine". *An Appraisal of Anthropology Today,* SolTax *et. al.* (eds.) Chicago : Chicago University Press, 175.

1953 : "On Anthropology in Government". *An Appraisal of Anthropology Today*, Chicago: Chicago University Press, 183-84.

1953 : "On Cultural-Social Anthropology". *An Appraisal of Anthropology Today,* SolTax *et. al.* (eds.) Chicago: Chicago University Press, 222.

1953 : "On Genetics and Social Selection". *An Appraisal of Anthropology Today,* SolTax *et. al.* (eds.) Chicago: Chicago University Press, 272.

1953 : "On Anthropology as a Field of Study". *An Appraisal of Anthropology Today,* SolTax *et. al.* (eds.) Chicago: Chicago University Press, 343-45.

1953 : "The Aboriginal Tribes of Orissa". *March In India,* Vol. 6, 54-56.

1953 : "Modern Trends and Anthropological Research". *Lucknow Orientation,* 40th Session, Indian Science Congress Souvenir, 23-37.

1953 : "India, Pakistan and Ceylone". *International Directory of Anthropological Institutions,* Williams L. Thomas, Jr. and Anna M. Pikilis (eds.), New York : Winner Gren Foundation for Anthropological Research, 67-77.

1954 : "Status of Women in Patrilocal Societies in South Asia". In *Status of Women in South Asia,* (eds.) Bombay : Oriental Longmans Ltd.

1954 : "The Religious Life of Ho". *Man In India,* Vol. 34, 346-50.

1954 : "Ethnic Frontiers and Caste Distance in Uttar Pradesh". In *31st All India Medical Conference Souvenir,* 19-33.

1954 : "Caste and Race". In Professor G.S. Ghurye Felicitation Volume (eds.) by K.M. Kapadia, Bombay : Popular Book Depot.

1955 : "Marriage and Family in Polyandrous Society". *Eastern Anthropologist,* Vol. 8, 85-110.

1955 : "Demographic Structure in a Polyandrous Village". *Rural Profiles,* Vol. 1, 32-44.

1955 : "Intercaste Relation in Gohana-Kalan". *Eastern Anthropologist,* Vol. 8, 191-214.

1955 : "Review of J.J. Honigmann's Culture and Personality". *Eastern Anthropologist,* Vol. 9, 63-67.

1955 : "The Dynamics of Social Change". Address of the Sectional President, Agra University, *Journal of Research,* Vol. 3, 39-43.

1955 : "The Chero Tribe of Bihar." *March of India,* Vol. 7, 39-43.

1955 : "The Eye and the Anthropologist". *Journal of Gandhi Eye Hospital and Aligarh Muslim University Institute of Ophthalmology, Special Number,* 65-69.

1955 : "Rural Analysis : Problems and Prospects". *Eastern Anthropologist,* Vol. 9, 92-103.

1956: "What Sociologist Can Do, What They Must Do, How They Can Do and How They Should Do It?". *Journal of Eastern Anthropologist,* Vol. 10, 130-43.

1956 : "Educated Unemployment : Nature and Extent of Unemployment in University Student". *Eastern Anthropologist,* Vol. 10, 43-51.

1956 : "Awadh Ke Ek Gram Me Parivarik Jivan". *Samaj*, Vol. 2, 525-30.

1956 : "A Little Community : A Polyandrous Village Jadi in Chakrata Tehsil, Dehradun District". *Journal of Sociology Association,* Christ Church College, Kanpur, 1-4.

1956 : "Anthropology and Primitive Medicine". *Manav Darpan,* Organ of Anthropology Club, Lucknow University, Vol. 1, 1-4.

1957 : "Functioning of School System in Polyandrous Society in Jaunsar Bawar" (with S.K. Anand). *Eastern Anthropologist,* Vol. 11, 36-41.

1958 : "Rural Life and Communication". *Eastern Anthropology,* Vol. 11, 175-88.

1958 : "Rupkhand in Rural Literature". *Eastern Anthropologist,* Vol.11, 36-41.

1958 : "Rupkhand Rahasya". *Prachya Manav Vaigyanik,* Vol. 3, 1-8.

1959 : "A Village School in Context of Tribal Education in Jaunsar Bawar". *Manav Darpan,* Vol. 3, 1-8.

1959 : "Rupkhand in Prospect and Retrospect, Uttar Pradesh". March, 1-12.

1959 : "Shramdan : An Aspect of Action Anthropology". *Indian Sociologist,* Vol. 1, 1-3.

1959 : "Indian Anthropologists in Action". *Journal of Social Research,* Vol. 2, 10-15.

1959 : "The Light that Failed." *Journal of Social Research,* Vol. 2, 907.

1960 : "Review of Thomas O Beidelman's 'Comparative Analysis of Jajmani System'." *Man,* Vol. 60, 80.

1960 : "Ho" in *Bihar Ke Adivasi*, edited by L.P. Vidyarthi, Patna College Centre, 111-25.

1960 : "Adivasi Aur Unki Samasyayen". In *Bihar Ke Adivasi* edited by L.P. Vidyarthi, Patna College Centre, 180-96.

1960 : "Lineage Structure in a Himalayan Society". *International Journal of Comparative Sociology.*

Books

1937 : *A Tribe in Transition : A Study in the Culture Pattern. Kolkata and London* : Longmans Green and Company.

1944 : *Fortune of Primitive Tribes.* Lucknow : Universal Publishers Ltd.

1944 : *Races and Cultures of India.* Allahabad : Kitabistan.

1946 : *Race Elements in Gujarat.* Bombay : Gujarat Research Society Publication.

1947 : *The Matrix of Indian Culture.* Lucknow : Universal Publishers Ltd.

1950 : *The Affairs of a Tribe : A Study in Tribal Dynamics.* Lucknow : Universal Publishers Ltd.

1956 : *An Introduction to Social Anthropology* (with T.N. Madan). Bombay : Asia Publishing House.

1958 : *Caste and Communication in an Indian Village.* Bombay : Asian Publishing House.

1958 : *Jati Parivartan Ke Prakran Men.* Bombay : Asia Publishing House.

1960 : *Race Elements in Bengal* (with C.R. Rao). Bombay : Asia Publishing House.

1960 : *Chor Ka Ek Gaon.* Bombay : Asia Publishing House.

1960 : *Social Contour of an Industrial City.* Bombay : Asia Publishing House.

1962 : *Himalayan Polyandry.* Bombay : Asia Publishing House.

Contribution in Cultural Anthropology

The major part of Majumdar's published work was in the area of ethnography. As a student of behavioural aspect of man, his approach was that of a cultural anthropologist, rather than that of social anthropologist. He regarded the works of man or products of human activity—language, magic, religion, art, groups, institutions, goods and services as a subject matter of cultural anthropology. In his opinion, social anthropology was a sub-discipline within cultural anthropology. His approach to the study of human culture was that of functionalists. He regarded functionalism as the best method for collection and interpretation of data concerning human behaviour. Majumdar made study of cultures, not of problems. In his all ethnographic works—articles and monographs—he included a discussion on cultural dynamics. He maintained and followed Malinowski's teaching that although changes are ever occurring in culture, yet it retains its character of being an integrated whole. But Majumdar did not make any distinction between content and function as Malinowski did. He was also influenced by Benedict's study of culture pattern. His Ph.D. thesis was published in the form of book under the title, "*A Tribe in Transition : A Study in Culture Pattern*" (1937). This book bears testimony that he was influenced by Benedict's theory of culture pattern. This book is regarded as the first scientific study of impact of modern civilization on an Indian tribe.

His another book, "*Fortunes of Primitive Tribes*" (1944) deals with ethnographic essays on various tribes of Uttar Pradesh. He also underscored the importance of studying the psychological dimensions of human behaviour particularly in the study of culture change. His book "*Affairs of Tribe : A Study in Tribal Dynamics*" deals with the change occurring in tribal cultures of India.

His contribution on cultural anthropology consisted of ethnographic accounts of Ho, Khasa, Korwa, Tharu, Criminal Tribes of U.P., Gonds of Bastar and Bhils of Gujarat. He published his books on the Hos and the Khasas whom he knew very well by his fieldwork. He wrote several articles on the above tribes in journals of national and international repute. He was a true fieldworker. He used to visit fields either alone or with his students whenever he got a chance of fieldwork. He had spent nearly 22 summers with the Khasas, totalling five years in them. All fieldwork was done through local dialect. In presenting his data, he covered all aspects of culture, such as language, folklore, religion, art, myth, marriage, family, kinship and economy of various tribes whom they studied.

Contribution on Village Study

Majumdar was the first Indian anthropologist to study and write about the impact of non-tribal culture on the ways of life of Indian tribes. His early interest in the study of culture change led him in 1950 to welcome the emergence of rural studies in India by anthropologists. He played valuable part in this new field of research on villages. Based on village studies, he published his two important books—*Caste and Communication in an Indian village* (1958) and *Chor Ka Ek Gaon* (1960).

The book, "*Caste and Communication in an Indian Village*", was based on fieldwork initially conducted under the auspices of Cornell-Lucknow Research Project financed by Ford Foundation under an agreement signed by Morris E. Opler and D.N. Majmudar. The period of fieldwork in the village Mohana near Lucknow was of two years. The fieldwork was started at the end of 1953 with the help of research investigators and continued till the end of 1955. The fieldwork was conducted with a purpose to analyse the process of culture change specially those induced by Community Development Programme. Majumdar had made a holistic study of the village Mohana. The village had a population of 603 at that time of study distributed into 15 castes. On the basis of an intensive study, the short range history of the village, the intercaste relationship, religious beliefs and practices, life cycle, rituals and other aspects of village cultures were explored and described. Majumdar considered the village as a concept, way of life. According to Majumdar, a village is a concept because it is a constellation of values which change slowly so that the village retains its identity. It is a way of life because people still lives more or less as they used to live before. Majumdar considered the village and town in India as two distinct constellation of values.

In his book, *Caste and Communication in Indian Village* (1958) Majumdar made an elaborate study of intercaste relationships and the process of mobility. He described the process of fusion and fission which had produced innumerable groups. He also gave evidences to support that the caste mobility was both vertical and horizontal. He also claimed that Indian village was not a self-contained unity. Rather village was integrated at different levels with the total social system of the country. But unfortunately, he did not illustrate this contention. Regarding castes and communication, he observed that the villagers used their mother tongue for the purpose of communication. Each individual caste followed the terms of reference and address according to its position in caste hierarchy. They use different languages for communication with their own caste members and for communication with other caste members. Even for communication with own caste group, they use different languages for male, female, boys, girls, adults and aged. Thus, each caste communicate with other caste according to position in the village society.

The next book, *Chor ka Ek Gaon* (1960) is based on research at village Chittora, in Mirzapur district of Eastern Uttar Pradesh, undertaken in 1955 under the direction of M.R. Goodal of Cornell University under Cornell-Lucknow Research Project. Professor D.N. Majmudar had supervised the fieldwork at Chittora village. It was a mixed village of tribals and non-tribals. It had a total population of 830 at the time of study which included 342 tribals. The whole population was distributed into 12 castes and 5 tribal communities. The tribal communities were Kherwar, Manjhi, Chero, Panikar, and Bhuiya. Manuscript was originally written in English by Majmudar but was translated into Hindi by one of his students Chandra Bhall Tripathy who was Deputy Director of Backward Class Commission. The book was published only in Hindi and presented a descriptive account of the village and also reflected the deep concern of the author regarding the process of acculturation which was operating in the village. Although the book claimed to describe all aspects of village life, but economic relationship between castes, festivals of tribals and political integration in the leadership of the village were not given adequate attention. The unity and extension of the village have also not been systematically analysed. But in spite of some of these gaps, the book is of special significance because it reflects Majmudar's attempt to study a village type in which tribals reside with Hindu caste, and who were detribalised and Hinduised. Secondly, this village was characterised by conspicuous absence of any dominant caste unlike most villages studied by anthropologists. Thirdly, it was only the village study of scientific nature available for in Hindi medium at that time. It is also regrettable that this book was not available for non-Hindi speakers and specially to the scholars of Cornell University who sponsored this project.

Contribution in Applied and Action Anthropology

Majmudar pleaded for the application of findings of Anthropology to the task of national development. As a member of Research Programme Committee of Planning Commission of India, he emphasised upon the role played by anthropologists and sociologists in helping the administration and Government by studying and exploring the problems of backward areas and their people and by assessing the impact of Government sponsored programmes of national reconstruction of the people at village level. His posthumously published book, "*Khasa Himalayan Polyandry*" (1962) also contained a detailed discussion of the Community Development Programmes in Jaunsar-Bawar, besides its polyandrous nature.

Contribution on City Study

D.N. Majumdar made a study of Kanpur city which was sponsored by Research Programme Committee and published a book entitled, "*Social Contours on an Industrial City*" (1960). His main purpose behind the study of Kanpur city was to assess the complex conditions of urban life in an industrial metropolis. In the light of his field inquiries as a social anthropologist, Majumdar made a departure from routine type of socio-economic surveys which were carried out in different parts of the country. For the purpose of study, a questionnaire was prepared to study social and cultural factors which bring changes due to industrialisation. The questionnaire was administered among 2000 informants of Kanpur city.

The book is divided into three parts with several chapters in each part : General, the Survey and Family Planning inquiry.

The book ends with an independent section on cultural content of Urbanisation.

In the first part, the Growth of Kanpur as an independent metropolis through decades, the present day civil problems, and nature and extent of industrial employment and unemployment was discussed. Presenting a historical appraisal, the report brought out as to how electric light came to Kanpur in 1909 with the increase in the number of factories. In the beginning, employment opportunity was increased in the city and a regular wage census was taken in 1906. According to this survey, the monthly wage of unskilled workers varied from Rs. 5.6 to Rs. 7.5. For Firemen it varied from Rs. 8 to Rs. 12 and for blacksmith it varied from Rs. 15 to Rs. 30. The improvement trust in Kanpur was established in 1919. In course of time, the industrial metropolis Kanpur continued to make its headway.

Reviewing the present day civic problems, Majumdar found the city full of slums, insanitation, poor public health, lack of planned market centres. He highlighted the absence of civic amenities in several village like settlements on the fringe of the city particularly southern border of Kanpur. In factual appraisal of the industrial employment, he found 273 factories in 1953 providing employment to 68,832 workers. He referred to growing unemployment among the educated young men and suggested several types of vocational training and effective services of Employment Exchange to combat the problem.

In the second part of the book, Majumdar presented field data collected on the basis of sample survey and analysed the data of both migrant and non-migrant as a masculine city. He observed that a total of 43.85 per cent immigrants came to the city due to pull factors. In the chapter on occupation and industry, he classified the people of Kanpur in 63 occupations which were divided further into 29 categories.

In the third part of the book, the author reported about fertility and family planning. For this purpose, 5 per cent married women were selected from the female population of the city. Data were gathered from a total of 1525 married women of different age groups. Data were gathered by the lady investigators trained in sociological and anthropological researches. From the data gathered, a number of tables were prepared for the purpose of explanation and analysis. Tables were related to childbirth indices, maternity pattern, mortality and survival, birth of twins, attitude towards family planning, mother's view on a family size and attitude towards contraceptives.

Unfortunately, cultural content of urbanisation could not attain closer attention. But it provided a statistical data on social life, such as marriage pattern, husband-wife relationship, attitude of husband towards the status of woman and a few casual comments regarding the caste clustering and social life of migrants as well as the impact of Kanpur on the neighbouring villages. In general, it was observed that the lower castes from the villages found an escape in the city from the old stigma of untouchability, while the upper castes from the villages had lost much of their importance in religious and other institutional fields. It was noticed that Kanpur could not change the face of the villages even adjacent to it in regard to various fields of activity, except that the educated persons of the village were the foci of new urban values. Majumdar closed this chapter with following advice :

> "Our towns and cities are growing, our vigilance must not wane, sociologists must line up for social research and help the administration in its assigned task of building an urban population socially aware and mentally conditioned for city life."

Contribution on Physical Anthropology

Majmudar conducted extensive anthropometric and serological surveys in Uttar Pradesh, Bengal, Gujarat, Bihar, and Madhya Pradesh. In this field of methodology, he realised quite early the importance of refined statistical treatment of data. His collaboration with Mahalanobis and Rao resulted in the formulation of D^2 or Generalized Distance Statistics which was recognised as an advanced and highly favoured statisco-taxonomic method in biometrical anthropology.

On the basis of serological studies, he demonstrated the genetic relationship of the population with Uttar Pradesh with those of Bengal in east and Punjab in the west. In the Uttar Pradesh itself, he showed that the caste hierarchy had a biometric basis. Castes showing clusters, being close to each other in hierarchical organisation, were shown to be also within a close range of biometric variation. It was H.H. Risley, the author of *Tribes and Castes of Bengal*—4 Volumes (1891) and *The People of India* (1908), who suggested a link between tribes, castes and race. Majumdar also got his idea from Risley, but he took it further and confirmed it by his own investigation.

In his book, *Races and Culture of India* (1944), Majumdar defined race as a group of people who on the basis of common physical traits can be distinguished from the other groups, even if the members of these biological groups are widely scattered.

Majumdar did not confine his attention to the distributional study of racial characters, but he was interested in the ontogenetic development of Indian children. His study on School Children in the City of Lucknow (1951) was an important landmark in the Physical Anthropological studies in India. At the time of his death, he was supervisor of a research project on, 'Cross-cultural Study of Growth Among Children in Uttar Pradesh'. Data on 30,000 cases were gathered by a team of investigators consisting doctors, physical anthropologists, social workers and statisticians. He was interested in determining purely physical as well as cultural determinants of growth.

At the time of his death, he was also engaged in the study of ABO and Rh blood groups among the Criminal Tribes of Uttar Pradesh. A.E. Mourant regarded Majumdar as pioneer in application of blood group testing of Anthropology in India.

IRAVATI KARVE (1905-1970)

Iravati Karve was born on 15th December, 1905 in Myingyan (Burma). She was educated at Poona in High School for Indian

Girls and later joined Fergusson College. She received her master degree in Sociology from Bombay University in 1927. Her master thesis was on Chitpavan Brahmans. She pursued her Doctoral Research at Berlin (1928-1931) with Dr. Eugene Fisher at Kaiser Wilhelm Institute for Anthropology.

Iravati Karve worked as Registrar of the S.W.O. College, University of Poona (1932-1937). She taught German in Fergusson College (1937-38). She was appointed as a Reader in Sociology and Anthropology at Deccan College, Poona in 1939. She was promoted to the post of Professor in 1966, a chair which she held till her death.

Publications of Research Papers

1932 : "The Parshurama Myth". *Journal of University of Bombay,* 1:5, 115-39.

1933 : "The Ethnic Affinities of the Chitpavanas-1'. *Journal of University of Bombay,* 1:3, 383-400.

1937 : "Normal Asymmetry of Human Body". *Journal of University of Bombay,* 6:1, 65-74.

1938-39: "Kinship Terminology and Kinship Usages in Rigveda and Atharva Veda". *Annals of Bhandarkar Oriental Research Institute,* 20:3&4, 213-34.

1939 : "Some Folk Songs of Maharashtra". *Bulletin of Dacca College Research Institute,* 1:1, 79-96.

1939 : "Kinship Usages and Family Organisation in Rig Veda and Atharva Veda", *Bhandarkar Oriental Research Institute,* 20:3&4, 213-34.

1939-40 : "A Note on Rig Veda". 111, 31, *New Indian Antiquity,* 2:2, 120-21.

1940 : "Kinship Usage in Rig Veda and Atharva Veda". *Man In India,* 20:1, 78-79.

1940 : "Kinship Terminology and Kinship Usages of Maratha Country". *Bulletin of Deccan College Research Institute.* 1:2-4, 327-89.

1941 : "Anthropometric Measurements of Sukla Ayurvedia Madhyandina Brahmins". *Man In India,* 21:1, 55-57.

1941 : "The Eternal Triangle in Some Marathi Folk Songs". *Abstract of Proceeding of Indian Science Congress,* 28:2, 215.

1941 : "Kinship System and Kinship Usages in Maharashtra". *Man In India.* 21:1, 68-69.

1941 : "Anthropometric Investigation of the Madhyandina Brahmins of Maratha Country". *Bulletin of Deccan College Research Institute,* 3:1, 1-74.

1942 : "Some Studies on Making of a Culture Pattern". In *Essays in Anthropology,* presented to Rai Bahadur Sarat Chandra Roy (ed.) by J.P. Mills and others, Lucknow : Maxwell & Company.

1942 : "Brother and Sister in Marathi Folk Songs". *Science and Culture,* 8:5, 214-17.

1943: "Kinship Terminology and Kinship Usages in Gujarat and Kathiawad". *Bulletin of Deccan College Research Institute.* 5:14, 61-148.

1942-44: "Kinship Terms and Family Organisations as Found in Critical Edition of Mahabharata". *Bulletin of Deccan College,* Research Institute, Poona.

1944: (Jointly with H.D. Sankalia) : "The Second Gujarat Prehistoric Expedition: A Preliminary Account of the Search of Microlithic Man in Gujarat". *New Indian Antiquary,* 7:1&2, 1-6.

1945 : (Jointly with H.D. Sankalia) "Preliminary Report on the Third Gujarat Prehistoric Expedition". Times of India Press for Deccan College Resarch Institute, p. 8.

1945 : (Jointly with G.M. Kurulkar) "A Preliminary Report on the Human Remains found in Lunghnaj". Times of India Press for Deccan College Research Institute, Poona.

1945 : "Prehistoric Expedition : A Preliminary Account of Search of Microlithic Man in Gujarat". *Indian Antiquary,* 7:1, 1-6.

1947 : "A Note on Incident in Ramayana". *Bulletin of Deccan College Research Institute,* 8:3-4, 422-24.

1947 : "Racial Conflict" in *Racial Problems in Asia* (ed.) by D.N. Majumdar.

1947 : "Some Problems of Indian Anthropology". *Proceeding of 34th Indian Science Congress,* Part 11, 1-12.

1948 : "Anthropometric Measurements of Marathas". *Deccan College Monograph Series, No. 2.*

1949 : (Jointly with Hasmukh Dhirajlal Sankalia) "Early Primitive Microlithic Culture and People of Gujarat". *American Anthropologists,* 51:1, 28-34.

1950 : "A Marathi Version of Oedipus Story". *Man,* 50 : 71-72.

1951 : "Cultural Process in India"'. *Man,* 232 : 135-38.

1951 : (Jointly with Vishnu Mahadeo Dandekar) "Anthropometric Measurement of Maharashtra". *Deccan College Monograph Series,* No. 8.

1952 : "Review of Cultural Anthropology of Rodiyas by M. D. Raghavan", *Man,* 52, 27-28.

1952 : Review of "Maria Murder and Suicide" by Verrier Elwin, *Man*, 52, 27.

1953 : "Dravidian Kinship Terminology and Marriage Customs". *Proceeding of Indian Science Congress,* 40:3, 37.

1954 : "Anthropometric Measurements in Karnataka and Orissa and a comparison of these two regions with Maharashtra". *Journal of Anthropological Society*, Bombay, 8:1, 45-75.

1955 : "Is happiness Mere Abstraction". *Fergusson College Magazine*, 47: 2.

1955 : "Castes in Modern Times and Some Measures to Combat its Evils". *Indian Conference of Social Work,* pp. 54-59.

1956 : "The Cultural Process in India". In *Society of India* (ed.) by A. Aiyappan and L.K. Balaratnam, Madras Social Science Association.

1957 : "Bhils of West Khandes". Anthropological Society, Bombay.

1957 : "The Indian Village". *Bulletin of the Deccan College Research Institute,* 18:73-106.

1957 : "Social Education of Scheduled Tribes". *Vanyajati,* 5:4, 164-69.

1958 : "What is Caste? I. : Caste as Extended Kin". *Economic and Political Weekly,* 10 : 4-5&6 : 126-38.

1958 : "What is Caste? II. : Caste and Occupation". *Economic and Political Weekly,* 10:12, 401-7.

1958 : "What is Caste? III. : Caste as a Status Group". *Economic and Political Weekly,* 10:26-28, 881-88.

1959 : "What is Caste? IV. : Caste Society and Vedantic Thought". *Economic and Political Weekly,* 11 : 149-63.

1959 : "Language Problem in India". Language Commission, Government of India.

1960 : "Succession in Matrilineal Royal House". *Bulletin of Deccan College Research Institute,* 20 : 1-4, 364-68.

1960 : "New Buddhism in Maharashtra". Department of Sociology, Bombay.

1961 : "Some Aspects of Organisation of Caste Society of Hindu". In *Changing India : Essay in Honour of Professor D.R. Gadgil,* Asia Publishing House, Bombay.

1961 : "Indian Social Structure". Seven Lectures delivered at the Institute of History and Culture, Poona University.

1961 : "Location and Organisation of Space". *Economic and Political Weekly,* 13:4, 5 & 6, 163-164.

1962 : "On the Road : A Maharashtrian Pilgrimage". *Journal of Asian Studies,* 22:1, 13:29.

1962 : "India as a Cultural Region". In *Indian Anthropology : Essays in Honour of D.N. Majumdar* (ed.) by T.N. Madan and Gopala Sarana, Bombay : Asia Publishing House.

1963 : "Grand Father in New Brahmins : Five Maharashtrian Families". Selected and Translated by the D.D. Karve, Berkley, University of California Press.

1963 : "Individual Case Study and Statistical Method in Social Organisation". *Economic and Political Weekly,* 15:17, 701-06.

1963 : "Communication and Anomie". *Economic and Political Weekly,* 15:49, 1995-1998.

1963 : "Family through Sex Generation". In *Anthropology on March* (ed.) by Balaratnam, Madras : Book Centre.

1963 : "Review of Indians in Plural Society". Written by B. Benedict, *Man,* 63 : 81-82.

1963 : "Notes on Problem of Acculturation in Tribes of India". *Indian Science Congress Golden Jubilee Volume*, Kolkata, Indian Science Congress Association.

1963 : (With Yashwant Bhaskar Damle) "Group Relations in Village Communities". *Deccan College Research Institute, Poona, Monograph Series No. 24.*

1964 : "The Family in India". In *Contemporary India* (ed.) by Baidya Nath Verma, Kolkata : Asia Publishing House.

1965 : (Jointly with J.S. Ranadive) "The Social Dynamics of a Growing Town and its Surrounding Area". *Deccan College Centenary and Silver Jubilee Series-29.*

1965 : "My 25 Years in Anthropology". In *Aspects of Indian Anthropology* (ed.) by P.C. Biswas and I.P. Singh.

1966-67 : "Language as a Social Factor". *Bulletin of Deccan College Research Institute,* 27 : 1-2, 20-26.

1967 : "An Analysis of Jointness and Non-Jointness of Family". *Anthropologist,* 14 : 1, 41-45.

1968 : (With K.C. Malhotra) "A Biological Comparison of Eight Endogamous Groups of Same Rank". *Current Anthropology,* 9 : 2-3, 109-23.

1968 : "Education and Social Change". *Economic and Political Weekly,* 3 : 122, 117-88.

1968 : "Maharashtra Land and Its People". Bombay : Director, Government Printing, Stationery and Publications.

1968 : "Kinship Organisation in India and the Place of Mundari Speaking People". *Adivasi*, 10 : 1, 1-25.

1968 : "What Urgent Anthropology Means to Me". *Bulletin of International Committee on Urgent Anthropological and Ethnological Research,* No. 10 : 15-16.

1969 : "Yuganta : The End of an Epoch". Poona : Deshmukh Prakashan.

1969 : (With Jai Nimbkar) : "A Survey of People displaced through Koyona Dam". Poona: Deccan College Post Graduate Research Institute, *Silver Jubilee Services–61.*

1969 : (With V.K. Kothurkar, G.M. Desai, N.V. Sovani, and S.D. Vanakudre) : "A Report on Health Status and Level of Living in Kolhapur Community Project". Shimla : Indian Institute of Advanced Study.

1970 : "Science and Society". Shimla : Indian Institute of Advanced Study.

1970 : "Social Structure and Human Genetics". Poona : National Congress of Human Genetics.

1971 : (With K.C. Malhotra) : "Biology of Split Community". National Congress of Human Genetics, Poona.

1971 : (With K.C. Malhotra) : "Population Biology of Three Split Gavda Groups of Goa". *Proceeding of International Symposium on Human Genetics,* Waltair.

1972 : "Kinship Patterns, Terminology and Behaviour in India". *Miami Florida, Field Research Project Study, No. 2.*

1972 : "Utilisation of Folklore and Myths in the Study of Ancient Indian Civilisation". Shimla : Indian Institute of Advanced Study.

Books

1953 : "Kinship Organisation in India." *Deccan College Monograph Series No. II,* 3rd (ed.) with three New Appendices, Kolkata : Asia Publishing House, 1968.

1961 : "Hindu Society : An Interpretation". Poona : Deccan College Postgraduate Research Institute. Second Edition, Poona : Deshmukh Prakashan, 1968.

Besides above publication of articles and books in English medium, she had written a number of articles and books in Marathi language.

A. AIYAPPAN (1905-1988)

A. Aiyappan was born on February 5, 1905 at Maurthayur Pavarathy, Kerala. He received diploma in Economics from Madras University in 1926 and then B.Sc. Hons. from the same university in 1927. He received M.Sc. degree in Economics from Madras University. For his doctoral research in Social Anthropology, he went to London University in 1937. At London University he got a chance to study with Malinowski. When he returned to India, he was appointed as Director of the Government Museum, Madras where he served from 1940-1958. In 1958, he was appointed as Head and Professor of Anthropology in the Department of Anthropology, Utkal University, Bhubaneshwar. Here he served till 1966.

Aiyappan also acted as Hon. Director of the Tribal Research Bureau, Government of Orissa (1958-1966). After his retirement from Utkal University, he served as U.G.C. Professor of Social Anthropology at Andhra University, Waltair (1960-1968). He was also Vice Chancellor of Kerala University since April 1969.

Aiyappan was visiting professor of Social Anthropology at Cornell University, Ithaca, New York (1953-1954). He was also the recipient of the Foreign Fellowship of Museum Association of Rochester for distinguished services as social anthropologist and museum administrator.

Aiyappan worked as Director of Seminars on Tribal Education (NCERT) and on Social Science Research Methodology sponsored by US Educational Foundation in India. He also organised first exhibition of Madras Museum Centenary Celebration (1951) and Buddha Jayanti Exhibition at Madras.

Aiyappan was also a member of Research Programme Committee, Planning Commission, Government of India, Rao Committee on Social Science Research, several Madras Government's Committees and Central Advisory Boards. He was the member of Central Advisory Board of Archaeology, New Delhi and Board of Trustees of Indian Museum, Kolkata. He was member of National Committee on Extension and Community Development, Ministry of Agriculture, Government of India. He was also a member of Planning Commission Panel on the Welfare of Backward Class, and Executive Association, Madras.

Books

1937 : "Social and Physical Anthropology of Nayadis of Malabar", *Bulletin of the Madras,* Vol. 2.

1942 : *The Manley Collection of Stone Age Tools (Memoirs of Archaeological Survey of India),* No. 68. Delhi : Manager of Publications.

1944 : "Iravas and Culture Change." *Bulletin of the Madras Government Museum,* General Section, Vol. 5.

1948 : *Report on the Socio-economic Conditions of Aboriginal Tribes and Backward Castes of the Province of Madras.* Madras Government Press.

1952 : *Guide to Buddhist Antiquities in Madras Museum.*

1955 : "Tribes of South-western India." Adivasi, Delhi : Government of India Press.

1959 : "Megalithic Survival Among the Mudugas of Attapadi Valley, Kerala." *Adivasi,* Bhubaneshwar : Government Press.

1960 : *Story of Buddhism with Particular Reference to South India.* Madras, Government Press.

1965 : *Social Revolution in Kerala Village.* Bombay : Asia Publishing House.

Papers

1932 : "Nayar Polyandry", *Man,* Vol. 32 : 99.

1934 : "Nayar Polyandry", *Man,* Vol. 34 : 155.

1934 : "Prehistoric Handmade Pottery". *Man,* Vol. 34 : 197.

1935 : "Fraternal Polyandry in Malabar", *Man In India,* Vol. 15 : 108-18.

1935-36 : "Blood Groups of Pre-Dravidians of Waynad Plateau". *Current Science,* Vol. 4 : 493-94.

1936 : "Primitive Medicine at Malabar Temple". *Man,* Vol. 36 : 80.

1936 : "Marriage by Elopement Among Paniyans of Waynad". *Man In India,* Vol. 16 : 27-37.

1937 : "Polyandry and Sexual Jealousy". *Man,* Vol. 37 : 130.

1939 : "Blood Groups of the Nayadis of Malabar". *Man*, Vol. 39 : 199.

1940-41 : "Rudestone Monuments of Perumal Hills, Kodai Kanal". *Journal of Mystic Society,* Vol. 31 : 373-79.

1945 : "Mesolithic Artifacts from Swayarpuram in Tinnevelly District, South India". *Spabia Leylanica*, Vol. 24 : 145-54.

1945 : "Megalithic Culture of Southern India". *Journal of Indian Anthropological Institute.*

1945 : "Handmade Pottery of the Urali Kurumbas of Wynad, S. India". *Man,* Vol. 47 : 54.

1955 : "Caste and Joint Family". *Indian Sociological Society Bulletin,* Vol. 5 : 2.

1955 : "Symposium on Caste and Joint Family : In Tamilnadu". *Sociological Bulletin,* Vol. 4 : 117-22.

1957 : (With C.J. Jayadeva). "Oil Lamps in South India". *Man,* 57 : 56.

1961 : "Thinking About the Hindu Way of Life". In L.P. Vidyarthi (ed.) *Aspects of Religion in Indian Society.* Meerut : Kedar Nath Ram Nath.

1963 : "A Pioneer : Some Reminiscences". In *Anthropology on the March* (ed.) by Balaratna. Madras : Book Centre.

1967 : "Patterns of Leadership". In *Leadership in India* (ed.) by L.P. Vidyarthi. Bombay : Asia Publishing House.

1969 : "Urgent Anthropology for Southern India". In *Urgent Research in Social Anthropology,* Shimla : Indian Institute of Advanced Study.

M.N. SRINIVAS (1916–1999)

Mysore Narasimbachar Srinivas (Iyyangar) was born on 16th November, 1916. He received B.A. (Hons.) degree in Social Philosophy in the year 1936 from Mysore University and M.A. in Sociology degree in the year 1939, LL.B. degree in 1940 and Ph.D. degree in Sociology in 1945 from Bombay University. Then he went to Oxford University, London, where he received D.Phil. degree in Social Anthropology in 1947.

Srinivas was a research fellow (1940-42) and Research Assistant (1942-44) in the Department of Sociology, Bombay University. At Oxford University London, he was awarded Carnegie grant (1945-47). He was also awarded Simon Senior Research Fellowship to visit Manchester University (1953-54), Rockefeller Fellowship to stay in American Universities (1956-57).

Srinivas held many appointments, University lecturer in Indian Sociology at Oxford University (1948-51), Professor : the M.S. University Baroda (1952-1959), Professor : University of Delhi (1959-1972), Joint Director : Institute of Economic and Social Change, Bangalore (1972-73), Simon Visiting Professor, University of Manchester (June 1963), and Fellow, Centre for Advance Study in Behavioural Sciences, Stanford, California, (1964-65) and (1970-71). He was appointed as Andrew D White Professor at Large, Cornell University, USA (September 1970 to November 1976).

He was awarded D.Sc. (Hons.) by Chicago University (1971), D.Lit. (Hons.) by the University of Mysore (1972), Doctorate Honoris Causa by University of Nice, France (1972), Foreign Honorary Member, American Academy of Arts and Science, Boston (1973), and Honorary Member of American Philosophical Society, Philadelphia (1976).

Srinivas had received several awards like Rivers Memorial Medal (1955), S.C. Roy Memorial Medal (1958), Honorary Fellow of the Royal Anthropological Society of Great Britain and Ireland (since 1964), Dadabhai Naoroji Memorial Prize for Social Science other than economics (1971), TH Huxley Memorial Medal for 1976 from Royal Anthropological Institute of Great Britain and Ireland, London (1976), Honorary Life Member, South Asia Association, Australia, and Padma Bhushan, Government of India (1977). He delivered lectures in several foreign universities including Tagore Memorial Lectures in the University of California, Berkeley. He was the President of Anthropology and Archaeology Section of 44th Indian Science Congress in 1957 and was President of Indian Sociological Society (1966-1969).

Srinivas did fieldwork in Coorg for two years (1940-42), Tamil Nadu for three months (1943), Andhra for three months (1944) and Rampura in Mysore for thirteen months (1948 & 1952). His chief interest lies in the study of regional culture of South India, social change and religion.

Publication of Papers

1942 : "The Family versus the State", *Aryan Path,* Vol. 13 : 68-70.

1942-43 : "Some Tamil Folk Songs". Part I and Part II, *Journal of University of Bombay,* Vol. 12, Part 1 & 4, July 1943 and January 1944.

1944-45 : "Some Telugu Folk Songs". Part I and Part II, *Journal of University of Bombay,* Vol. 13, Part I & IV, July 1944 and January 1945.

1946 : "The Social Organisation of Coorgs of South India". *Man,* Vol. 46 : 86.

1947 : "Sociology and Social Work in England". *Silver Jubilee Volume of the School of Economics and Sociology,* Bombay.

1951 : "The Social Structure of a Mysore Village". *The Economic Weekly,* October 30, pp. 1951-56.

1952 : "A Joint Family Dispute in Mysore Village". *The Journal of M.S. University Baroda.* Vol. 1:1, 7-31.

1952 : "Social Anthropology and Sociology". *Sociological Bulletin,* Vol. 1:28-37.

1953 : "Prospects of Sociological Research in Gujarat". *Journal of M.S. University,* Baroda, Vol. 2:1, 21-25.

1954 : "A Brief Note on Aiyappan : The South Indian Deity". In *Professor G.S. Ghurye Felicitation Volume* (ed.) by K.M. Kapadia. Bombay, Popular Book Depot.

1954 : "Varna and Caste". In *Essays in Philosophy Presented to A.R. Wadia* (ed.) by S. Radhakrishnan *et.al*, Bangalore.

1954 : "A Caste Dispute Among Washermen of Mysore". *Eastern Anthropologist,* Vol. 8:3 & 4, 148-68.

1955 : "The Social System of a Mysore Village". In *Village India* (ed.) by McKim Marriott, Chicago, University of Chicago Press.

1955 : "The Village Studies and their Significance". *Eastern Anthropologist,* Vol. 8 : 3&4, 215-28.

1955 : "Castes : Can They Exist in India of Tomorrow". *Economic Weekly,* October 15, pp. 1230-32.

1956 : "A Note on Sanskritisation and Westernisation". *The Far Eastern Quarterly,* Vol. 15:4, 481-96.

1956 : "The Industrialisation and Urbanisation of Rural Areas". *Sociological Bulletin,* Vol. 5:2, 79-88.

1956 : "Radcliffe-Brown : The Man and His Work". In *Society in India* (ed.) by L.K. Balaratnam and A. Aiyappan, Madras. Social Science Association Publication.

1956 : "Regional Difference in Customs and Village Institutions." *The Economic Weekly,* February 18 : 215-20.

1957 : "Caste in Modern India". *Journal of Asian Studies,* Vol. 16:4, 529-48.

1958 : "Hinduism". *Encyclopedia Britannica* : 574-77.

1958 : "Caste and Its Future". *Akashvani,* October 19, pp. 10-11.

1959 : "Study of Disputes in An Indian Village". Kolkata : UNESCO Research Centre.

1959 : "The Caste of Potter and Priest". *Man In India,* Vol. 39:3, 190-209.

1959 : "Dominant Caste in Rampura". *American Anthropologist,* Vol. 61:1, 1-16.

1959 : "The Changing Social Pattern in India". *Illustrated Weekly of India,* January, 25:20-25.

1959 : "Social Anthropology and Study of Rural and Urban Societies". *The Economic Weekly Annual,* Vol. 11:4, 5 & 6, 133-140.

1960 : "Indian Road to Equality". *Economic Weekly Special Number,* June, 867-72.

1960 : "The Myth of Self Sufficiency of Indian Village". (With A.M. Shah) *Economic Weekly,* September, 10:1375-78.

1961 : "Changing Attitudes in India Today". *Yojana,* October, 25-28.

1961 : "The Changing Faces of the Villages". *Yojana,* Special Number, *Illustrated Weekly of India,* January, 22.

1961 : "There is Vested Interest in Backwardness". *The Statesman,* October 9.

1961 : "Sociological Aspects of Indian Diet". In *Agricultural Situation in India,* Ministry of Food and Agriculture, Vol. 16:3, 246-48.

1962 : "Pursuit of Equality". *The Times Survey of India,* London, January 26.

1962. "Changing Institutions and Values in Modern India". *Economic Weekly,* Annual Number, February : 131-137.

1963 : "National Integration : Can We Take It for Granted". *Yojana,* Republic Day Special Number, pp. 24-38.

1964 : "Changing Indian Villages". *Indian and Foreign Review,* Vol. 1:7, 11-12.

1964 : "Social Structure". *Sociological Bulletin,* Vol. 13:1, 12-21.

1964 : "Network in Indian, Social Structure" (With Andre Beteille) *Man,* Vol. 64, Art. 212, November-December, 165-68.

1965 : "The Untouchables of India" (With Andre Beteille) *Scientific American,* Vol. 213:6, 13-17.

1965 : "Social Structure". *The Gazetteers of India,* Publication Division, Government of India.

1965 : "Reducing the Inequalities". *The Times Supplement of India*. August, 14.

1973 : "Itineraries of an Indian Anthropologist". *International Social Science Journal,* Vol. 25 : 1/2, 129-48.

1975 : "Indian Village : Myth and Reality". In *Studies in Social Anthropology : Essays in Honour of E.E. Evance Pritchard,* Oxford University Press, Oxford, (ed.) by JHM Beteille and G. Lienhardt.

Publication of Books

1942 : *Marriage and Family in Mysore.* Bombay : New Book Company.

1952 : *Religion and Society Among Coorgs of South India.* Oxford : Clarendon Press. Reprinted 1962, Bombay : Asia Publishing House.

1955 : *India's Village.* West Bengal Government Press, Kolkata, (Reprint) 1960, 1963 and 1966, Bombay : Asia Publishing House.

1959 : *Method in Social Anthropology.* (With A.R. Radcliffe-Brown), Chicago : University of Chicago Press. 1961 Indian Edition, Bombay : Asia Publishing House.

1962 : *Caste in Modern India. Berkeley* : University of California Press.

1962 : *Caste in Modern India and other Essays.* Bombay : Asia Publishing House. Reprint in 1964.

1966 : *Social Change in Modern India. California* : University of California Press. Allied Publisher Delhi (Indian edition). Also Published in Hindi.

1969 : *India's Social Structure.* Delhi : Oxford University Press.

1976 : *The Remembered Village.* Berkeley : University of California Press, Delhi : Oxford University Press.

1976 : *Nation-building in Independent India.* Delhi : Oxford University Press.

1977 : *Dynamics of Social Change in India* (ed.). Delhi : Allied Publisher.

1986 : *Dominant Caste and Other Essays.* Delhi : Oxford University Press.

1989 : *The Cohesive Role of Sanskritisation.* Delhi : Oxford University Press.

1992 : *On Living in Revolution.* Delhi : Allied Publisher.

1996 : *Village, Caste, Gender and Method.* Delhi : Oxford University Press.

1997 : *Caste : Its Twentieth Century Avatar.* Delhi : Oxford University Press.

Concept of Sanskritisation

Concept of Sanskritisation was propounded by M.N. Srinivas in his book, "*Religion and Society Among Coorgs of South India*" (1952). He developed the concept of Sanskritisation in order to understand the process of social-cultural change in Indian society. He conceived Sanskritisation as an upward process of social-cultural change. The book "*Religion and Society Among Coorgs of South India*" is a published version of his doctoral dissertation submitted to Oxford University for the award of Ph.D. degree. In this book, he postulated for the first time the idea that Sanskritisation spread vertical and horizontal unity in a village in India. In course of field enquiry, he stayed in Rampura village for 10 months in 1948 and three months in 1952. Besides these two long duration visits, he had visited the village several times for short duration.

This village was also his Nana's (maternal grandfather's) village. Its original name was Koddhahalli but Srinivas had made a change in its name as Rampura in order to show a difference between Rampura village of North India studied by Oscar Lewis, an American anthropologist and the village Rampura of South India studied by himself. Among the 18 castes of the village Rampura, Srinivas observed the existence of hierarchy according to which individual castes behaved with each other. But each individual caste was maintaining vertical and horizontal unity.

Brahminical Model of Sanskritisation

Srinivas found that the position of Brahmins was at the top in structural status of the village society. The Brahmins had their own style of life. They used to get up early in the morning, performed bath in tank, rivers or wells, put *tilak* on forehead, offered water to Sun God and mother *Tulsi,* did worship in temples, wore neat and clean dresses, and took breakfast after accomplishing these tasks in their daily lifestyle. They did not take wine and non-vegetarian food. They were sacred and ceremonial specialists of the village. Hence, the Brahminical model of lifestyle was a model to be followed by castes having lower position in caste hierarchy and by tribals of Indian village. By following the Brahminical model of lifestyle, the low caste Hindus and Tribals of Indian villages, did not claim that they had become a Brahmin. But they attempted to show their status high in their own community. They proudly said that they had adopted Brahminical model of lifestyle, therefore, they are superiors to other members of their own community. Hence, Sanskritisation did not make any change in vertical and horizontal unity of the village. This process had not brought any kind of jealousy, hatred, conflict and tension in Indian Society. This change was not induced by any missionary. It was self-induced. The main purpose of this upward change in Indian village was to lead a clean, pure and pious life in society. Brahminical model of lifestyle was definitely difficult for those who loved non-vegetarian food and intake of wine and for those who liked to share breakfast and food without bathing and offering water and worship to Sun God and *Tulsi* plant. Therefore, the members of different castes began to think over another model of lifestyle under Sanskritisation.

Kshatriya Model of Sanskritisation

In his book, "*Social Change in Modern India*" (1966) Srinivas propounded the Kshatriya and Vaishya models of Sanskritisation and the concept of desanskritisation in order to show changes in modern India. As Brahminical model was very difficult and not practicable by all members of a particular low caste, hence members of low castes and tribals began to think for an another model of change which did not require formality of bathing, putting *tilak* on forehead, offering water to Sun God and mother *Tulsi,* worshipping in village temples, sharing vegetarian food and not sharing wine in daily life. For this purpose, the members of low Hindu castes and tribals looked towards Kshatriyas, whose position in caste hierarchy was next to Brahmins. In adopting this model, there was no need to give up non-vegetarian food and wine. There was also no need to share breakfast and food after performing bath. The only need was to add title Singh or Thakur and claim their descent from Raja, Maharaja and mythical kings and dynasties. Following this model of change, a good number of low caste Hindus and Tribals began to claim themselves as Kshatriya and added title Thakur and Singh with their name. Kahar began to call themselves as Ravani Kshatriya, Rajwar as Rajvanshi Kshatriya, Dusadh as Gehlot Kshatriya, Kurmi as Lava Kshatriya, Koeri as Kusha Kshatriya, Ahir or Yadvas as Yaduvanshi Kshatriya, Barahi, Lohar and Kumhar as Vishwakarma Kshatriya and Gareri as Chandravashi Kshatriya. Kshatriya model of Sanskritisation was followed more and more by those Hindu castes whose position was lower in caste hierarchy. Not only low caste Hindus, but Tribals of our country, too, have adopted Kshatriya model of Sanskritisation. For example, Munda, Bhumij, Ho, Chero, Kharwar, Gond, Bhil, Kisan, Banjara, Pando, Bharia, Paharia and others claim themselves as Kshatriya and add Singh title with their names.

Vaishya Model of Sanskritisation

In Hindu castes after Brahmins and Kshatriya, the position of Vaishya was third in hierarchy. Hence, the Vaishya model of Sanskritisation was also followed in Hindu society. This model was very easy to follow because it needed only to follow the occupation of Vaishya caste and to offer daily worship to Lord Ganesha and Goddess Lakshmi before opening the shop. Following Vaishya model of Sanskritisation, a number of not only low caste Hindus and Tribals, but castes having higher position in caste hierarchy have also established small or big shops and entered in business and trade. This model does not emphasize upon food taboos. It also does not require a change in title. The only thing required in this model was to establish shops, business and/or enterprises. While Brahminical model and Kshatriya model of Sanskritisation have brought upward social mobility in Indian society, Vaishya model has brought social and economic mobility in society. This model of Sanskritisation opened the path for establishing shops, business, trade and enterprises by any individual of any caste. Thus, this model has also brought occupational mobility in Indian society.

Desanskritisation

Contrary to the concept of Sanskritisation, Srinivas propounded the concept of Desanskritisation to show downward changes in stratified position of caste system. Desanskritisation is a process in which High caste Hindus give up their lifestyle and adopt the life ways of low caste Hindus or Tribals. This change is not only in lifestyle, but also in occupations. For example, a good number of Brahmins, whose position in stratified caste system has been at the top, but they have started sharing breakfast and meals without performing bath, and worship. Not only this, they have started taking wine, egg and non-vegetarian foods. They have given up the role of religious and ceremonial specialists. They are found working in shoe and leather industries on different posts. Many Brahmins are incharge of Sulabh Sauchalaya in our country as well as in foreign countries.

Now-a-days effects of Sanskritisation can be found in almost all Hindu villages of India. In all Hindu houses, one finds a flag of Lord Hanumana, Chaura of *Tulsi* plant and a *Hanuman Chalisa* book to recite after performing bath. This shows Brahminical ways of life. This way of life has become common for all castes occupying different positions in structure of Hindu society. A number of castes having adopted the title of Brahmins like Pandit, Mishra, Bhatta and others. Some have started adding the title of Brahmin Rishi Munis after whom the name of Hindu Gotra have been established. For example Garg, Gautam, Bhardwaj, Vishwamitra, Vashishtha, Atri, Sandilya, Kaudilya and Kashyapa. Now-a-days, a caste member cannot be identified with a title. Singh, Kumar, Thakur have become common titles for all castes having different positions in caste hierarchy. Some have started adding the title Raj, Krishna, Balrama, Gopala, Shiva, Das and others. A number of castes have no title with their names. They write only name, not title. For example, Gajanand, Panchanand, Ananta, Vishwanath, Santosh and others. Some castes have started adding two names. For example, Sanjiv-Rajiv, Shashi-Prabha, Shashi-Bhushan and others. These types of changes show upward social mobility. It is not concerned with occupational and economic mobility. But Vaishya model of Sanskritisation has brought economic and occupational mobility in Hindu caste society. There is no doubt that Sanskritisation has brought mobility in Indian society, but mobility may also occur without Sanskritisation. However, mobility associated with Sanskritisation results only in positional changes in the system, and does not lead to any structural change. That is a caste moves up, above its neighbours, another comes down, but all this takes place in an essentially stable hierarchical order. The system itself does not change.

Westernisation

Srinivas in his book, "*Social Change in Modern India*" (1966), dealt with the concept of Westernisation. According to him, Westernisation is related to those changes which were brought in India during British rule. He was of opinion that Indian people came in contact with British rulers during British rule. British rulers were agents of Western ideology and philosophy. They started making changes in Indian society from their Western approaches. British rulers introduced changes in traditional, social, economic, political, religious, health, sanitation, education, transportation, communication, art, culture, sports and other areas of Indian society.

Of two processes, Sanskritisation and Westernisation, Sanskritisation seems to have occurred throughout Indian history and still continues to exist. Westernisation, on the other hand, refers to changes introduced into Indian society during British rule and which continue in some cases with added momentum during independent India. Westernisation, unlike Sanskritisation is not combined to any particular section of Indian population. Its importance both in the number of people it affects and the way in which it affects them is steadily increasing. The achievement of independence has in some ways quickened the process of westernisation. It is not unlikely that independence was a necessary precondition for such acceleration.

It is beyond doubt that the British rule produced radical and lasting changes in Indian society and culture. It was unlike any previous period in Indian history because British brought with them new technology, institutions, knowledge, beliefs and values. The new technology and the revolution in communication enabled the British to integrate the country as never before in its history. During the 19th century, the British slowly laid the foundation of modern state by surveying land, setting the revenue, creating a modern bureaucracy, army, police, courts, schools, colleges, universities, railways, airways, waterways, roadways, postal and telegraphs, canals, printing press and industries. The profound and many-sided changes brought about by them in Indian society and culture deserve a volume in itself. One obvious result was that books and journals with schools made possible the transmission of modern as well as traditional knowledge to a large number of Indians. Knowledge was now no longer the privilege of a few hereditary groups. Newspapers made the people of different parts of the world aware of each other.

Railways, postal and telegraph services connected the people of different parts of India. Waterways and seaways connected the people of India with foreign countries.

Christian missionaries from Europe knew India long before the arrival of British. During the early days of East India Company, the entry of European Missionaries into India was banned. This ban was lifted in 1813, when British Parliament permitted Christian missionaries entry into India under a new system of licensing. This eventually threw the entire subcontinent open to missionary activity.

In the first half of 19th century, the British with the support of enlightened Indian opinions, abolished such institutions as *Sutee* or *Sati* (1829), female infanticide and human sacrifice and slavery (1833). The Indo-British impact was profound, many-sided and fruitful.

Thus, Srinivas had used the term Westernisation to characterise the changes brought in Indian society and culture over a period of 150 years of British rule. The term also subsumes at different levels—technology, institutions, ideology and values.

Westernisation, Urbanisation and Industrialisation

Srinivas had made a conceptual distinction between the concepts of Westernisation, Urbanisation and Industrialisation. The common consensus among the scholars was that industrial revolution resulted in an increase in the rate of urbanisation and highly industrialised areas were treated as highly urbanised. But in our country we have references about the urbanity of Indus Valley Civilisation, and ancient towns and cities like Gaya, Varanasi, Prayagraj, Haridwar, Mathura, Ayodhya, Vrindavan, Badrinath, Kedarnath, Puri, Dwarika, Rameshwaram, Somnath, Tirupati, Vaishnav Devi and others. Thus, urban cities were flourishing even in pre-industralised world. While the most Westernised groups are found generally in big cities, but a caution is needed while equating urbanisation with Westernisation. Even in country like India, it is possible to come across groups inhabiting rural areas which are more Westernised in their lifestyle than many urban groups. The former are found in areas where plantation and commercial crops were grown or which had a tradition of supplying recruits to Indian army.

Westernisation results not only in the introduction of new institutions, for example newspapers, elections, Christian Mission etc., but it also makes fundamental changes in old institutions. For example India had schools long before the arrival of British, but they were quite different from the schools introduced by the British. The traditional schools were restricted to only upper caste children and transmitted mostly traditional knowledge. Other institutions such as laws, courts, army, civil services were similarly affected.

Westernisation and Modernisation

A popular term for the changes brought about in a non-Western country by contact, directly or indirectly is 'modernisation'. Daniel Learner in his book, "*The Passing of Traditional Society*" (1958:45-49) had opted modernisation over Westernisation after considering the suitability of both. According to him, modernisation includes a disquieting positive spirit touching public institutions as well as private aspirations. But positive spirit is not enough, a revolution in communication is essential. Modernisation is also marked by increasing urbanisation which has, in turn, resulted in the spread of literacy. The urbanisation has tended to enhance media exposure and finally enhanced media exposure is associated with wider economic participation (per capita income) and political participation (voting). Modernisation also implies social mobility. A mobile society has to encourage rationality for calculus of choice. It shapes individual behaviour and conditions it rewards. The people come to see social future as manipulatable rather than ordained and their personal prospects in terms of achievement rather than heritage.

Modernisation means only an increased effectiveness in goal attainment with no increase in the rationalisation of the goal setting process. Thus, modernisation involves rationalisation of ends, which means goal chosen by society must be rational and the subject of discussion. It needs to be pointed out here that the social goals are the expressions of value preferences and hence, non-rational. The public discussion of goals can in no way guarantee to their rationality. Rationality can only be predicted of means, but not of the ends of social action. The term Westernisation, unlike modernisation, is ethically neutral. It does not carry the implication that it is good or bad. But modernisation is always seen as good and used in the sense that it is good.

Secularisation

Srinivas was of the opinion that British rule brought with it a process of Secularisation of Indian Society and Culture. Secularisation developed a tendency that gradually became stronger with the development of communication, growth of towns and cities, increased spatial mobility and spread of education. The two World Wars and Mahatma Gandhi's Civil Disobedience Campaigns, both socially and politically mobilised the masses and contributed to increase secularisation in India. After Independence, the process of secularisation was deepened and broadened. It was witnessed in such measures as declaration of India as a secular state, declaration of fundamental rights and citizenship, constitutional recognition of equality of all citizens before law, introduction of universal adult suffrage and undertaking a programme of planned development.

It is significant to mention here that Sanskritisation is also spreading and it seems paradoxical that both Sanskritisation and Secularisation are gaining ground in modern India. But of two processes, Secularisation is a more general process affecting all Indians, while Sanskritisation affects only Hindus and Tribals. It will be true to say that Secularisation is more marked among urban and educated groups, and Sanskritisation is more marked in lower Hindu castes and tribals. It is necessary here to reiterate that one of results of Secularisation of India is reinterpretation of Hinduism in which Sanskritic elements are predominant.

The term Secularisation implies that what was previously regarded as religious is now ceasing to be such. It also implies as a process of differentiation, which results in various aspects of a society—economic, political, legal and moral, becoming increasingly discrete in relation to each other. The distinction between church and state and the Indian concept of secular state both assume the existence due to such differentiation.

Another essential element in Secularisation is rationalisation, a comprehensive expression applied to various theoretical and practical tendencies which aim to interpret the universe purely in terms of thought. Rationalism also aims at regulating individual and social life in accordance with the principles of reason and to eliminate everything that are irrational. Rationalism involves removal of traditional beliefs and ideas by modern knowledge.

Hindus were more affected by the process of secularisation than other religious groups in India. The concepts of purity and pollution of Hinduism were greatly weakened due to variety of factors. Different sections of Hindus are affected in different degrees. The effect of secularisation can be seen in daily life, rituals, ceremonies, occupations, travelling, treatment and others.

Concept of Dominant Caste

M.N. Srinivas had made a study of a village Rampura in Karnataka state. On the basis of his field researches in Rampura village he propounded the concept of Dominant Caste. He published a paper entitled, "Dominant Caste in Rampura" which was published in the *Journal of American Anthropologist* (1951 : 16:1, 1-16). According to Srinivas, a feature of Indian village is existence of dominant caste. The dominant caste is decided by the ownership of rural resources particularly land, high position in caste hierarchy and strength of number. When a caste has all attributes of dominance, it is termed as a dominant caste. Occasionally, there may be one dominant caste in a village. Srinivas held that a caste may be dominant when it has numerical strength, ownership of local resources like land, high status in traditional caste hierarchy, and political power. A large and powerful caste group can be most easily dominant in the village, if its position in local caste hierarchy is not too low. In the light of caste hierarchy in Rampura, Srinivas suggested that the peasants in Rampura enjoyed all the elements of dominance in the village. Identification of dominant caste was providing a better understanding of characteristics of rural social organisation because the council of dominance tried to create structure of authority within each group it has to deal with. Dominant caste played very significant role in settlement of disputes in the village. The leaders of dominant castes were not only settling disputes between members of different castes, but were also frequently approached by non-dominant castes of the village for settlement of their intercaste and even domestic disputes.

According to Srinivas, there were four factors of dominance. They were: numerical strength, control of resources, i.e. land, possession of political power and socio-religious status in local caste hierarchy. Thus, there was numerical dominance, economic dominance, political dominance and socio-religious dominance. Traditionally, these factors were related to dominance in the village. But after achievement of independence, implementation of secular constitution, voting rights, modern education, modern administration and urban sources of income like new factors have emerged in the way of concept of traditional caste dominant. Now prestige and powers are determined by new factors in the village. The introduction of adult franchise and Panchayati Raj (Local Self-Government) in village, Prakhand and Zila level has resulted in giving a new sense of respect and power to low castes particularly untouchables and women because they are enjoying reservations in Panchayati Raj Institutions and also in MLA and MP elections. In traditional system, it was possible for a small number of people belonging to high Hindu castes to weild authority over the entire village, when they owned a large quantity of village land and enjoyed a high position in caste hierarchy. But now, in many parts of India, power had shifted in the hands of numerically dominant caste groups, irrespective of high or low position in caste hierarchy. Factionalism in traditional dominant castes has also emerged which is also responsible for shift of power. Caste alliance is also taking place at the time of Panchayati Raj Institution's elections.

No longer is dominance purely a local matter in rural India. A caste group which has only a family or two in particular village, but enjoys decisive dominance in the wider region, is still count locally because of network of ties binding it to its dominant relatives. The other castes of the village are equally aware of the existence of this network. Countrywide a caste which enjoys dominance in only one village has network with regional dominance.

The concept of dominant caste propounded by Srinivas have been subjected to severe criticism by anthropologists like S.C. Dube and B.K. Roy Burman. Dube propounded the concept of dominant individual in place of dominant caste of the village. He was of the opinion that all members of a caste did not enjoy dominant position in the village. Rather few individuals were holding this position. Hence, the concept of dominant caste was not true in practical. B.K. Roy Burman had propounded the concept of dominant community in place of dominant caste of the village of Srinivas. According to Roy Burman, Dominant Communities have several dimensions, such as control over resources, social status and maintenance of law and order.

Concept of Spread

Srinivas in his book, "*Religion and Society Among Coorgs of South India*" (1952), developed the concept of spread in order to understand the spread of Hinduism in India. According to him, Hinduism has a long history of existence in India. In course of its long history, it has spread over the whole India. Buddhism, a Hindu schism in origin is now a religion of Asian countries. While explaining the concept of spread, Srinivas talked about four types of spread of Hinduism. They are as follows:

- Local spread of Hinduism
- Regional spread of Hinduism
- National spread of Hinduism
- Peninsular spread of Hinduism

According to Srinivas, local Hinduism has a local spread in which all Hindus of a local area share common beliefs, rituals, and performances. The spread of this Hinduism is local. The regional spread of Hinduism can be found out on the basis of practice of a common belief, rituals and performances by all Hindus living in a particular region. The regional spread of Hinduism covers more geographical area than local spread. The national spread of Hinduism covers the entire country. When Hindus of entire country share some common belief, rituals and practices, it is called as national spread of Hinduism. For example, ancient places like Gaya, Kashi, Prayagraj, Ayodhya, Mathura, Puri, Dwarika, Badrinath, Kedarnath, Tirupati, Ganga Sagar and Rameshwaram had a national spread among the Hindus residing in all parts of India. Because these places are called *Dham* (Pilgrimage Centre) where people from all parts of India come to share common belief, rituals and performances. The great festivals like Holi, Durga Puja and Diwali are celebrated in all parts of India. The peninsular spread of Hinduism shows common beliefs, rituals and practices by the Hindus of peninsular India. For example, Pongal is observed in Kerala and South Indian states. Ganesha festival is observed in Maharashtra. These two festivals show the peninsular spread of Hinduism.

Concept of Vertical and Horizontal Caste Solidarity

M.N. Srinivas in his books, "*Caste in Modern India*" (1962) and "*Caste in Modern India and Other Essays*" (1962) opined that *Varna* model produced a wrong and distorted image of caste. He made a request to sociologists and anthropologists to free themselves from the hold of *Varna* model in the study of castes and to know the caste system in India. M.N. Srinivas did not provide a clearcut definition of caste, but he believed that the structural basis of Hindu society is caste. He examined the interrelationship between various facets of castes and sub-castes in community and region-wise setting.

Observing the diversities in castes, he propounded the concept of 'Vertical' and 'Horizontal' solidarity of Indian caste system. He observed some common elements of local culture shared by all Hindu castes living in a region from the top to the bottom position. Thus, the Brahmins, Scheduled Castes and other castes of a region speak a common language, observe common festivals, and share common deities and beliefs. Srinivas has called this type of unity in Indian caste system as 'Vertical' solidarity. In 'horizontal' solidarity, contrary to vertical solidarity, members of a single caste share common beliefs, traditions, and rituals, irrespective of their region and language. Thus, Brahmins of all parts of India share common sanskriti and rituals. Srinivas has termed it as 'Horizontal' solidarity. Thus, according to M.N. Srinivas, caste system in India should be understood in terms of horizontal solidarity and vertical solidarity.

In his book, "*Caste and its 20th Century Avatar*" (1992), Srinivas opined that attempts were made to break vertical and horizontal caste solidarity of Indian caste system by various developmental experiments and equality based programmes of the Government. Due to developmental experiments and programmes, castes have incarnated in new form. Castes were changing into class. Upper class, middle class and lower class had emerged in all castes. In place of caste endogamy, class endogamy appeared. But these changes in caste appeared only in urban and industrial areas where people were engaged in non-agricultural occupation. In agriculture based rural society vertical and horizontal caste solidarity was still a reality.

Contribution on Village Study

Srinivas in course of his field enquiry in Rampura, he stayed in village for a period of 10 months in 1948 and 2 months in 1952. Besides these two visits of long duration, he had made several visits time to time of short duration in Rampura. At the time of his study, the village Rampura had a population of 1523 persons distributed in 18 castes. The village Rampura was located at a distance of 25 miles south-east of Mysore city. Based on study of Rampura, several research papers were published on the social system of Rampura. Srinivas was greatly influenced by British structuralist functionalist anthropologist A.R. Radcliffe-Brown. Under the influence of A.R. Radcliffe-Brown, Srinivas made structural study of relationships of roles and status of castes and their occupation.

Srinivas emphasized upon the unity of the village. He observed that a village was a vertical entity made up of several horizontal layers each of which was a caste. The unity of the village was expressed by village officials supervising the rituals, the village elders and the dominant caste.

In an another paper on dominant caste in Rampura, Srinivas attempted to redefine and clarify the concept of dominant caste. He observed disputes in village Panchayat organisation. In his book, "*Dominant Caste and Other Essays*" (1986) Srinivas added two more criteria for dominant caste. They were Western education and occupation. Thus, there was sex criteria of dominant caste. They were numerical strength, control over land, high socio-religious status, political power, Western education and occupation. These were elements of dominance in the rural villages in India.

Srinivas's (ed.) book, "India's Village" (1955) consisted of 13 articles on Indian village contributed by 5 American anthropologists, 5 British anthropologists and 3 Indian anthropologists. American anthropologists were Beals, Mandelbaum, Gough, Marriott and Martin. British anthropologists were Bailey, Collin, Carstairs, Miller and Newell. Indian anthropologists were Dube, Sharma and Srinivas. Except the paper of Mandelbaum, all papers were based on fieldwork done in Indian villages. These papers provided several important concepts as well as preliminary methodological and theoretical leads in concerning rural life in India.

S.C. DUBE (1922-1996)

Shyama Charan Dube had received his master degree in Political Science with Social Anthropology as a special group. He received his Ph.D. degree from Nagpur University. His doctoral dissertation was on Kamar, a tribe of Madhya Pradesh. He was awarded with K.E.M. Scholarship and Morris Memorial Scholarship from Nagpur University.

Dube served as lecturer at Nagpur, Lucknow and Osmania Universities. He was also visiting professor at Oxford University, London and Cornell University, USA. He had served for some time in Anthropological Survey of India and National Institute of

Community Development, Government of India, as Director and Principal respectively.

He did field researches in Chhattisgarh, Telangana, West Orissa and North Andhra Pradesh.

Dube had attended World Congress of Anthropological and Ethnological Sciences at Vienna and the UNESCO Working Group on Human Progress and Technological Change held at Paris in 1953. He was invited to several major international conferences and seminars to each of which he had contributed substantive papers. He had attended seminars at London, Paris, Burg, Wafenstein and Moscow. He went to Pakistan in 1962 to advice on a major study on rural leadership in the country in 1962 as a UNESCO Consultant. In 1963, he had attended a UNESCO Expert Working Group Meeting in Cyprus on 'Social Prerequisites of Economic Growth'. In the same year he had attended a seminar at Manila, Philippines on 'Religion and Economic Progress'. He had contributed a substantive paper to the Rehoboth, Israel, conference on, 'Comprehensive Planning of Agriculture'. In 1964, he had attended a six weeks International Development Workshop at East-West Centre, Hawaii. He had also served as Director of Indian Institute of Advanced Study, Shimla. He was also Vice Chancellor of Sagar University.

Publication of Books

1954 : *The Kamar.* Lucknow : Universal Publisher.

1955 : *Indian Village.* London : Routledge and Kegan Paul. Ithaca : Cornell University Press.

1958 : *India's Changing Villages : Human Factors of Community Development.* London : Routledge and Kegan Paul, Ithaca : Cornell University Press.

1958 : *Power and Conflict in Village India.* London : Routledge and Kegan Paul, Ithaca : Cornell University Press.

1968 : *Institution Building for Community Development.* (ed.) Hawaii, East-West Centre Press.

1971 : *Essays on Modernisation.* New Delhi, Vishal Publisher.

1973 : *Contemporary India and its Modernisation.* New Delhi, Vishal Publisher.

1977 : *Tribal Heritage of India.* New Delhi, Vishal Publisher.

1988 : *Modernisation and Development.* New Delhi, Vishal Publisher.

1990 : *Tradition and Development.* New Delhi, Vishal Publisher.

Contributions to Books and Journals

1961 : 'Indian Cillage Communities and Social Anthropology' in *Sociology, Social Research and Social Problems in India* ed. by R.N. Saxeana, Bombay Asia Publishing House.

1962 : 'Social Anthropology in India' in *Indian Anthropology* ed. by T.N. Madan and Gopala Sarana. Bombay : Asia Publishing House.

1962 : 'Considerations of Social and Political Structures and Agricultural Traditions Influencing Agricultural Development' Rehovoth', Israel : Conference on Comprehensive Planning of Agricultural.

1964 : 'Bureaucracy and Nation Building in Traditional Society' in *Political Development and Change* ed. by Jason L. Finkley and Richard Gable, New York : John Wiley and Sons Inc. 1960. Also in *International Social Science Journal*, Vol. XVI, No. 2 1964.

1965 : 'Cultural Problems in Economic Development of India' in *Religion and Progress in Modern Asia* ed. by Robert N. Bellah, New York : The Free Press.

1965 : 'Men's and Women's Roles in India : A Sociological Review', in *Women in New Asia* ed. by Barbara Ward, Paris : UNESCO.

1965 : 'The Study of Complex Culture', in *Towards a Sociology of Culture in India*, ed. by TKN Unnithan, Indra Deva and Yogendra Singh, New Delhi : Prentice Hall of India.

1965 : 'A Framework for the Study of Rural Leadership in Transitional Society' in *Emerging Pattern of Rural Leadership in Southern India* by UNESCO and Hyderabad : National Institute of Community Development.

1966 ; 'Bureaucracy and Economic Development', *Indian Journal of Public Administration*, Vol. XII, No. 2.

1967 : 'A Note on Communication in Economic Development' in *Communication and Change in Developing Countries* ed. by Daniel Lerner and Wilbur Schram.

1967 : 'Modernisation and its Adoptive Demands on Indian Society' in *Sociology of Education in India* ed. by M.S. Gore, I.P. Desai and Sumachituis, New Delhi : National Council of Education Research and Training.

1967 : ' Human Problems of Economic Development', *Eastern Anthropologist*, Vol. XX No-1.

1967 : 'Social Factors in National Integration' in *Education for National Integration* ed. by T.S. Avinashilingam; Coimbatore : Sri Ram Krishna Mission Vidyalaya.

1968 : 'Strategies of Community Development' in *Institution Building for Community Development* ed. by self, Honolulu : East-West Centre Press.

1968 : 'Possibilities and Limitations of Institution Building for Community Development' in *Institution Building for Communit Development* ed. by self, Honolulu : East-West Centre Press.

1968 : 'Strategies for Influencing Change' in Professor P.C. Biswas Felicitation Volume. The Anthropologist, Delhi.

1968 : 'Caste Dominance and Factionalism', Contribution to Indian Sociology, New Series, Vol. II.

Contribution on Tribal Study

Dube in his book, "*The Kamar*" (1954) has presented an ethnographic description of Kamar tribe of Chhattisgarh. He has described in detail about social, economic, political, religious organisations of the Kamar. He has also dealt with magical behaviours of the Kamar.

In his another book, "*Tribal Heritage of India*" (1977) Dube has dealt with knowledge and arts, music, dance, songs and folklores of tribals of Madhya Pradesh. This is a edited book in which different eminent anthropologists have contributed their papers on tribal heritage of India.

Contribution on Village Study

Dube is famous for his village study applying scientific research methodology. Dube had carried on fieldwork in Shamirpet, a village in the region of Telangana. He had published his first full length monograph in 1955 under the title, "*Indian Village*". His book, "*Indian Village*" is based on data collected from the village Shamirpet. Data were gathered by five research investigators under the guidance of Professor Dube who was the Director of this project. He was also assisted by five other faculty units who did social work in their area of interest and possessed technical competence. This interdisciplinary collaboration was sponsored and financed by the Social Service Extension Project of Osmania University in 1951. For this purpose, Dube had chosen the village Shamirpet of Telangana for the study.

The village Shamirpet located about 25 miles from Hyderabad had a population of 2494 persons at the time of study. There were 19 different Hindu castes. Muslim caste was also found who had a total population of 340 persons. Thus in total population of 2494, 340 were Muslims and 2154 were Hindus. Hindu population was distributed in 19 castes. In the light of field data an integrated picture of the village was presented, and historical, geographical and sociological perspectives were taken care of properly. Morris E. Opler, in the foreword of the book had introduced it as a solid study which would doubtlessly take its place among the standard community study made in various parts of the world. In the same foreword, Morris E. Opler observed that in a number of ways this volume was specially valuable and challenging and was a tonic to present day research on Indian village life.

Although this book is one of the earliest monographs on a village, but it presents a comprehensive picture of the functioning of village institutions. Dube has noted that the economic system of rural India is found mainly on castes' functional specialisation, interdependence and occupational mobility. He also found that the elements of classical Hinduism of an all India spread are mingled with the regional religious beliefs and practices of the Hindus of Deccan plateau. Three major types of religious services and festivals were observed in the village. They were as follows:

- Family ceremonies.
- Village ceremonies.
- Caste ceremonies.

The Muslims had their own familial beliefs and communal festivals.

The interaction between Hindus and Muslims was observed at village festivals.

Dube also attempted to give a short account of the worldview, intergroup relation, inter-caste attitudes and stereotypes. He went to discuss the three significant stages of life, namely childhood, youth and old in a generalised biography.

In addition to this full length book "*Indian Village*", Dube wrote few papers on village studies. Among them mention may be made of one, "Remaking of Castes in Telangana Village" published in *Rural Profiles of India* (ed.) by D.N. Majumdar. According to Dube, the fundamental principle of caste ranking is a concept of pollution and purity. The caste ranking in Shamirpet was also determined by traditions and myths. The caste ranking was based on ascribed system of status. He established that the observance of prescribed daily rituals, hierarchy of food eaters, occupation allowed and practised and observance of rules connected with life cycle rituals also determined rank. He made repeated emphasis that the main criteria used for caste ranking were ritual and not economic. He did not consider the economic basis of dominance suggested by Srinivas as effective in ranking the castes. McKim Marriott also observed the ranking of castes on the basis of interactions among them instead of attributes.

Under the Cornell-Lucknow Village Study Project, S.C. Dube had supervised the fieldwork in two villages of western Uttar Pradesh. With the help of four research Associates, fieldwork was done in two villages—one Rajput village and other a Tyagi village in the Rani-Khani block of western Uttar Pradesh. The fieldwork was started in the end of 1954 and continued till 1956. The Rajput village had a population of 5142 at the time of study. It was the largest village of the block where 21 Hindu castes and seven castes like Muslims were living. The Tyagi village represented a smaller settlement with a population of 757. The results of the fieldwork were published in the form of book, "*India's Changing Villages : Human Factors in Community Development*" (1958). The book attempted to discover cultural changes experienced by technologically underdeveloped Indian villages specially under the influence of externally induced community development plans. Dube tried to analyse human factors in community development. He applied two very general principles of anthropology, which are as follows:

- Culture is a functionally integrated whole in which a change at any point would have repercussions throughout the system.
- The traditionally achieved organisations and culture is mediating screen for all innovations and would have selective effects on these innovations.

The work of Dube was of evaluative nature. It was of limited value. With the passage of time, it has gone out of date. It tells us about the initial stage of Community Development Programme on Rural areas of western U.P.

Contribution on Family Planning

Dube in monograph No. 6 and No. 8 of National Family Planning Institute, Government of India (1969) presented the description of his researches done on family planning. In monograph No. 6, he had presented the propagation of IUCD. He had also dealt with the lifestyle of users. He was of opinion that in the transmission of family planning programmes, special emphasis should be given on time and acceptance of the programme. In monograph No. 8, he has described the media related to transmission of family planning programme.

Contribution in Political Anthropology

His book, "*Power and Conflict in Village India*" (1958), is regarded as a very significant contribution in the field of political anthropology. On the basis of data collected from a Rajput village and a Tyagi village, he had attempted to explore the emergence of power and conflict in Indian villages. He observed that before independence, power in Indian villages was enjoyed as per structural positions of castes in caste system and there were no conflict and village system functioned. But after independence, attempts have been made to abolish the hierarchical positions of the castes. As a result, the conflict for power has started appearing in modern political system of the village.

Contribution on Modernisation

Dube's book, "*Essays on Modernisation*" (1971) is an edited book which presents collection of essays written by different eminent sociologists and anthropologists. All papers deal with impact of modernisation on Indian village life.

Dube's book, "*Contemporary India and Its Modernisation*" deals with the processes of modernisation in contemporary Indian Society.

In his book, "*Modernisation and Development*" (1988), Dube had attempted to show the role of modernisation in development of Indian Societies.

In his book, "*Tradition and Development*" (1990), Dube attempted to show that development is not anti-tradition. Rather development had brought changes in tradition. As a result, traditions have emerged in new form. Thus, traditions are not anti-development. Rather they make a change to accommodate with development. Thus, development has made the tradition a dynamic concept and a changing concept.

Dube was general editor of *Bhartiya Samaj Parichaya Mala*, Delhi, a Raj Kamal Prakashan in which three volumes were published. They were as follows:

- *Bharat Ki Samudayik Vikas Yojnayen* : Vol I by Sachchidananda.
- *Adivasi Bharat*, Vol II, L.P. Vidyarthi.
- *Bharatiya Nagar*, Vol-III, L.P. Vidyarthi.

SACHCHIDANANDA (1925-2015)

Sachchidananda was born on October 28, 1925 at a place Chhapra in Bihar state. He was founder head of the Department of Anthropology at Ranchi now in Jharkhand state. He was educated at Patna Collegiate School. After school education, he was admitted to Patna College, Patna for undergraduate education. He passed his M.A. Examination in History from Patna University in 1947 with first division. In his college life, he had received a number of gold medals and merit scholarships. In 1948, he was appointed as a lecturer in the Department of History at Patna University. In 1950, he got scholarship to study Anthropology at London University. He was awarded M.A. degree in Anthropology from the School of African and Oriental Study, London in 1952. At London, he had made study in anthropology under the guidance of C. Von Furer Haimendorf. When he returned from England, he was appointed as Reader and Head, Department of Anthropology at Ranchi in July 1953 under the then Bihar University.

In December 1957, Sachchidananda resigned from the Department of Anthropology at Ranchi and joined Social Education Organisers' Training Centre Ranchi as Director. This Centre was running under Ministry of Community Development and Extension, Government of India. This Centre imparted training to Social Education Organisers for working in tribal areas and Tribal Development Blocks of the country.

In the year 1961, he was awarded D.Litt. degree by Patna University, Patna.

In 1962, he was appointed as a Director of Bihar Tribal Research Institute, Ranchi. He served on this post for four years. During this period, he made intensive and extensive studies of tribals of Chotanagpur and Santhal Pargana. He was able to publish his research data on tribals in the form of books.

In 1966, he was appointed as a Professor of Social Anthropology and Sociology at A.N. Sinha Institute of Patna. He became Director of this Institute in 1971.

In 1973, he visited City University, New York as Assistant Professor in Anthropology. He was President of Archaeology and Anthropology Section of Indian Science Congress in 1978. He was closely related to a number of national and international sociological and anthropological institutes. He was also deeply and closely related to Indian Social Research Council, Delhi and National Education and Training Council, Delhi. He served as Chairman, A.N. Sinha Institute of Social Studies, Patna, even after his retirement till his death.

Under his guidance three and half dozen students had received Ph.D. degree in Sociology and Social Anthropology. Under his supervision, a number of research projects funded by Planning Commission, Government of India and Indian Social Science Research Council, Government of India were completed successfully.

He had authored more than one and half dozen books and nearly six dozen articles in journal of national and international repute.

Publications

1964 : *Culture Change in Tribal Bihar.* Kolkata : Bookland and Private Limited.

1966 : *Profile of Tribal Culture in Bihar.* Kolkata : Punthi Pustak.

1968 : *Tribal Village in Bihar : A Study in Unity and Extension.* Delhi : Munshi Ram Manohar Lal.

1972 : *Social Dimension of Agricultural Development.* New Delhi : Munshi Ram Manohar Lal.

1976 : *Tribal Voters in Bihar.* New Delhi : Munshi Ram Manohar Lal.

1977 : *Sarvodaya and Development.* Kolkata : Munshi Ram Manohar Lal.

1977 : *Harijan Elite.* New Delhi : Concept Publishing Company.

1980 : *Changing Munda.* New Delhi : Concept Publishing Company.

1984 : *Status of Women in India.* New Delhi : Concept Publishing Company.

1986 : *Scheduled Castes.* New Delhi : Concept Publishing Company.

1987 : *Industrialisation and Social Disorganisation.* New Delhi : Concept Publishing Company.

1987 : *Swidden Cultivation in India.* New Delhi : Concept Publishing Company.

1997 : *Tribal Studies Series.* New Delhi : Serial Publication.

2001 : *Dalit Women on Road.* New Delhi : Serial Publication.

2005 : *Water Supply Management in Bihar.* New Delhi : Serial Publication.

Besides above books, he had to his credit nearly 100 articles published in the journal of national and international repute.

Contribution on Tribal Studies

Being founder Head, Department of Anthropology at Ranchi, Director of Training Programme on Study of Tribal Areas and Tribal Development Blocks, Department of Welfare, Government of India and Director, Tribal Welfare Research Institute, Ranchi, Sachchidananda got opportunity to study tribals of Chotanagpur and Santhal Pargana, and published books dealing with tribal culture of Bihar. His book, "*Profile of Tribal Culture in Bihar*" (1966) presents a holistic picture of tribal culture of Bihar. He had shown that 30 types of tribals of Chotanagpur and Santhal Pargana were identified as Scheduled Tribes in Bihar. But a tribe was a cultural unit. Each tribe had its own culture on the basis of which each tribe maintained its separate existence. There is no doubt that each tribe had some common features, but they did not show cultural similarity. Therefore, the culture of each tribe should be studied and recorded for the welfare of the tribes.

In his another book, "*Culture Change in Tribal Bihar*" (1964), he attempted to show changes occurring in two major tribes of Jharkhand—Munda and Oraon. According to him, no culture was static. Changes in culture occurred with passage of time. It is also true for the tribals of Bihar. With the passage of time, new needs were created and the creation of new needs brought changes in material and non-material aspects of culture. Factors like sanskritisation, Westernisation, modernisation, secularisation and democratisation were responsible for changes in Munda and Oraon cultures of tribal Bihar. Changes were observed in social, cultural, economic, political, religious, and material aspects of tribal life. In this way, he presented a change oriented ethnography and monograph on tribes of Bihar.

In his book, "*Shifting Cultivation*" (1987), he has dealt with the practice of Jhum Cultivation by the tribals of North-East India. As they do Jhum Cultivation so they are termed as Jhumia. Processes involved in Jhum Cultivation have been described in very detail.

In tribal study series (1997), he had published a series of books dealing with various aspects of tribals of India.

Contribution on Village Study

Sachchidananda made a study of a tribal village in detail and published his book, "*Tribal Village in Bihar : A Study of Unity and Extension*". He had made study of tribal village with a purpose to understand its unity and extension. He observed the existence of village institutions like Akhra, Sasan, Youth dormitory (Dhumkhuria), Sarana, Munda, Pahan, forest, river, mountain and other village resources were contributing significantly in maintenance of unity in the village. Besides the unifying elements, the tribal village was not self-sufficient. It was dependent on other villages for marriage, education, work, occupation, markets, fairs, festivals, and inter-village political organisation. Thus, a tribal village shows social, cultural, economic, political, religious and educational extension. In this study, he had tested the concept of unity and extension propounded by American anthropologist Morris E. Opler and Indian anthropologist R.D. Singh (1956).

Contribution on Agricultural Anthropology

One of significant contribution of Professor Sachchidananda was contribution in Agricultural Anthropology. In his book, "*Social Dimension of Agricultural Development*", he dealt with beliefs, rituals, innovations, technology and attitudes related to the practice of agricultural development in rural India. He observed that in the beginning agricultural innovations like tractor, HYV seed, chemical fertilizer, pesticides, weedicides, soil testing were not accepted by the agriculturists of India. It was due to a myth prevalent in the mind of villagers that their use would destroy the fertility value of the agricultural land. But gradually trained agriculturists began to adopt agricultural innovations for assured yield from the field.

Contribution on Political Anthropology

In his book, "*Tribal Voters in Bihar*" (1977), he made a detailed study of tribal voters with a view to observe their voting behaviour at the time of M.P. and M.L.A. elections. He showed that tribal voters were very much interested in casting their votes. Not only male tribal voters, but female tribal voters also participated interestingly in casting their votes. But their voting behaviour was manipulated by tribal elites and village leaders. For tribals, voting was a festive occasion because meat and rice party was organised on the day of election for casting votes in favour of a particular candidate.

Contribution on Scheduled Castes Study

In his book, "*Harijan Elite*" (1977), he had made study of Harijan elites to understand their roles in development of Harijan communities. No doubt, the welfare schemes launched by Government for upliftment and betterment of Harijan Communities had resulted in building a good number of elites. Elites were in a position to take more and more advantages of reservational and welfare schemes for their own and their relatives' benefits. But they did politics in the name of their own Harijan Community. In this way, a class of elites had emerged. Elite class people opposed the term Harijan and in place of Harijan they wanted to be identified as *Dalit* (Depressed).

In his book, "*Scheduled Castes*" (1986), he presented a status oriented description of Scheduled Castes in Bihar. He attempted to explore social, economic, political, religious, educational, health and sanitational status of Scheduled Castes of Bihar.

Contribution on Women Study

In his book, "*Status of Women in India*" (1988), he attempted to explore the social, cultural, economic, political, religious, educational, health and sanitational status of women in India. He also dealt with women development programmes and women problems in detail. He also describes the constitutional provisions and Acts for women upliftment. The book was informatory, exploratory and of descriptive nature.

In his book, "*Dalit Women on Road*" (2001), he attempted to show the organised efforts of Dalit women against their exploitation, oppression and Deprivation.

Contribution on Industrialisation and Social Disorganisation

In his book, "*Industrialisation and Social Disorganisation*" (1987), he attempted to present disorganising effects of industrialisation in tribal belt of Chotanagpur. He observed that industrialisation resulted in family disorganisation, sex trade, sex crime, beggary, and others which were not prevalent before industrialisation. It is also true that tribals were reorganising themselves to meet the challenges of industrialisation.

LALITA PRASAD VIDYARTHI (1931-1985)

L.P. Vidyarthi was born on February 28, 1931 in a village of Patna District of Bihar state. He matriculated from City High School, Gaya, now known as Rajendra Vidyalaya, Gaya in 1946 with first division. He passed his Intermediate examination from Patna College of Patna University in 1948. He passed his Bachelor of Arts examination with Geography Hons. in 1950 from Patna College of Patna University with first class in 1950. He was admitted to Patna University for his M.A. course in Geography. He passed M.A. Part-I examination of Patna University in Geography in 1951. In 1951, he was awarded Government of Bihar Scholarship for M.A. in Anthropology. He left M.A. Geography Part-II course of Patna University and joined the M.A. course of Anthropology in Lucknow University. He passed M.A. in Anthropology Examination from Lucknow University in 1953 and topped the list of successful candidates. He received award of Indrajeet Singh Gold Medal of Lucknow University.

Vidyarthi was appointed as lecturer in the Department of Anthropology at Ranchi under the then Bihar University, Muzaffarpur in 1953. He was awarded the Ford Foundation Fellowship and Chicago University Fellowship in 1957-58 to complete his doctoral Research Programme. He selected Sauria Paharia, the Maler, for researches to complete his doctoral dissertation at Chicago University under the guidance of Julian H. Steward. He did intensive and extensive field researches among Sauria Paharia (The Maler) and submitted his doctoral dissertation under the title, "Maler : Nature-Man-Spirit Complex in a Hill Tribe of Bihar" in 1958. In the same year, he was awarded his doctoral degree from Chicago University. After receiving his doctoral degree, he returned and joined the Department of Anthropology at Ranchi as Lecturer and Head. In the same year, he became Reader and Head, Department of Anthropology at Ranchi University, Ranchi. In 1968, he became University Professor and Head, Department of Anthropology, Ranchi University, Ranchi.

Vidyarthi's continuous successful efforts raised the status of Department of Anthropology as Department of Special Assistance, University Grants Commission, Government of India in 1978. Vidyarthi became Director of this U.G.C. funded D.S.A. Scheme. After proper evaluation, D.S.A. was raised to the status of Centre of Advanced Study (CAS) October 2, 1985. This was the only department in the country in Anthropology which was crowned with the status 'Centre of Advanced Study'. Thus, Professor Vidyarthi was successful in his attempt in raising the status of the Department of Anthropology as Centre of Advanced Study, University Grants Commission, Government of India. Now, he was Director of CAS, UGC, Government of India.

When University Grants Commission, Government of India, declared the Department of Anthropology as Centre of Advanced

Study on October 2, 1985, it was the happiest moment in the life of Professor Vidyarthi. He was very much overwhelmed by this grand success. But this happiness in his life could not continue for long. He fell ill seriously and breathed his last on December 1, 1985 in RMCH. Thus, the rising star of Indian Anthropology made departure for his heavenly abode at an age of 55 years leaving the Department and C.A.S. to maintain its rich heritage by his colleagues and students. Although, Professor Vidyarthi is no more but his valuable contribution in Indian Anthropology will keep him always alive and immortal. His academic gene is still continuing in teachers and students of the Department. His death was mourned over the whole country by the social scientists as well as anthropologists of abroad. The sorrowful news of his death was broadcasted by All India Radio and B.B.C. London.

Professor Vidyarthi was a very good teacher and he used to teach anthropological theories very clearly.

He was winner of several fellowships and awards such as Government of Bihar fellowship for M.A. Anthropology (1950), Indrajit Singh Medal of Lucknow University (1953), Fullbright and Smithmundt Scholarship (1956-57), food Foundation Fellowship (1957), University of Chicago Fellowship (1957), Foreign Fellow American Association (1958), Indo-GDR Cultural Exchange Fellowship (1959), Indo-USSR Cultural Exchange Fellowship (1959), and Rome Civic Reception Bronze Medal (1976).

He was Chairman of All India Social Science Congress, USEFI, New Delhi (1960), Study Team on Tribal Labour, Indian Commission on Labour (1968), Standing Committee on Anthropology, Indian Council of Social Science Research (1966-1975), Task Force on Development of Tribal Areas, Planning Commission, Government of India (1972), and Committee on Identification of Primitive Tribes of India, Ministry of Home Affairs (1974).

He was President of Folklore Section, All India Folk Culture Conference, Bombay (1959), Anthropology and Archaeology Section, Indian Science Congress, Varanasi (1968), Indian Social Science Association (1959-1974), Indian Anthropological

Association (1970-till death), International Union of Anthropological and Ethnological Science (1973-1978), and International Congress of Anthropological and Ethnological Sciences.

He was member of Panel on Backward Classes, Planning Commission, Government of India (1964), Founder member of Indian Council of Social Science Research, New Delhi (1974), Advisory Committee, Anthropological Survey of India (1968-1971), Steering Committee on Backward Classes, Planning Commission, Government of India (1972), Committee for the Development of Primitive Tribes of Andaman and Nicobar Islands, Government of India (1976), and Panel on Scheduled Castes, Ministry of Home, Government of India (1978).

He was Editor of *Journal of Social Research* (Ranchi) since 1958 till his death, *Indian Anthropologist,* Delhi (1971), *Research Journal of Ranchi University* (1964), *Sociological Bulletin,* Ghaziabad (1966) and *Folklore,* Kolkata (1966).

He directed many a large scale research projects like, Urban Pattern of Ranchi (1960), from Simple Economy to Industrialisation : A Techno-Cultural Implication of Change in India (1958), Tribal Indebtedness (1962), The Birhor Action Research Project (1966), Monographic Study of Munda Village : Ghaghra (1965), Changes in Leadership Pattern in Tribal Society in India (1966-68), Student Unrest in Chotanagpur (1969-1970), Sacred Complex in Kashi (1972-1976), Restudy of Kharia (1975-1977), Cultural Linguistic Zones of Bihar (1976), Revival of Indigenous Nutritive Dietary Habit and Recipes in four Cultural Linguistic Zones of Bihar (1975-77), from Cradle to Playground Socialisation Process in Tribal Bihar (1982-84), and Techno-Cultural Implications of Industrialisation in Central India (1982-84).

Publication of Books

1961 : *Sacred Complex in Hindu Gaya*. New Delhi, Concept Publishing Co. (reprinted in 1978).

1963 : *Maler : Nature-Man-Spirit Complex in a Hill Tribe of Bihar.* Kolkata. Bookland Private Limited.

1963 (With K.S. Mathur & I.P. Singh) : *Manav Shastra Ki Rupa Rekha*. Meerut. Ram Nath Kedar Nath.

1964 : *Cultural Contours of Tribal Bihar*. Kolkata : Punthi Pustak.

1966 : *Ghaghara : A Village in Chotanagpur.* New Delhi : Census of India, Ministry of Home Affairs.

1966 : *Bhartiya Nagar.* New Delhi : Rajmahal Prakashan.

1969 : *Cultural Configuration of Ranchi.* New Delhi : Planning Commission Publication Division.

1970 : *Socio-Cultural Implication of Industrialisation in India : A Case Study of Tribal Bihar.* New Delhi : Planning Commission Publication Division.

1976 (With K.N. Sahay) : *Dynamics of Tribal Leadership in Bihar.* Allahabad : Kitab Mahal.

1976 : *Students Unrest in Chotanagpur.* Kolkata : Punthi Pustak.

1976 : *Bhartiya Adivasi : Unaki Samajik Ewam Sanskritik Prishtha Bhumi.* Lucknow : Hindi Samiti.

1976 (With B.K. Rai) : *Tribal Culture of India.* New Delhi : Concept Publishing Company Pvt. Ltd.

1977 : *Peasant Organisation in India : A Study of Voluntary Organisation in Tribal Bihar.* Ranchi : Council of Social and Cultural Research Bihar.

1977 (With N. Mishra) : *Harijan Today.* New Delhi : Classical Publishers.

1977 : *Rise of Anthropology in India : A Social Science Orientation* (Two Volumes). New Delhi : Concept Publishing Company.

1978 : *Sacred Complex in Kashi* (with B.N. Sarasvati & M. Jha). New Delhi : Concept Publishing Company.

1979 : *The Kharia : Then and Now* (with U.S. Upadhyay). New Delhi : Concept Publishing Company.

1980 : *Trends in World Anthropology.* Concept Publishing Company, New Delhi.

1980 : *Rise of World Anthropology.* New Delhi : Concept Publishing Company.

Edited Books

1960 : *Anthropology and Tribal Welfare in India.* Ranchi : Council of Social and Cultural Research, Bihar.

1960 : *Indian Anthropology in Action.* Ranchi : Council of Social and Cultural Research, Bihar.

1961 : *Bihar Ke Adivasi* : Patna : College Centre.

1961 : *Aspects of Religion in Indian Society.* Meerut : Kedar Nath Ram Nath.

1967 : *Leadership in India.* Bombay : Asia Publishing House.

1968 : *Applied Anthropology in India.* Allahabad : Kitab Mahal.

1968 : *Tension, Conflict and Social Change in India.* Kolkata : Punthi Pustak.

1968 : *Tribal Labour : Agricultural and Industrial.* New Delhi : Manager of Publication, National Commission on Labour.

1970 (With B.N. Sahay & B.K. Srivastava) : *Gandhi and Social Science in India.* New Delhi : Book and Hive.

1971 (With G. Choubey) : *Bihar in Folklore Study.* Kolkata : Indian Publication.

1973 (With B.C. Agarwal) : *Researches in Complex Society in India.* New Delhi : Indian Academy of Social Science.

1976 : (With B.K. Rai) *Tribal Culture of India.* New Delhi : Concept Publishing Company.

1973 : *Essays on Indian Folklore.* Kolkata : Indian Publication.

1978 (With B.B. Lal and I.P. Singh) : *Researches in Prehistory and Physical Anthropology in India.* (Three Volumes). New Delhi : Classical Publication.

1978 : *Growth and Development of Anthropology in Bihar.* New Delhi : Classical Publication.

1979 (With B.N. Sahay) : *Applied Anthropology and Development in India.* New Delhi : National Publication.

Besides above books, Vidyarthi had published nearly150 research papers in journals of national and international repute and edited books. Throughout his life, he attempted to establish anthropology as integrated subjects of Social-Cultural Anthropology, Biological Anthropology, Prehistoric Archaeological Anthropology, Linguistic Anthropology and Applied and Action Anthropology.

Contribution on Sacred Complex Study

Vidyarthi in his book, "*Sacred Complex in Hindu Gaya*" (1961) propounded the concept of Sacred Complex in relation to a

Sacred Hindu City Gaya about which descriptions are found in Vedas, Puranas, and Dharmashastras. He was greatly influenced by the concept of Folk-urban Continuum propounded by Robert Redfield, Concepts of Cultural Complex, Cultural Centres, Cultural Specialists and Cultural Media of Milton Singer and also the Concept of Cultural Role of City propounded by Redfield and Milton Singer of Chicago University, USA.

Vidyarthi in this book propounded three analytical concepts : Sacred Geography, Sacred Performances and Sacred Specialists. He observed that the above three analytical concepts together were forming a complex at a great traditional Hindu City of Gaya. He formulated Sacred Complex Study Methodology and applied it over the Sacred City Gaya which was an example of Primary Urbanisation and great tradition in Redfieldian terminology. Vidyarthi had formulated following research hypotheses to be tested in course of his study:

- that Sacred Complex—a happy synthesis of sacred geography, sacred performances and sacred specialists— of a Hindu place of pilgrimage reflected a level of continuity, compromise and combination between great tradition and little tradition.
- that the sacred specialists of a place with their distinctive style of life transmit certain elements of great tradition to the rural population of India.
- that the sacred complex has been in the process of modification and transformation.

Vidyarthi observed that the city of Gaya was orthogenetic in origin. Hence, it was an example of Primary Urbanisation. It had patronage of the Great Kings and their dynasties. They had established it as a great cultural, religious and administrative centre. It was managed by the literate class—the Panda and Pujari. Panda and Pujari were literate people. They had distinctive lifestyle and offered daily worship in temple. They were connecting link between the Gods and Goddesses of the temple and the rural people. The temples were excellent examples of art, architecture and aesthetic behaviour. Thus, the sacred city Gaya was fulfilling all criteria of a great traditional city in Redfieldian terminology. It was regarded as a *Dham* by the local, regional and on some occasions national people. Cultural role of Gaya was witnessed in transmission of myths, prayers, songs, Bhajan, Kirtan, dance, *Puja-path*, offering of *Prasad* and worship from morning to evening among the rural masses of local, regional and national areas who had little traditions, but had very high regard for the great tradition of Gaya city. In this way, the great traditional city Gaya was showing a level of continuity, compromise and combination between Great tradition and little tradition.

He observed that the lifestyle of Panda and Pujari was distinctive. They maintained their routine according to activities of temple from morning to evening and for whole night on some specific occasions of worship. They teach the rural people about the religious value of the place and benefit of making pilgrimage of Gaya Dham. Thus, the elements of Great tradition of Gaya Dham reach among rural people who had little tradition. The Panda and Pujari visit to villages of their *Jajmans*. They receive good hospitality and *Dan-Dakshina* from the villagers. Thus, Panda and Pujari act as a connecting link between great tradition and little tradition.

Vidyarthi also observed changes and modifications in Sacred complex. The Sacred City of Gaya was witnessing a secondary urbanisation. Now-a-days, sacred complex was managed and maintained by District Administration and Management Committee.

In the study of sacred complex, Vidyarthi was clear in his stand with certain necessary specifications. He had used the term Hindu civilisation and not the Indian Civilisation. In place of culture, he had used the term sacred to evolve the analytical concepts of sacred geography, sacred performances and sacred specialists. He introduced the term sacred complex to indicate the integrative pattern envisaging all sacred elements.

The period of author's visit in field was 1948 to 1956. He found the sacred complex of Gaya was predominantly a great traditional centre. He observed a peculiar process of combination and compromise in the past leading to the development of Hinduism. The sacred complex provided a meeting place for different kinds of people, traditions, castes, sects, status, and flourished a sense of Indian Unity; even at a time when spirit of nationalism was lacking. And finally, he observed that sacred complex was undergoing secondary urbanisation which needs to be studied in future. A number of rich and valuable appendices attached at length, further enhanced the utility of the book.

Under the analytical concept sacred geography, Professor Vidyarthi included a number of sacred centres and sacred spots which were regarded as pure and pious by the people and they possessed abode of Gods and Goddesses. Vidyarthi had observed 51 such sacred spots spreads over Gayadham. Here people visit to offer rituals and worship after performing bath and without shoes and slippers and leather belt. Sacred areas and spots were demarcated from the secular areas.

Under the analytical term sacred performances, Vidyarthi dealt with rituals, worships and offering done at each sacred centres by pilgrims, devotees and visitors.

Under the analytical concept sacred specialists, Vidyarthi described the lifestyle and roles played by Panda and Pujari. At each sacred centre, there was a priest termed as Panda and Pujari who mediated between deities and devotees and pilgrims. Sacred specialists were involved in getting the rituals and worship performed for which they were paid *Dan* and *Dakshina* by the devotees and pilgrims.

Thus, in a Hindu place of Pilgrimage or Dham like Gaya, the three sacred elements—Sacred geography, Sacred performances and Sacred specialists—were integrated together to form a Sacred complex. Thus, Vidyarthi's hypothesis related to Sacred complex was proved theoretically and methodologically as truth.

After study of Professor Vidyarthi on Sacred complex in Hindu Gaya, a number of his students field tested the concept of Sacred complex in different fields like Janakpur, Kashi,

Deoghar, Rajgir, Ayodhya, Prayagraj, Mathura, Haridwar, Puri, Badarinath, Kedarnath, Somnath, Dwarika, Vaishnav Devi, Tirupati, Rameshwaram and others.

Later on Sacred complex model was applied to Buddist, Jain, Sikh and Muslim civilisations.

Contribution on Nature-Man-Spirit Complex

Vidyarthi had propounded the concept of Nature-Man-Spirit Complex in his book, "*Maler : Nature-Man-Spirit Complex in a Hill Tribe of Bihar*" (1963). He was deeply influenced by the ecological Anthropologist at America Julian H. Steward who was also Supervisor of his doctoral Dissertation at Chicago University, USA in 1956-58. According to Steward, man developed his technology, economy, social organisation and religious organisation according to ecology in which he lived. Ecological conditions were not same all over the world. Rather ecology, i.e. Man-Habitat interaction varied in different environments, such as hills, forests, deserts, coastal, islands and plains. Hence, cultural evolution had followed multi-linear course of evolution. Vidyarthi observed the ecological conditions of Sauria Paharia—hills and forests—evolving a particular type of technology, economy, social organisation and religious organisation. He found that the ecology, i.e. social organisation and religious organisation were forming a complex in the lifestyle of Malers. He was very much clear in his stand. He used the term Nature in place of ecology, Man in place of social organisation and Spirit in place of spirit world of Maler. The three elements—Nature, Man and Spirit of Maler lifestyle were integrated together and presented a complex pattern in lifestyle of Maler. Hence, theoretically and methodologically, Vidyarthi was quite clear and successful in his stand on Nature-Man-Spirit Complex. Thus, he formulated a methodology to record the present oriented ethnography of tribal communities living in different ecological conditions of the country.

Vidyarthi observed that Sauria Paharia, who is also known as Maler because they speak Malto, a language of Dravidian family, lived in hills and forests of Rajmahal. Their ecological conditions were such in which their entire economic needs were fulfilled by hills and forests, i.e. nature. Thus, under the analytical term 'Nature', Vidyarthi described the economic relation between Sauria Paharia and hills and forests. Maler possessed very simple technology of gathering, hunting and shifting cultivation. Maler did collection of edible roots, shoots, stems, leaves, flower, fruits, and seeds from the forest. They collected timber and bamboo to erect houses. They gathered dry woods and cow dung to be used as fuel for cooking food. They collected fodder from the forest. They collected Chop fibres and Sevai grass from the forest to prepare rope, mat, cot and other articles. They also collected Jari-buti or herbal medicines from the forest. Thus, forest was fulfilling their varieties of needs. Hills and forests were also abodes of their spirits.

The Malers were practising shifting cultivation or Jhum cultivation which is known as Khalu or Kalu cultivation in local term. Their cultivation is also known as Swidden Cultivation. This cultivation involved cutting and clearing of the bushes, leaving them to dry, burning them to ash, sowing after first rain of rainy season with spade, weeding, watching, harvesting, thrashing and merry making. They did shifting cultivation on collective basis. The yields were distributed among families after thrashing and winnowing. Thus, the nature was playing significant role in the lifestyle of Malers.

Under the analytical term 'Man', Vidyarthi described the social organisation of the Maler. Under social organisation, he had described marriage, family and kinship organisations of Maler. He observed that Maler practised village exogamy rule. The boys and the girls of the same village are never married. There was no totemic clan organisation. Hence, marriage in mother's village was also tabooed. The most common ways of acquiring marriage mate was bride price, Raji-Khusi, elopement, service and exchange. Generally, boy's parents or anyone of his relatives approach the parents or guardian of the girl for marriage settlement. Maler boys and girls of neighbouring villages met frequently in forest, hills and markets. Hence, they develop attraction towards each other. They convey their choice to their parents. The parents accept the choice, if they were not of same village and of mother's village. Marriages are held in simple way and manners followed by a marriage feast of rice and meat.

The family of Maler is patriachal, patrilocal, patrilineal and nuclear. Family is centre of cultural, social, economic, political, religious, health and sanitational activities. It is also chief agency of socialisation of Maler children. The lineage is also patrilineage. On the basis of marriage and blood relations, kins were divided into affinal and consanguial kins. Avoidance and joking relations were also in existence. Birth, marriage and death rituals were held collectively. Worships were also organised collectively. Thus, a village as a unit was collection of families of consanguial kins. Villagers were organised under the guidance of village head and village priest.

Under the analytical term 'Spirit', Vidyarthi described the spirit world of the Maler. Maler called their spirits as Gossaiyans. Gossaiyans had their abodes at hills, in forest, rivers, bushes, mud hills, old trees, root of old trees, stone pieces, bamboo poles, below bridges, tanks, wells and others. Every Maler had in mind the concept of spirit and supernatural world. Maler children are instructed about the Gossaiyans from very beginning of life. The term Gossaiyan was a household word and used to denote a group of spirits that were believed to guide their destiny.

Vidyarthi observed that Malers had deep faith in spirits of their ancestors. The ancestral spirits played significant role in deciding the destiny of Malers. Malers were very cautious in performing rites and observing ceremonies. The spirits of ancestors were worshipped annually collectively. Ancestral spirits appeared in dreams and demanded worship and sacrifice. Malers have too many Gossaiyans like Beru Gossaiyan (Sun God), Belpu Gossaiyan (Moon God), Bindke Gossaiyan (Star God), Chal Gossaiyan, Rakshi Gossaiyan, Kando Gossaiyan.

In order to describe the spirit world of Maler, Vidyarthi applied his methodology of sacred complex. He attempted to explore and describe sacred geography, sacred performance and sacred specialists of Malers. In sacred geography, he described sacred centres and sacred areas of Malers. The sacred area of Maler envisaged the whole village and its vincity. The household deity, who is generally an ancestral spirit, resided in kitchen or a part of the hut. The God of village resided at the outskirt of the village. The God of forest lived in forest situated nearby the village. The God of mountain resided at the top hill. The God of tree resides in root of the tree. The God of snake resided in mud hills or root hills. Similarly tanks, streams, rivers, trees, ditch, hills, and others were the abodes of numerous other deities.

Sacred centres were sacred spots where varieties of rituals and religious activities were carried on. The three valuable village deities were Chal Gossaiyan, Raksi Gossaiyan and Kando Gossaiyan. Chal Gossaiyan resides in Jaherthan or sacred grove of the village. On every occasion sacrifices were offered to him for the wellbeing and prosperity of the village. Raksi Gossaiyan resides in Raksithan somewhat away from the village. He controls the entry of evil spirits in the village. On the occasion of annual worship, sacrifices were offered in his name by the village priest. Kando Gossaiyan was presiding deity of the village. He was marked by a wooden seat placed in the house of Kanho Manjhi or placed centrally in the village under some thatched structure. The other sacred centres were Manjhithan where the village deity Jhanda Gossaiyan resides. Singpate Nadu was represented by two black stones and was worshipped on the occasion of Bandana festival. Chal Gossaiyan was located at hill top. Maler Gossaiyan was represented by 11 cylindrical stones. Kanhaiya Nadu was the spirit of stream and Tudu Nadu was spirit of Tiger.

Among Maler, there were three sacredotal functionaries at village level. They were Kando Manjhi, Kotwar and Chalwa. Kando Manjhi was religious head of Maler village. He controlled and directed the ritualistic life of the people. He was supposed to be chosen by the God. For his selection villagers gathered in the middle of the village in front of the house of the village head man. Incense was burnt. Kotwar offered prayers and worships to invoke the deity for the selection of Kando Manjhi. If everything was found well, it was believed that the Gossaiyan had accepted him as village priest. He was then formally declared as village head priest or Kando Manjhi.

Kotwar is assistant to Kando Manjhi or head priest. He performed the actual worship including offering of sacrifices to the deity. A Kotwar had life tenure and was selected in the same manner as that of Kando Manjhi, the head priest. At the time of selection of Kotwar, Kando Manjhi invoked the name of Gossaiyan. Chalwe is assistant to Kotwar. He was also selected in the same manner as the other two religious dignatories.

The sacred performances of Malers included worships offered to Gossaiyans on different occasions and rituals observed in those connections. The help of sacred specialists were taken on the occasion of village level collective worships and sacrifices. Sacrificial objects were goat, sheep, cock, egg, buffalo and pigeon. The other articles of *puja* were vermilion, sunfried rice, flowers, fruits, loaf sugar, liquor, new cereals.

Thus, Vidyarthi evolved a methodological approach—Nature-Man-Spirit Complex—to describe and analyse the tribal way of life in terms of their ecological setting, social institutions and spirit world or supernatural world.

After Vidyarthi, a good nmber of his students had followed this methodology to explore present day enthography of tribals in different parts of India.

The concepts of sacred complex, great tradition and little tradition were criticised by a French scholars—Lucy Dumont and Pecock. According to them, the concepts of sacred complex, great tradition and little tradition are mental construct and ideal types. It is very difficult to find great tradition, little tradition and sacred complex in the same way as were mentally constructed by the scholars of sacred complex and great tradition and little tradition. Sacred complex is found even in villages which have little traditions. Similarly, elements of literacy, artistic and asthetic behaviours are also found in villages which have little traditions. Similarly, magical performances and illiteracy, which have been identified as elements of little tradition, are also found at great traditional centres having sacred complex. According to these two French scholars, it is very difficult to draw a clear cut distinction between great tradition and little tradition on the basis of two different places—rural and primary urban.

Contribution on Tribal Studies

Vidyarthi studied a village Ghaghra under Census operation in 1961. The study of this Munda village reflected that Manjhi, a section of Munda tribe had adopted the Hindu style of life and had become a caste. This study presented an example of tribe caste continuum.

Vidyarthi had edited a book, "*Aspects of Religion in Indian Society*" (1961). In this book, Vidyarthi had contributed a paper on, 'Sacred Complex of a Tribal Village'. The other contributors were Gopala Sarana, McKim Marriott, A. Aiyappan, K.N. Sharma, R.S. Srivastva, Carstairs, Mathur, I.P. Singh, T.N. Madan, Yogesh Atal, Chattopadhyay, T.R. Singh, Surjit Sinha and K.N. Sahay. The book covered a wide range on the way religion was practiced by Indian folk in different parts of India. Analysis of certain complex present among tribal people and which were modified under the influence of Hinduism were also done.

In his book, "*Cultural Contours of Tribal Bihar*" (1966), Vidyarthi presented the historical, geographical and social background of the tribes of Chotanagpur. Some concepts like unity and extension, Sanskritisation, desanskritisation, tribalisation, detribalisation, retribalisation were attempted to explain in the context of tribal Bihar. The book also dealt with changes occurring in tribal societies of Bihar and factors responsible for them.

In his paper, 'Cultural Types in Tribal India with Special Reference to Tribal Bihar' (1966), Vidyarthi developed the concept of cultural types and attempted to classify the tribes of Bihar into four cultural types which were as follows:

- Hunting and gathering type – Birhor
- Hill cultivation type – Sauria Paharia

- Artisan type – Lohra, Karmali, Mahli and Chickbaraik.
- Urban and Industrial Labour type – All tribes living in and around urban and industrial areas.

In evolving the concept of cultural types, Vidyarthi paid special attention on economy, ecology, socio-religious adaptations, religious beliefs and emerging contemporary situation.

Vidyarthi made a field visit of Andaman and Nicobar Islands with a team of post-graduate students in 1970. On the basis of his field experiences, he published his two research papers in *Journals of Social Research,* published by the Department of Anthropology, Ranchi University in Vol. 1 & Vol. 2 in 1971. His first paper, 'Cultural Diversities in the Andaman and Nicobar Islands' explained the existence of diverse cultural groups of the islands and made a comparison of their social, cultural, religious, political and linguistic ways of life. His another paper, 'Ranchi Tribals in Andaman and Nicobar' described the migration of Munda and Oraon tribal group to Andaman and Nicobar islands to work their as migrant labourers. They were popularly known as Ranchiwala. They settled there since generations. They had played significant role in making of modern Andaman.

Vidyarthi in his book with B.K. Roy, "*Tribal Culture of India*", presented in detail about life ways of Tribal India. Historical backgrounds, social organisation, economic activities, political organisation, religious beliefs and practices, life cycle and personality development, tribal villages, tribal folklores, polyandry, matriarchy, planning, approaches and plans of welfare and development were presented elaborately and scientifically in the book. This book is still regarded by Indian anthropologists as a base book for understanding tribal culture in India.

Contribution on the Phases of Growth of Indian Anthropology

Vidyarthi in his paper, 'Social Anthropological Researches in India' published in the *Journal of Social Research,* Vol. 9, No. 1, (1960) had made a review of the rise of Social Anthropological Researches in India. According to him, the rise of Social Anthropological Researches in India had progressed through three successive stages of development, which were as follows:

- Formative Period (1774-1911)
- Constructive Period (1920-1949)
- Critical or Analytical Period (1950 onwards).

According to Vidyarthi, the formulative period of Indian anthropological researches began in 1774 with the establishment of Royal Asiatic Society of Bengal by Sir Willium Jonnes, Chief Justice of Kolkata High Court. With his efforts, the publication of a Research Journal entitled, '*Journal of Royal Asiatic Society of Bengal*' was started. In this journal, researches on man, culture and society made by social scientists were published. The formulative or formulatory period continued till 1919. In between 1774 to 1919, there were no basic changes in nature of researches on man, society and culture. British anthropologists, British administrators and some anthropologically oriented Indian scholars made study of man, society and culture of Indian people in this formulatory period. They published papers, articles, reports and monographs on Indian tribes and castes of different parts of India.

According to Vidyarthi, the constructive phase of Social Anthropological Researches began in 1920 and continued till 1949. In this period, the Department of Anthropology was established at Calcutta University in 1920 and first Anthropological Journal '*Man in India*' was started in 1921. Now Indian scholars trained in subject of Anthropology and anthropological researches began to appear. They were taught different papers of anthropology and trained in anthropological researches. They started studying different aspects of tribes and castes in India. They published their results in the form of monographs and research papers in *Journals of Royal Asiatic Society of Bengal* and *Man In India*. The constructive phase of social anthropological researches in India continued till 1949.

According to Vidyarthi, Critical and Analytical Phase of Social Anthropological Researches in India began in 1950 and continuing even today. In this period, Anthropology as a subject of study and research was established in almost all Universities of States of India. Tribal Research Institutes and Cultural Research Institutes were also established. Now, Indian anthropologists came in contact with American anthropologists. The traditions of village studies, caste studies, urban studies, religion study, power structure study, folklore study, social psychological study, community development programmes study, development and change study, applied anthropological researches, action anthropological researches, development anthropological researches were started. A number of methods, techniques, approaches, concepts, theories and methodologies were developed based on village, caste, urban development, applied and action studies. Anthropology became an integrated discipline of Socio-Cultural Anthropology, Biological Anthropology, Prehistoric Archaeological Anthropology, Linguistic Anthropology and Applied and Action Anthropology.

In his another paper, 'Researches in Social Science in India' published in the *Journal of Social Science Information,* International Social Science Council, Paris Vol. 5, No. 1 (1966). Vidyarthi presented the recent trend in Social Anthropological Researches in India. He highlighted the approaches of anthropologists to integrate the knowledge of various disciplines for proper understanding of man and his society. He made special mention of the various efforts of social scientists to study the problems of rural and tribal societies of India.

In another paper, 'Social Anthropology in India Since Independence' published in the journal *Man and Society* (1972), Vidyarthi examined the rise and growth of Social Anthropology in India. He concluded that social anthropological researches in India were organised and developed under the British influence, but flourished under the influence and stimulus from American and other countries of the West. The administrative anthropology of colonial period was getting an orientation of academic interest. With this, a new quest for interdisciplinary approach to understand the various dimensions of complex Indian Societies had become evident.

In his trend report submitted to ICSSR on Tribal Studies in India, Vidyarthi viewed elaborately researches in different tribal zones of India. As regard anthropological researches in north-eastern Himalayas, he observed that this area was relatively better explored and a series of ethnographic publications were made by British administrators, Missionaries, and anthropologists. The ethnographic works in central and north-western Himalayas revealed that very little ethnographic work was done in this area till independence. In post-independence era, the ethnography of these regions received attention of scholars of University of Lucknow, Chandigarh and Delhi, Census operation and Anthropological Survey of India. The tribal belt of Central India had been exposed to anthropological researches and extensive ethnographic works were done. About tribal studies in West India, he felt that the research tradition of Gujarat was quite strong. Regarding tribal studies in South India, he viewed that they had early beginning, but anthropology at analytical level could not flourish there due to lack of academic recognition till recently. While reviewing the existing materials, Vidyarthi pointed out the gaps in tribal studies and priority of tribal researches to be undertaken in different zones.

In his book, "*Rise of Anthropology in India : A Social Science Orientation*", Vol. 1 (1977), Vidyarthi presented a critical appraisal of researches done by Indian social scientists in general and social anthropologists in particular. The book aimed at highlighting source of the basic factors of genesis and development of socio-cultural researches in India. An attempt was made to record and examine the researches conducted by Indian social scientists on Indian tribal societies and cultures. Besides reviewing ethnographic researches on tribal communities of India living in different parts of the country, the Vol. 1 of the book presented the theoretical and methodological appraisal of studies on socio-cultural change in tribal societies in India.

In his book, "*Rise of Anthropology in India*", Vol. 2, (1977), Vidyarthi attempted to review and present the results of researches on village studies, caste studies, urban centre studies, industrial cities studies, religion study, psycho-social studies, medical anthropological studies, Applied and Action anthropological studies and profiles of Indian social scientists. The book attempted to fill-up the long felt gap in the knowledge of social anthropological researches in India.

Contribution on Urban and Anthropological Researches

Under the influence of Chicago School of Cultural Anthropology, the need was felt to study the cultural roles of cities and their contributions in the development of India's civilisation. Vidyarthi in his paper, 'Thinking About Sacred City' published in the *Journal of Eastern Anthropologist,* Vol. 13, No. 4 (1960), highlighted the anthropological approach to study the Indian Civilisation in terms of various dimensions including traditional and urban industrial centres. His approaches to the study of Indian Civilisation attracted a good number of scholars to study the complex societies in India.

His book, "*Sacred Complex in Hindu Gaya*" (1961) dealt with study of a traditionally emerged urban centre—Gaya. In this book, he attempted to throw light on interaction between the great community having literacy, religious, artistic, aesthetic and orthogenetic organisation and little community having illiteracy, magical and simple organisation. He also highlighted the complex organisation of Sacred geography, Sacred performances and Sacred specialists of a traditionally emerged primary urban centre Gaya which had patronage of ancient kings and dynasties and whose management and maintenance was in the hands of Sacred specialists—Panda and Pujari.

Vidyarthi's concepts and methodological approaches of Sacred Complex of Hindu Gaya had attracted a number of his students and colleagues to study Sacred Complex of almost all traditionally emerged primary urban centres of India.

In his paper, 'Historical Factors of Urbanisation in Ranchi' published in *Journal of Social Research,* Vol. 7, No. 2 (1964), Vidyarthi attempted to show the emergence of Ranchi as an urban centre historically. According to him, Ranchi was a tribal town of local haat bazar. But it was developed into hill station by Britishers. They established army cantonment. Then a number of offices, schools, hospitals, station, bus stand were established. A number of businessmen came here from different parts of India to run their business. As a result, now, Ranchi had emerged as a tribal and non-tribal town.

In his book, "*Cultural Configuration of Ranchi*" (1969), Vidyarthi attempted to highlight origin, morphology, function and influence of Ranchi as a city as a link between interactions of two distinct cultures—folk and urban, or the tribal and non-tribal. He also observed Ranchi as a tribal city acting as a centre of transformations of various tribal societies in the midst of which it was located. In fact, his attempt was to present a monographic study of the city bringing out historical, geographical, demographic, socio-economic and religio-political characteristics of Ranchi city as a whole.

Considering the importance of industrial urbanisation and consequent implications, Vidyarthi took up the study of industrial complexes of Chotanagpur with a view to develop a new branch of anthropology. His book, "*Socio-cultural Implications of Industrialisation in India : A Case Study of Tribal Bihar*" (1970), dealt with the study of Hatia Industrial Complex. Hatia Industrial Complex was an excellent case study for understanding the form and process of culture change caused by the emergence of factory in an underdeveloped area. The study of Hatia Industrial Complex provided a case for a longitudinal analysis of the various phases of industrialisation such as formulatory, constructive, productive and elaborative phases. The formulatory phase of urbanisation included the uprooting of folk and peasant societies having social and cultural base, their rehabilitation and reaction. The constructive phase included the establishment of factories, township, commercial network, educational centre, hospitals and others. In the productive and elaborative phase, the full-fledged development of industrial complex, means industrial production and industrial style of living came into existence.

Taking the special expansion of the industrial complex and its radiating influence, Vidyarthi noted that the industrial core had undergone geographical expansion. Even at the second phase of development, three concentric regions of expansion and influence could be established. These three regions were as follows:

- The Core of Industrial Complex.
- The Fringe of the Industrial Complex.
- The Margin of Industrial Complex.

The first circle with a radius of five miles covered all the factories, townships, dam, railway station, official buildings, eight uprooted villages and also the village Hatia which is even now standing in the core of industrial complex.

The second concentric circle extended beyond this circle but up to a radius of 10 miles from the industrial core. It included 150 villages. Four villages belonging to fringe industrial complex were selected for intensive study. The impact of successive phases of industrialisation on these villages were recorded to provide a comparative analysis of demography, economy, and socio-religious customs of the pre-industrial and industrial periods.

The third concentric circle which extended up to 20 miles from the industrial core and covered more than 200 villages constituted the industrial marginal circle. This belt seemed to be less affected by the industrial core. Its impact was recorded again by an intensive study of four villages selected at different distances within the margin of the industrial complex.

Vidyarthi's book, "*Bhartiya Nagar*" (1961) reviewed the historical growth of urban centres in India, classified them from different angles and examined the cultural life of urban centres with two illustrative accounts of sacred city of Gaya and emerging industrial city of Ranchi. The book based on both literary and fieldwork, was proved useful for giving a picture of urbanisation in India and in view of its utility. The book was translated into Gujarati by two eminent sociologists of Bombay University—A.R. Desai and Meera Desai.

Contribution on Political Anthropology

Vidyarthi's edited book, "*Leadership in India*" (1967) was a result of All India Seminar on 'Tribal and Rural Leadership in India' held at Ranchi in 1962 under the joint auspices of Council of Social and Cultural Research, Bihar and Department of Anthropology, Ranchi University, Ranchi. This book was a valuable contribution in Political Anthropology because it covered papers on various aspects of rural and tribal leadership in India. The volume also provided certain theoretical and methodological leads relevant to leadership studies. The book was divided into two parts. The first part of the book dealt with problems of leadership in India at theoretical and methodological levels. The second part of the book had thirteen chapters in which attempts had been made to explore the authority and leadership pattern of tribal India.

Vidyarthi in his book with K.N. Sahay, "*Dynamics of Tribal Leadership in Bihar*" (1976), had attempted to explore and present the dynamics of leadership in tribal Bihar. The book explored and presented the genesis and development of Tribal leadership in Bihar. Jharkhand movement in post-independence period, ecological, economic and social-structural background of tribal typologies, biographical analysis of tribal leaders, pre-election study of tribal voters, tribal leadership as reflected in elections, village level leader's attitude towards modernity, urban leaders in comparison to village and sub-regional level leaders, followers' attitude towards leadership, modernity and political consciousness.

In his book, "*Student Unrest in Chotanagpur*" (1976), Vidyarthi attempted to explore certain political issues related to student leaders and the functioning of their unions. He also highlighted the causes of student unrest in Chotanagpur.

Contribution on Psychological Anthropology

Vidyarthi's book, "*Sacred Complex in Hindu Gaya*" (1961) had analysed in detail the biographies of the priestly community Gayawal to highlight the process of personality formation among Gayawals. Gayawals were associated with the pilgrimage of the Gaya Dham and offering of Pinda for the salvation and peace of the ancestors. The children of Gayawal priestly community were dependent on the income of their fathers' priesthood. Their parents met every demands of their children from the income they had from the priesthood. But after adolescence, they were left to deal with Jajmans and pilgrims coming from different parts of India for their livelihood and survival. In the light of biographical materials Vidyarthi attempted to explore the personality structure and lifestyle of Gayawal. The personality of Gayawals was characterised by caste consciousness, profession consciousness, conservatism and ritualism.

Vidyarthi in his book, "*Nature-Man-Spirit Complex*" (1963), also attempted to explore the personality type and personality structure of Maler, Sauria Paharia, on the basis of biographical study of Malers. He devoted a chapter on personality type of Maler. He observed the usefulness of biographies in understanding the ethos and worldview of a particular cultural situation at the axis of self.

Contribution of Folklore

Professor Vidyarthi was the president of the folklore section of all India Folk Culture Conference, Bombay (1951). He was also editor of the journal *Folklore* (1966). He was very much interested in the study of folkloric tradition of Bihar which had broad dimensions like Bhojpuri, Magahi, Maithili and tribal languages. He had included linguistics and folklore as a special paper taught under the subject anthropology. According to Professor Vidyarthi, folklores are our traditional heritage continuing generation after generation as oral traditions. They include our prehistory, history, psychology, sociology and culture. Vidyarthi used to collect data on folkloric traditions of different parts of India with the help of his students. He used to send his students for 45 days of fieldwork as a part of M.A./ M.Sc. Anthropology syllabus. In fieldwork, students used to collect data on folklores such as songs, ballads, myths, tales, proverbs, riddles, idioms, phrases, and other oral aspects of the community concerned. In his book, "*Maler : Nature-Man-Spirit Complex of Tribal Bihar*" (1963), Vidyarthi had collected folklores of Maler habitat, social organisation, economy, religion, festivals, fairs and cultural history. He had edited a book, "*Folklore Researches in India*" (1973). This book dealt with collection of essays on Indian folklore written by eminent anthropologists, sociologists and social scientists of India.

Contribution on Scheduled Caste Study

Professor Vidyarthi was very much interested in the study of Scheduled Castes of Bihar. In his book, "*Harijan Today*" (1977) with Dr. N. Mishra, he attempted to explore and analyse socio-cultural, religious, economic and political aspects of Scheduled Castes of Bihar. Changes taking place in Scheduled Castes also get significant place in this book. Several reservational and welfare schemes had brought changes in social, cultural, political, religious and educational status of Scheduled Castes.

Contribution on Applied and Action Anthropology

As referred earlier, Professor Vidyarthi was Chairman of Several Committees set up by the Government of India for the upliftment of Scheduled Tribes, Scheduled Castes, Backward Castes, primitive tribes and rehabilitation scheme meant for them. As an anthropologist, he made several suggestions which were of applied value. He also evaluated the rehabilitation schemes of Birhor and stressed upon the importance of Applied and Action Anthropology.

Vidyarthi had organised series of All India Level Seminars on the practical problems of the Scheduled Tribes. The proceedings of the Seminars were published in the form of books. As a result of these publications, it became possible to initiate the teaching of Applied and Action anthropology in universities as a paper in the subject Anthropology.

His edited book, "*Anthropology and Tribal Welfare in India*" (1960) dealt with various anthropological aspects related to tribal welfare in India. It also presented the anthropological approaches, theories and methodology related to tribal welfare programmes. The book was a collection of papers written by eminent anthropologists on various aspects and problems of tribal welfare.

Vidyarthi's book, "*Indian Anthropology in Action*" (1960) dealt with collection of papers contributed by anthropologists on Action Anthropology. Through research papers attempts were made to highlight the role of anthropologists in bringing anthropological knowledge in action.

Vidyarthi's book, "*Applied Anthropology in India*" (1968), included 38 valuable and thoughtful papers covering a wide range of research in the field of applied anthropology. The book was divided into four parts:

1. General concepts, principles, problems and postulates of applied and action anthropology;
2. Problems of tribal welfare;
3. Caste studies collected from specific tribes, and
4. Few problems of Applied physical anthropology.

The another edited volume, "*Conflict, Tension and Cultural Trends in India*" (1968), consisted of 28 papers on various themes of conflict, tension and cultural trends in tribal and rural societies in India.

His edited book, "*Prefarming and Marginal Farming Tribes of India*" (1978) consisted of collection of research papers by anthropologists on different aspects of prefarming and marginal farming tribes of India. He highlighted various problems faced by prefarming and marginal farming tribes and also suggested ways and means to uplift their condition.

Contribution on Restudy

Vidyarthi in his book, "*Kharia : Then and Now*" (1979) with V.S. Upadhyay studied the Kharia tribe of Chotanagpur in which he had applied restudy method to know the continuity and changes in Kharia Tribe. The Kharia Tribe was studied by S.C. Roy and the book was published under the title, "*Kharia*" in two volumes in 1937. Vidyarthi took baseline data from S.C. Roy's book and made a restudy of the tribe in 1977-78. The book was published in 1979 under the title, "*Kharia : Then and Now*". The book presented continuity and changes in Kharia culture, society, economy, religion and education.

R.K. MUKHERJEE (1919-)

Ram Krishna Mukherjee was born in Kolkata on 28th October, 1919. He did graduation in Science from Kolkata University in 1939. He received M.Sc. degree in Anthropology from the same university in 1941. He received Ph.D. degree from Cambridge University, London, in 1948.

Mukherjee had served in several countries and in different capacities. Her served as Chief Research Officer in his Majesty's Social Survey, London in 1948-49. He was consultant to the Government of Turkey, Central Statistical Office, Ankara in 1949. He served as Director, Field Research Methods and Specifications for the Government of India, National Sample Survey, Indian Statistical Institute 1950-51, Consultant, London School of Economics, 1952, Professor for Indian Studies, Humboldt University, Berlin, 1953-1957, Research Professor, Indian Statistical Institute, since 1957. He was deeply involved in conducting and guiding researches on social change in India. He was specially interested in research methodology and application of statistical principles and methods of sociology.

Publications

1941 : "The Khasi Huts on Mawphlang". *Journal of Letter,* New Series, Calcutta University, 6(6) : 177-87.

1944 : "Destitution at Contai Thana : Midnapur". *Modern Review.* Kolkata, 26:6, 296-303.

1944 : "Effects of the Food Crisis of 1943 on the Rural Population of Naokhali, Bengal". *Science and Culture,* Kolkata, Vol, 10:5, 185-191 and Vol. 10:6, 231-38.

1945 : "Scarcity of Milk in Bengal", *Modern Review,* Vol. 77:6, 294-96.

1945 : "The Famine and Disintegration of Education in Rural Bengal" (with K.P. Chattopadhyay). *Science and Culture,* Kolkata, Vol 11:1, 20-26.

1946 : "A Note on the Concentration of Income in Bengal Villages" (with M.M. Mukherjee). *Sankhya,* Kolkata : Vol 7:3, 327-328.

1946 : "A Sample Survey of After effects of Bengal Famine of 1943" (with P.C. Mahalanobis and A. Ghos) *Sankhya*; Kolkata, Vol. 7 : 4, 337-46.

1946 : "Note on Concentration of Agricultural Wealth in Bengal". *Sankhya,* Kolkata, Vol. 7:4, 442-444.

1946 : "A Plan for Rehabilitation of Bengal" (with K.P. Chattopadhyay). Statistical Publishing Society.

1946 : "Famine and Rehabilitation of Bengal". (with three co-authors), Statistial Publishing Society, Kolkata.

1948 : "The Economic Structure in Rural Bengal : A Survey of Six Villages". *American Sociological Review,* USA, Vol. 13:6, 660-72.

1949 : "The Economic Structure and Social Life in Six Villages of Bengal". *American Sociological Review,* USA , Vol. 13:6, 415-425.

1949 : "Economic Structure in Two Breton Village" (with F.K. Girling), *Rural Sociology,* USA, Vol. 14:4, 295-305.

1950 : "Communal Tension in Uganda". *Man In India,* Ranchi, Vol. 30 : 2&3, 1-28.

1950 : "Tagore and Class Forces in India". *Science and Society,* USA Vol. 14:2, 97-114.

1950 : "Breton and Economic Structure" (with F.K. Girling), *Rural Sociology,* Vol. 15:1, 49-62.

1951 : "A Study of Difference in Physical Development by Socio-economic Strata". *Sankhya,* Kolkata, Vol. 11:1, 47-56.

1951 : "Cotton Economy of Uganda Protectorate". *Interagra,* Prague, Vol 5:1&2, 1-15.

1952 : "Peasant Problem in Uganda". *Interagra,* Prague, Vol. 6:2, 178-92.

1953 : "Caste in Bengal". Wissenchaftliche Zeibechriff der Humboldt Universitat Zu Berlin, Vol. 3:1, 13-23.

1954 : "A Note on Analysis of Data on Social Mobility" (with J.R. Hall). In *Social Mobility in Britain,* Routledge and Kegan Paul, London, 266-90. (ed.) by G. Glass.

1954 : "A Further Note on the Analysis of Data on Social Mobility". In *Social Mobility in England* (ed.) by G. Class, Routledge and Kegan Paul, London.

1954 : "A Study of Social Mobility between Three Generations". In *Social Mobility in Britain,* Routledge and Kegan Paul, London.

1954 : "Social Mobility and Age at Marriage". In *Social Mobility in England,* Routledge and Kegan Paul, London.

1955 : "Tribes in Pre-British Uganda". *German Academy of Sciences,* Berlin, Vol. 3:1, 99-128.

1955 : *The Physical Characteristics of Ancient Inhabitants of Jebel Moya Sudan* (with two co-authors), Cambridge University Press, Cambridge, U.K.

1956 : *The Problem of Uganda : A Study in Acculturation.* Academic Verlag, Berlin.

1957 : *The Dynamics of a Rural Society.* Academic Verlag, Berlin.

1958 : *The Rise and Fall of the East India Company.* Academic Verlag, Berlin.

1958 : *Six Villages of Bengal : A Socio-economic Study.* Asiatic Society of Bengal, Kolkata.

1959 : *A Note on the Classification of Family Structures*, UNESCO Research Centre, Kolkata.

1960 : "Some Considerations on Social Research". *Eastern Anthropologist,* Lucknow, Vol. 13:3, 121-131.

1961 : "A Note on Village as Unit or Variable for Study of Rural Society", *Eastern Anthropologist*, Lucknow, Vol. 14, No 1, pp. 3-29.

1961 : "Caste and Economic Structure in West Bengal in Present Time". In *Sociology, Social Research and Social Problems in India* (ed.) by R.N. Saxena, Asia Publishing House, Bombay, 157-67.

1962 : "On Classification of Family Structure : Dimension—Kinship Composition, Indian Anthropology : Essays in

Honour of D.N. Majumdar". Asia Publishing House, Bombay, 352-98.

1962 : "Sociologist and Social Change in India Today". *Sociological Bulletin*, Indian Sociological Society, Bombay, Vol. 9:2, 4-13.

1963 : "On Village Studies in India". *Indian Journal of Social Research,* Meerut, Vol. 4:2, 1-14.

1963 : "Socio-economic Factor in Children's Body Development". Ranchi, *Journal of Social Research,* Vol. 6:122, 12-14.

1963 : "Urbanisation and Social Transformation in India". *Dharwad International Journal of Comparative Sociology,* Vol. 4:2, 178-210.

1963 : "Social Research and Mahalanobi's D^2" (with Suraj Bandopadhyay), *Contributions to Statistics.* Kolkata : Statistical Publishing Society and Bergaman Press, Oxford.

1963 : "A Note on the Measurement of Kinship Distance". Meerut : *Indian Journal of Social Research,* Vol. 4:1, 12-14.

1963 : "A Note on the Use of Societal Factors for Stratification in Social Surveys". Kolkata : *Bulletin of Cultural Research Institute.*

1964 : "Comments on Ethnic Unit Classification by Naroll". USA : *Current Anthropology,* Vol. 5:4, 301.

1964 : "A Minority Marginal Group in Kolkata". Louvaina, Belgium, *International Sociological Association,* Vol. 111, 157-68.

1964 : "Sociology and Folklore". Kolkata, *Proceedings of All India Folklore Conference.*

1965 : "A Minority Refugee Groups in Kolkata". In *Minority Problems* (ed.) by A.N. Bose and C.B. Bose, New York : Harper and Row, 93-97.

1965 : "Indian Tradition and Social Change". In *Towards a Sociology of Culture in India, Essays in Honour of Professor D.P. Mukherjee,* New Delhi : Prentice Hall of India, 189-211.

1965 : "On Major Stocks, Grand Races, Hauptrassen". Paris : *International Social Science Journal,* Vol. 17 : 124-25, 130-32.

1965 : *Sociologist and Social Change in India*. New Delhi : Prentice Hall.
1966 : *Recent Trends of Sociological Studies on Rural Society in India*. Tokyo : The Institute of Asian Economic Affairs.

G.S. GHURYE (1893-1983)

Govinda Shadashiva Ghurye did M.A. in Sociology from the University of Bombay. He received Ph.D. degree in Sociology from Cambridge University, London. He was the first Indian to become Head, Department of Sociology, University of Bombay after Sir Patrick Geddes. He was appointed as Reader in the Department of Sociology, Bombay University in 1924. He became Professor in Sociology at the Department of Sociology, Bombay University in 1934. He retired from his post in 1959. But he continued as UGC Retired Professor in the Department of Sociology, Bombay University for two years. In his 37 years of service in this institution, he contributed more than hundred articles and one and half dozen books. In all his time, he was busy in anthropological and sociological researches, besides teaching assignment.

His some of publications are as follows:

1932 : *Caste and Races in India.* London : Kegan Paul.
1938 : *Sex Habit of Middle Class People.* Pune : Gokhale Institute of Politics and Economics.
1943 : *Aboriginal So called and their Future.* Pune : Gokhale Institute of Politics and Economics.
1945 : *Culture and Society.* Bombay : Popular Book Depot.
1957 : *The Mahadeokolis*. Bombay : Popular Prakashan.
1959 : *The Scheduled Tribes.* Bombay : Popular Book Depot.
1960 : *After a Century and Quarter.* Bombay : Popular Prakashan.
1961 : *Caste, Class and Occupation.* Bombay : Popular Prakashan.
1962 : *Family and Kinship in Indo-European Family.* Bombay : Popular Prakashan.
1963 : *Anatomy of a Rural-Urban Community.* Bombay : Popular Book Depot.

1964 : *Indian Sadhu. Bombay* : Popular Prakashan.
1968 : *Religious Consciousness.* Bombay : Popular Prakashan.
1968 : *Social Tension in India.* Bombay : Popular Prakashan.
1973 : *I and Other Explorations.* Bombay : Popular Prakashan.
1974 : *Wither India.* Bombay : Popular Prakashan.
1978 : *India Recreates Democracy.* Bombay : Popular Prakashan.
1979 : *Vedic India.* Bombay : Popular Prakashan.
1980 : *The Burning Kaldrom of North-East.* Bombay : Popular Prakashan.

Contribution on Scheduled Tribes

Ghurye in his book, "*Aborigines so called*" (1943) did not accept the isolationist approach of Verrier Elwin who had propounded a National Park Theory for the development of tribals. He propounded assimilation theory for the development of tribals. He was of opinion that tribals are backward Hindus and without assimilation a proper development of tribals could not take place.

The book "*Aborigines so called and their future*" was published later on as "*The Scheduled Tribes*" (1959). This book was re-edited several times. In this book, Ghurye divided tribals into three classes, which are as follows:

- Tribals with high status in Hindu society for example Raj Gond.
- Partially Hinduised tribes for example Pahariya.
- Hill sections of tribes for example Sauria Paharia.

The assimilation theory of tirbals for development had attracted a number of anthropologists to study the Hindu influence upon tribes in India. Ghurye had characterised the tribals as Backward Hindu and argued that any attempt to isolate tribals from mainstream of Indian life would be meaningless. While sections of these tribes are properly integrated into Hindu society, but bulk of them are loosely integrated. Very few tribes living in hills and forests have been more than touched by Hinduism. According to Ghurye, tribals are imperfectly integrated classes of Hindu Society. He was of view that for the sake of convenience they may be designated as tribal classes of Hindu society. Tribals had retained much more of tribal creeds and organisations than many castes of Hindu society. But in reality they were backward Hindus. The Gonds were best illustration of assimilation and the Raj Gond ranked with the Hindu cultivating castes.

Contribution on Village Study

Ghurye had made study of a village named Haweli Taluka in four seasons in 1954-1958. Based on fieldwork, he published a book, "*After a Century and Quarter*" (1960). He had made study of this village with the assistance of his two research scholars L.K. Chapekar and M.G. Kulkarni. This village was studied by Major Coats in 1819.

The study was undertaken with two fold purposes. Firstly to test the concept of folk-urban continuum and secondly to plot out the socio-economic changes which had occurred in village life since 1819. That is why he had given the title of the book, "*After a Century and Quarter*".

Ghurye had vast learning in ancient Hindu scriptures and gave the historical perspectives of the village communities and then presented comparative picture of the changes in the village. The unity of the village was demonstrated by the working of the village council, common shrines, and their mutual participation in the festivals of the village. However, the picture of village life was incomplete since many topics such as Baluta system, life cycle, caste structure, and kinship system were not described. Although Ghurye attempted to bring out the fact that the local community was an integrated whole, but he failed to do so in the absence of ethnographic materials.

The next book of Ghurye on Rural life was published under the title, "*Anatomy of a Rural-Urban Community*" (1963). The book embodied the results of pilot study of the whole Haweli Taluka in Maharashtra. The fieldwork was carried out by research assistants for about three months in each year during 1954-1960. Ghurye had surveyed 117 villages including 8 agricultural towns, 9 super villages, 34 big villages, 39 standard villages and 21 small villages.

The project was undertaken to provide empirical information about rural-urban continuum so as to help welfare agencies and facilitate industrialisation. Although the book was dominated by statistical analysis, but also provided description of socio-religious and socio-economic aspects of life of various communities. With particular emphasis on urbanising influences, Ghurye made a successful attempt in conducting such a large anthropologically oriented survey of a type which was so rare in India at that time. The book is, to some extent, comparable to Redfield's book, "*Folk Culture of Ucatam*" (1941). However, the statistical orientation interfered with a true depiction of life of communities. The book failed to analyse adequately the concept of folk urban continuum.

Contribution on Caste Study

Ghurye's interest in the study of caste dates back to 1921, when he chose caste as a subject of study at Cambridge University. His first paper on caste, 'Ethnic theory of Caste' was published in *Man In India* as early as in 1924. Since then he was writing about different asspects of caste in India. In his two books, "*Caste and Race in India*" (1932) and "*Caste Class in India*" (1934), Ghurye highlighted the historical, ethnological, occupational and other aspects of caste system.

In his another book, "*Caste Class and Occupation*" (1961), Ghurye attempted to combine and expand his two earlier books. This book covered all aspects of castes and was rather up-to-date. It provided an excellent general reading on the subject. The book running into twelve chapters discussed the features of caste system, nature of caste groups, history of caste through the ages, relationship of race with caste, elements of caste outside India, origin of caste system, caste under British rule, Scheduled Castes, occupation in relation to caste class and finally, the future of caste system. As the book was written by a sociologist who was well acquainted with both textual and field data, it presented authentic appraisal of the history as well as the actual functioning of caste system in modern India. He had devoted an exclusive chapter on the analysis of Scheduled Castes in India. This chapter brought out the stages and events in the transformation of Scheduled Castes and highlighted contemporary problems.

The chapter on future of caste summarised some of the contemporary developments in different parts in India and took into consideration the caste movements specially in south India. Ghurye's study proved that the caste system had some of its features, for example occupational specialisation. But, it was disappearing fastly. Caste solidarity was increasing and the vitality of caste system had also become stronger.

Regarding the definition of the caste, Ghurye was of view that caste was the most general form of Social Organisation in India and any attempt to define it was bound to fail because of its complexity. Reviewing the philosophy of caste, he concluded that in each linguistic area, there were 200 groups called as caste with distinct names. Each one of which determined the status of individuals in society. They were divided into about 2000 smaller units generally known as sub-castes. The sub-castes were fixing the limits of marriage and effective social life. They were also responsible for specific cultural traditions.

SURJIT CHANDRA SINHA (1926-)

Surjit Chandra Sinha did M.A. in Anthropology from Calcutta University. He received Ph.D. degree from Chicago University. He did his doctoral researches under the supervision of Robert Redfield. He was closely related to the Department of Anthropology, Calcutta University and Anthropological Survey of India. He was also related to other academic institutions for study and researches. He retired from the post of Headship of the Department of Sociology and Anthropology from Vishwa Bharati Shanti Niketan University, West Bengal. His main area of research was Bhumij of Manbhum. On the basis of his researches among Bhumij of Manbhum, he propounded the concept of Tribe-Caste continuum, Tribe-Peasant Continuum and Tribe-Rajput-continuum. He attempted to show that Bhumij of Manbhum had become caste through these processes of acculturation. They felt pride in calling themselves as caste. The Bhumij had adopted the Kshatriya model of caste.

Publications

1957 : "Tribal Culture of Peninsular India : Dimensions of Little Tradition in the Study of Indian Civilisation". Ranchi : *Man In India,* Vol. 37.

1957 : "The Media and Nature of Hindu-Bhumij Interaction". Kolkata : *Journal of Asiatic Society of Bengal*, Vol. 23:1.

1958 : "Changes in the Cycle of Festivals in a Bhumij Village". Ranchi : *Journal of Social Research,* Vol. 1:1.

1959 : "Bhumij-Kshatriya Movement in South Manbhum". *Bulletin of Anthropological Survey of India,* Vol. 3:2.

1961 : "Agricultural Crafts and Weekly Markets in South Manbhum". *Journal of Anthropological Society,* Vol. 10:1.

1962 : "State Formation and Rajput Myths in Central India". *Man In India,* Vol. 42:2.

1965 : "Tribe-Caste and Tribe-Peasant Continuum in Central India". Ranchi, *Man In India,* Vol. 45:1.

B.K. ROY BURMAN (1922-2012)

Roy Burman was a visiting fellow in the Centre for the Study of Developing Society. Before this, he was Professor in the Department of Rural Development, Vishwa Bharati Shanti Niketan. He was also Deputy Secretary of the Department of Census, Government of India. He was also Commissioner, Census of India.

He was closely related to the Department of Census, Government of India. Being closely related to the Department of Census, Government of India, he gathered data and informations about the tribes of India. He had published a number of papers on tribes of India. His publications were as follows:

1961 : "Barmoing : An Ao Naga Village". Monograph Series, Part-VI, Census of India, New Delhi.

1966 : "Structure of Bridge and Buffer Communities in Border Areas". *Man In India,* 46:2.

1969 : "Tribal Demography in India : A Preliminary Appraisal". *Census of India,* New Delhi.

1970 : "Modernisation Process in the Hills of North-East India". *Journal of Institute of Defence Study,* January 1970.

1970 : "Demographic and Socio-economic Profiles of Hill Areas of North-East India". *Journal of Institute of Defence Study.*

1971 : "A Preliminary Appraisal of Scheduled Tribes of India". Manager Publication, New Delhi.

1973 : "Chetlat Village Monograph", *Census of India,* New Delhi.

Contribution on Geographical Distribution of Tribes

Roy Burman in his book, "*A Preliminary Appraisal of Scheduled Tribes of India*" (1971), presented the geographical classification of Indian tribes. He divided tribes of India into five geographical groups. They were as follows:

- *North-East India* : In this group, he included tribes of Assam, Meghalaya, Nagaland, Manipur, Arunachal Pradesh, Mizoram and Tripura.
- *Sub-Himalaya of North and North-West India Region* : In this geographical group, he included the tribes of northern region of Uttar Pradesh and Himachal Pradesh.
- *Central and Eastern India Region* : In this geographical group, he included tribes of West Bengal, Bihar, Orissa, Madhya Pradesh, and Andhra Pradesh.
- *South India Region* : In this geographical group, he placed the tribes of Kerala, Karnataka and Tamil Nadu.
- *Western India Region* : In this geographical group, he placed tribes of Rajasthan, Gujarat and Maharashtra.

Contribution on Cultural Classification of Tribes

Roy Burman presented a cultural classification of Indian tribes on the basis of their adaptation with Hindu Social order, which were as follows:

- *Tribes Included in Hindu Social System* : Under this group, he cited examples of Bhils and Bhumij tribes.
- *Positive Adaptation with Hindu Social System* : Under this group, he placed Munda, Oraon and Santhal.
- *Negative Adaptation with Hindu Social System* : Under this group, he placed Naga and Mizo tribes.
- *Neutral towards Hindu Social System* : Under this group, he placed the example of tribes of Arunachal Pradesh.

Concept of Bridge and Buffer

In his paper, "Structure of Bridge and Buffer Communities in Border Areas" (1966), Roy Burman propounded the concept of bridge and buffer. He studied the border tribes Toto of Bengal and Bhutan. The Toto tribe supplied rice, salt and spices from plain area to the villages of border areas. They also supplied fruits and forest produce to border areas. Thus, the Toto tribe acted as a bridge between plain and border areas people. As a bridge connects the two borders of a river, similarly Toto tribe connected the people of two border areas by supplying rice, salt, spices, fruits and other forest produce.

Contrary to Toto tribe, he observed the behaviour of tribes of Manipur acting as a buffer. For example Naga and Luchay, Naga and Kachari, Luchay and Kachari and Naga and Maitey. In this way, Roy Burman observed the behaviour of tribals acting as bridge and buffer.

R.D. SINGH

Rudra Dutta Singh was an Indian Scholar. He was closely associated with Morris E. Opler of USA. Morris E. Opler was scholar of Cornell University. He came to India to undertake and supervise the village studies in India for effective implementation of Community Development Programme. In course of fieldwork in Indian village, he came in contact with an Indian scholar R.D. Singh. R.D. Singh and Morris E. Opler both studied a village Senapur in western Uttar Pradesh. Singh studied the Senapur village with a purpose to know various aspects of unity in the village. He wrote a paper, 'Unity of an Indian Village' and published it in the *Journal of Asian Study* (1956). In this paper, he observed that in Indian Village life unity had several dimensions such as social, cultural, economic, political and religious. Villagers have face to face relation. They knew each other by name and face. They have we-feeling and high regard for their village. Although they were divided into different castes and sub-castes, but they call each other by kinship terms. They have daily interactions and cooperate each other on the occasion of marriage, death and other needs.

The villagers speak a common language, sing common songs and *Geet,* celebrate common festivals and perform similar types of dances. They observe village exogamy rule at the time of marriage.

The villagers follow vertical and horizontal solidarity. They have their own village Panchayat and they also have caste Panchayat. The village level leaders keep the villagers united by their guidance.

The villagers have common Gods, Goddesses, Sacred Centres, Sacred Specialists and festivals.

The villagers have common history, tank, wells, roads, boundary, playground, cremation ground, pasture land, means of irrigation and common occupation of agriculture and allied work.

Thus, villagers show unity in their social, cultural, economic, religious and political behaviour.

R.S. KHARE

R.S. Khare was an Indian Scholar who had made village study in Uttar Pradesh under Lucknow-Cornell Research Project. He had made study of a village named Gopalpur. This village was located at a distance of 22 miles south-east of Lucknow. He had studied the village Gopalpur during 1958-60 and published few research papers.

In his first paper, 'Ritual Purity and Pollution in Relation to Democratic Sanitation'. Published in *Eastern Anthropologist,* Vol.

15:2, 125-139 (1962)' he attempted to establish that a relationship exists between the ritual status of purity and sanitation and physical status of cleanliness and uncleanliness. He also underlined the importance of studying it from the viewpoint of public health. He had done a new type of village study in the context of health and culture. There had been some type of relationship between ritual concept of purity and pollution and physical cleanliness. However, there were differences between the two, too. Pollution was observed at the time of birth and death by relatives but no physical cleanliness occurred. He had given a new dimension to the concept of purity and pollution. Generally, pollution was transmitted at the time of sharing meal by sitting in the same line.

In another article, 'Folk Medicine in a North Indian Village' published in *Human Organisation,* Vol. 22 (1963), Khare established that beliefs were determined by religious sophistication as well as by social hierarchy. The village folk medicine had an important function since it served to overcome intercaste tension and insulations. Its practice overrided traditional code of conduct and adhered to ordinarity as the art was transmitted through verbal and physical behaviour and experiences of elders and specialists. Khare's analysis of folk medicine was of practical significance and threw light on the neglected aspect of village study.

GAURANGA CHATTOPADHYAY

Gauranga Chattopadhyay was son of Late K.P Chattopadhyay who was Head, Department of Anthropology, Calcutta University. He was also a teacher of Anthropology at Calcutta University. He had done fieldwork in a village named Ranjana and published a full length monograph based on the study of this village in 1964 under the title, 'Ranjana'. He had done fieldwork in Ranjana village between November 1956 and January 1960 with the financial assistance of Ministry of Education, Government of India. He had worked under the guidance of his father K.P. Chattopadhyay.

The purpose of research was to find out changes occurring in village society in India. In course of description of the villages, the author clearly brought out the fact that all rural values and ideas were changing under the impact of new attitude first forming at towns and then spreading in villages among young people. The Government agencies and contact of villages from urban centres were responsible for transformations in villages. In this process of transformation, the unity and integration of the village was adversely affected. He observed that kinship was a strong bond among the village population. He also observed the influence of Sanskritisation and Westernisation in the village. The author observed the Santhals had adopted two Hindu festivals.

K.S. MATHUR

K.S. Mathur was Professor of Anthropology at Lucknow University. He had conducted field study in Madhya Pradesh in Malwa. The name of the village was Potlod. The fieldwork at Potlod village was sponsored by the Australian National University. The fieldwork research result was written under the guidance of S.F. Nadel, a British Social Anthropologist. The period of fieldwork was from April 1955 to April 1956. The village had a population of 1037 Hindus, 23 Muslims and 2 Jains divided into 28 castes. Potlod village was located at a distance of 17 miles south-west of Ujjain. It was a religious centre of Hinduism because of famous Shivalingam. In this study, Mathur had attempted an analysis of the function of Hinduism in the integration of caste society. He had thrown light on problem raised by Redfield as to how religion contributed to the existence of society as an ordered and continuing system of relationships among human being. In the light of his field researches, Mathur described castes' ritual status and observed in his book, "*Caste and Ritual Status in Malwa Village*" (1964) that religion provided the philosophy of social system in the form of doctrine dogma, myths, rites and rituals prohibition and sustained the social system. In the light of Potlod materials, he established that the fundamental system of Hindu Social Organisation was caste. The entire system was bound up with notion of ritual purity and pollution. The concept of purity and pollution was discussed at two levels—the intracaste and intercaste relationship. The various types of pollution were also analysed.

Mathur had examined the structural network of the village in relation to the rituals which according to him tended to perpetuate the system of religious ideas and beliefs and constituted the machinery which maintained the efficient working of the society in its traditional structure.

Mathur went on to analyse as to how social structure based on caste system was perpetuating through the system of religious beliefs and rituals. Mathur did not concern himself much with details of castes and caste system. But he described the rituals of different caste groups with a view to establish the role of religion in social integration.

However, in analysing the social function of religion, he failed to describe the ways in which different castes were integrated to form a solidarity. He had mentioned communal rituals or festivals of the village. The social function of religion in maintaining law and order in village life was not examined, though it was an important aspect of village life.

B.R. CHAUHAN

Brij Raj Chauhan possessed first-hand knowledge of rural Rajasthan. He had made study of a small village named Sadari. The village Sadari was located in the district of Chittorgarh in Rajasthan. With his first-hand knowledge of rural Rajasthan, he had made an intensive study of the village Potlod. The village was small in size. It consisted of 640 persons distributed in 130 families. In the background of rich ethnographic materials, he established that the village was characterised by smallness, distinctiveness in the sphere of ritual festivals and village deities. However, the village was not so homogenous as a caste was. The village was also not self-sufficient. But it could be viewed in wholistic sense because it had an identity and smallness of its own.

Chauhan criticised the concept of Peasant Society because it limited the attention to that section of the village which was dependent on agriculture and brought to focus only the economic status of the village. He considered that the term little community coined by American anthropologist Robert Redfield was more acceptable in case of the village Sadari. It was because the village had wholistic nature. He pointed out the linkages of the village with outside world. He had talked about both types of links—traditional and modern village links. He referred to the concept of peasantry in eliciting information regarding relationship. He had described these features of a Rajasthan village in his paper, 'An Indian Village : Some Questions' in *Journal of Social Research,* Vol. 4, Ranchi (1961).

YOGESH ATAL

Yogesh Atal was a student of B.R. Chauhan. Atal was encouraged by B.R. Chauhan to undertake village study in Rajasthan. Atal studied the importance of Bheru deity of a Mewar village with reference to their specialised function and mode of worship. He had attempted a comparison of Bheru worship in Malwa village reported by A.C. Mayer, a British anthropologist. Unlike in Malwa, the shrine Bheru in Mewar was a Centre of Corporate Worship. This was because in Malwa it was a lineage deity, but in Mewar it was a deity of the village which had sometimes intervillage significance.

Since the cult of Bheru had both Brahmanic and non-Brahmanic attributes, it was difficult to apprehend whether Bhairav of great tradition was a universalised version of Bheru or Bheru was the parochialised form of Bhairava. Atal considered that its parochially universalised form and modes of worship were more significant than the universalised traits. He postulated that in two regions of Malwa and Rajasthan, the process of universalisation had followed different paths. He concluded that since Bheru worship was not reported from other villages of North India, it was a local deity. Bheru and Bhairava were two separate deity with only name resemblance.

Atal's analysis of Bheru cult provided an insight for understanding the process of Hinduism. The concepts of parochialisation and universalisation developed by McKim Marriott of Chicago University, USA, were utilised here for analysing the relationship of cult of Bheru with Bhairava of great tradition. In Atal's analysis the two terms—universalisation and parochialisation—were synthesised into one term as parochially universalised. But in absence of any definition and clarification, his concept remained functional and vague. He had published his findings in *Journal of Social Research,* Ranchi, Vol. 4, 1961.

Y.V. LAKSHMANA RAO

Y.V. Lakshmana Rao had made study of two villages in Andhra Pradesh. The name of one village was Kathuru and the name of another village was Pothuru. The meaning of Kathuru in Telugu is new and the meaning of Pothuru in Telugu was old. The residents of Kathuru village possessed progressive characters. It was more developed and industrialised. The village Pothuru possessed traditional characters. The residents of Pothuru village were less developed and not industrialised.

On the basis of researches in these two villages, Rao had published his book, "*Communication and Development : A Study of two Indian Villages*" (1972). In this book, Rao was mainly concerned with relationship between communication and development. He was of opinion that the progressive characteristics of Kathuru was a result of communication. The increased flow of communication had made the people of Kathuru aware of alternative way of earning a livelihood and promoted the diversification of their economic pursuit. In the social sphere communication had led to the breakdown of old caste prejudices and practices. In the light of facts and statistics collected from the two villages, Rao made a quite simple and straight forward conclusion. He opined that communication familiarised people with new and alternative ways of earning a livelihood. It reduced the pressure on land, created demands for goods, encouraged local initiative to meet those demands, enlarged the entrepreneurship base, encouraged a shift from heredity to achievements as status criteria and promoted accumulative acceleration of economic growth. Politically and socially, Rao showed that communication had reduced the gap between elite and mass. It promoted egalitarian ideas, encouraged the breakdown of old caste prejudices and increased the political participation by a large mass of people in the affairs of community. It was also clear from Rao's analysis that local and regional development programmes should be based on the particular needs of an area and not on some general economic plans.

H.S. DHILLON

Dhillon had studied a village Haripura in Malvali Taluka in Mandya district of Mysore state. The study of Haripura village of Mysore state was undertaken under the auspices of Programme Evaluation Organisation of the Planning Commission, Government of India. The pattern of Haripura village study was similar to Rampura study conducted by Oscar Lewis of Cornell University, USA near Delhi. Dhillon attempted to delineate factions and leadership pattern in the village Haripura. The result of researches carried out in Haripura was published in the form of a book under the title, "*Leadership and Groups in a South Indian Village*" (1955).

On the basis of field data, it was established that the village Haripura had more peaceful and tolerant behaviour than the north Indian village Rampura. Unlike north Indian village, the position of women was higher and marital relations were largely combined within the circle of few villages. 21 per cent marriages were settled within the village itself. This factor was responsible for weakening factionalism in the village. It prevented factional network from spreading and reduced the rigidity of factional behaviour.

The study of social, economic, and ceremonial relationships in the village revealed the existence of six factional groups in the village. Factions were running along kinship ties and caste was not an important factor. It was because Haripura was a single caste village. The leadership in the village was not symbolised by one or two individuals, but by a group having own leadership. The factors contributing to leadership were economic and social status of the family and individual personality traits, enterprise, education and innovations were less important than conservative factors.

The study was significant because it showed that the pattern described by Lewis in Rampura was not applicable on all India level. Kinship was less important factor in factions in South Indian village.

K. ISHWARAN

K. Ishwaran had made a study of a village named Shivapura. The village Shivapura was located near Dharwad in Karnataka state. He had studied economic activities of the villagers in relation to their social activities. Based on intensive field study, in Shivapura village, Ishwaran published his book, "*Tradition and Economy in Village India*" (1966). The book consisted of eight chapters namely The Scene, Social Structure, Aya and the Caste, Rights and Responsibilities, Strength and Values, Conflicts and Tensions, Changing Scenes and Evaluation. The book focused its attention on the economic aspect of the village in framework of the social context.

In this book, Ishwaran had proposed to formulate a sociology of exchange. The Aya explained the exchange aspect of the village society. To the author Aya was the unmeasured and unconditional gifts and reflected the motif of sharing one's possession with others. In the legal sphere, the traditional Aya system recognised rights of individuals, groups, community and of community in the sphere of politics. The jajmans whether of street, caste or village got leadership and headship automatically. The author observed a very close correspondence of the Aya system with the Potlach Institution of Polynesia and Kwakiutl, and Kula exchange of Trobriand islanders.

In a true scientific spirit, the author started doubting many established concepts like Sanskritisation and dominant caste.

These two concepts were based on the study of Rampura, an another Mysore village by M.N. Srinivas. The study of Shivapura had led to set of conclusions which were quite different from the conclusions of Srinivas. However, the contentions of author were not thoroughly indicated for want of a comparative analysis as well as the inadequacy of substantive data.

His next book, "*Shivapura : A South Indian Village*" (1968) was also based upon the study of same village located at a distance of 20 miles from the city of Dharoa and 10 miles from Hubli. The village possessed wide range of castes specially of Lingayats, Marhathas, and Muslims. In a monographic style, Ishwaran described the styles of life of various caste groups and concentrated on the intercaste and intervillage relationships. He referred to the solidarity within the village as well as to intervillage corporation. But he could not show as to how it worked.

While describing religious beliefs and practices of villages, he termed religion as an integrating force.

Although he was quite conscious that sometimes it could be a source of division, too. Taken on the whole like his first book, his second book was also an odd mixture of good description and dubious theory.

Ishwaran's third book, "*Change and Continuity in India's Village*" (1970) was an edited book. It consisted of ten articles written by different authors dealing with communities widely distributed over the country. The papers on varied aspects of village life were based on fieldwork done-by the contributors during sixties. In the words of Ishwaran, the book was specially offered to help the planners in locating the channels of social change and also the barriers to change while the volume included important papers written by American and British anthropologists.

K.N. DIKSHIT

Ray Bahadur K.N. Dikshit was Director General of Archaeological Survey of India after John Marshal. He had placed special emphasis on excavations of archaeological sites. He had attracted the attention of educational institutions towards the excavation of prehistoric sites in India. A teacher in the P.G. Department of History and Linguistics had submitted a proposal before him for the purpose of excavating the sites of prehistoric importance. The concerned teacher had collected stone tools near Pune. Dikshit accepted the proposal of explorations and excavations of stone tools in prehistoric sites. Under his able guidance prehistorical and archaeological researches achieved progress. Deccan College Pune and Gujarat Research Society started research works in prehistoric archaeology. The researches done by scholars put a full stop on the hiatus between Palaeolithic and Neolithic period as propounded by Robert Bruce Foote. He had also sanctioned the project on excavation at Bangarh in Kolkata.

H.D. SANKALIA

H.D. Sankalia was Professor in Deccan College, Postgraduate and Research Institute, Pune. He was described as student par excellence by Sir Martimer Wheeler. He was known for his prompt reporting of archaeological investigations. His book, "*Prehistory and Protohistory of India and Pakistan*" (1974) presented a critical account of prehistory and protohistory of Indian subcontinent, covering a period of nearly half a million years. Much of informations in this book was based on his own work.

NARMADESHWAR PRASAD

Narmadeshwar Prasad was Professor of Sociology at Patna University, Patna, Bihar. He was also Director of Tribal Welfare Research Institute, Ranchi. His major contributions were as follows:

1957 : *Myth of Caste System.* Patna : Samjana Prakashan.
1964 : *Land and People of Tribal Bihar.* Ranchi : Tribal Welfare Research Institute.

Narmadeshwar Prasad in his book, "*The Myth of Caste System*" (1957) had suggested that the caste functioned on the levels of rituals and ideology. He was of opinion that there was no considerable change in the Domain of caste rituals, but when different castes were organised to fight election, it was one step more towards the crystallisation of caste ideology. In the view of this, the two way traffic between the two levels of caste system as such, remained very much same. Due to such situation, he concluded that the changes within the system took place, but not beyond the system. This happened because caste was not merely a process but was also a product of our social, economic and political thinking and behaviour.

Narmadeshwar Prasad also formulated the concept of Kulinisation to explain caste dynamics in India. He felt the necessity of proposing such a term as somewhat approximate concepts of Sanskritisation and Westernisation, though useful in cultural connotation failed to explain the structural contents of social system. He gave further limiting the unity of these two terms and suggested that Kulinism practised in Bengal may be expanded to include within itself the process of status change within the caste system. He indicated two types of Kulinisation, which were as follows:

- Sanskritic Kulinisation.
- Western Kulinisation.

The dialectical situations would be as follows:

- Non-Kulinised (N.K.).
- Sanskritic Kulinised (S.K.).
- Western Kulinised (W.K.).

He further observed that caste as a dominant ideology to be used for social, economic and political purposes started functioning immediately after Sanskritic Kulinisation. Democracy became some sort of Castocracy.

Along with emphasis on study of caste dynamics in relation to different variables and social situations, Prasad had also furnished excellent background materials for the study of caste system in terms of its origin, growth and its historical stages. In the light of field researches, he also examined the functioning of castes in rural areas as well as in urban and industrial areas. He noted that there were changes in caste patterns, theories and practices of caste system were very much the same in spite of urbanisation and industrialisation. As no attempt was made to destroy the caste system, the caste stereotypes continued to flourish and functioned as primary and reference groups in industrial and urban centres.

In conclusion, Prasad considered caste system as myth. It was myth in the sense that it was not true, but people used to take it as true and their thinking, willing and feeling behaviours were shaped and guided by it. The myth of caste system was made to continue from the days of *Purusha Sukta* and for the interest of the group—caste or class they belonged persistently and tenanciously, they went on building up one myth after the other about the caste system. Owing to such a series of powerful myth-plasm, the caste system as a myth continued and only social revolution in India would affect it.

In his another book, 'Land and People of Tribal Bihar', Prasad was able to furnish in brief ethnological and ethnographical accounts of each thirty Scheduled Tribes of the then Bihar state.

KUMAR SURESH SINGH (1935-2006)*

Dr. Kumar Suresh Singh graduated with first class first in History and completed Master's degree from Patna University. He started his career as a Lecturer in Department of Humanities at the famous Indian School of Mines, Dhanbad, in 1956. He was selected as an Indian Administrative Officer (IAS) in 1958 and opted for the Bihar State cadre. His first posting was in 1959 as an Assistant Settlement Officer in Singhbhum. This was his first exposure to a Ho tribal community to study its agrarian system and social

* This profile is contributed by Prof. H.K. Singh (Rtd.) with Xavier Institute of Social Service, Ranchi.

structure. He learnt the Ho language and surveyed 100 villages. This study was converted into village notes. Kumar Suresh Singh worked as Sub-Divisional Officer in Khunti (at present district), which is predominantly inhabited by the Munda tribe. He learned the Mundari language and started participating in tribal festivities. It was a remarkable exposure for K.S. Singh to the tribal world, which provided him with a holistic view of the tribal society. This may be treated as 'love at first sight'. He registered for his Ph.D. on the topic 'A study of Birsa Munda and His Movement in Chotanagpur, 1874-1901' at Patna University.

Academic Contribution

K.S. Singh transformed his Ph.D. Thesis into a book, titled '*The Dust Storm and the Hanging Mist: A Study of Birsa Munda and His Movement in Chotanagpur, 1874-1901*'. The first edition of this book was published by Firma K.L. Mukhopadhayaya, Calcutta in 1966. A combination of religious and political movement; it represents the struggle and aspiration of their life, sowing the stirrings of nationalism among the tribes. In a larger perspective, the Birsa movement shared with the national movement an anti-British credo. It also shared with the Indian renaissance, a spirit of reform, a faith in individual dignity and effort. Birsa's religious philosophy was influenced by both Christianity and Hinduism (Singh, 1995: 27-45).

The second revised edition of the book titled '*Birsa Munda and His Movement*' was published by Oxford University Press, Calcutta, in 1983. Birsa Munda has emerged as the icon of the tribal people all over India. The statue of Birsa Munda was unveiled in the precincts of Parliament House, by the President of India and Birsa Munda became the first tribal leader to get recognition at the galaxy of national leaders on 28 August, 1988. The legend of the lad from Chalkad village in Khunti District has travelled far and wide and finally reached the Parliament House. The credit goes to Kumar Suresh Singh, a versatile scholar, an administrator and an ardent practitioner of historical ethnography.

The centennial edition of the same book was published to mark the centenary of the Birsa Munda by K.S. Singh in 2006. This is the third edition published by Seagull Books, Calcutta. It includes more photographs of Birsa Munda, contemporary missionary accounts, a fresh updating of the Birsa and a revised bibliography.

K.S. Singh's book on '*Birsa Munda and his Movement*' has gone into six editions. The book is translated into different languages and has inspired various forms of creative adaptation in contemporary folk and regional literature, including Mahasweta Devi's major novel '*Aranyer Andolan*'. He adopted a combined methodology of historical research and anthropological fieldwork in his work.

Dr. Singh worked as Deputy Commissioner of Palamau during 1965-1968. Palamau was known for drought and famine. He was the key person in monitoring the Palamau relief network at the state, national and international level. He successfully dealt with the famine of 1967. Dr. Singh shares his experiences of famine management in a book titled '*The Indian Famine,1967*', which was published by the Peoples Publishing House, New Delhi, in 1975. This book was received by the Nobel Laureate Prof. Amartya Sen. According to Prof. Sen, the book is a judicious mix of theory and practice on famine and relief. The book is a model for relief work and a case study of how bureaucracy can avert large-scale starvation deaths.

K.S. Singh was fellow at Indian Institute of Advanced Study Shimla (IIAS) in 1970. The IIAS, in collaboration with the Centre for Advanced Study in Sociology, Delhi University, convened a seminar on the Tribal Situation in India from 6 to 19 July, 1969, at IIAS, Shimla. Prof. S.C. Dube, a renowned sociologist and the then Director of the IIAS gave the editorial responsibility of the seminar papers to K.S. Singh. This volume brought together the papers presented at the seminar under the title '*Tribal Situation in India*'(1972). S.C. Dube complemented K.S. Singh as a brilliant and a dedicated officer of the IAS who handled his editorial task with great responsibility and imagination (Singh,1972). The editor has mentioned that the tribal scene was becoming rapidly politicalised and the tribal unrest had turned violent at a few places. A new tribal identity was emerging. It was time to take stock of the situation and evolve a guideline that could promote the development of emerging forces within the framework of the unity, strength and integrity of the country. There were two papers by K.S. Singh, namely 'Agrarian Issues in Chotanagpur' (pp. 374-85), and 'Famine, Scarcity and Economic Development in Tribal Areas' (pp. 388-95). K.S. Singh highlighted the concept of *dikus*, land alienation, amendment of the agrarian laws and discussed their implications for the tribal society.

Singh facilitated the Indian research scholars to collaborate with the Russian counterparts to understand the phenomenon of ethnicity, identity and nation building. This effort led to the publication of '*Ethnicity, Caste and People*' (1992). The book was edited by K.S. Singh and it contained 36 papers presented at the two Indo-Soviet seminars held in Kolkata in July 1990 and in Leningrad in October1990.The volume embraced wide ranging problems, such as ethnic processes of the Russians and other peoples in the USSR in the past and present, ethnicity and people of different regions of India, national policy with regard to small ethnic groups in India and the Soviet Union, ethnicity at the level of modern political and social life, ethnos and caste, regional situation and specific communities in the two countries.

K.S. Singh had special academic interest on tribal movements in Chotanagpur. He started studying this topic during the Jawaharlal Nehru Fellowship project on 'Tribal Society' in 1973. The Anthropological Survey of India conducted a survey of ongoing tribal movements in different parts of the country in 1976 and organised a seminar in September 1976 to evaluate its findings. The papers were presented by Anthropologists, Historians, Sociologists, Political Scientists and Administrators. Besides, there were tribal scholars who provided the insiders' views. All these papers were edited by K.S. Singh and published under the title '*Tribal Movements in India*' in two volumes (1983). K.S. Singh contributed three articles in the second volume. The first article titled 'Tribal Autonomy Movement in Chotanagpur' was revised and published in 1977, 1979 and 1980 (see detailed references in the books edited by K.S. Singh).

He was the Divisional Commissioner of South Chotanagpur Division from February 1978 to June 1980. He officiated as Vice Chancellor of Ranchi University for a short duration in 1980. He converted his visionary thought of Tribal Development into practice and set up Post Graduate Department of Tribal and Regional Language (TRL), and invited Dr. Ram Dayal Munda from USA and appointed him as Head of the Department. Whenever K.S. Singh visited his house at Ashok Nagar, Ranchi, he invited me too. One fine evening while we were seated in his house, I asked K.S. Singh what motivated him to establish the Department of TRL. He narrated the story of the Red Indians in the USA and emphasised that this department would create a history for the development of Tribal and Regional aspirations. This was the strong administrative and academic vision of K.S. Singh in the creation of new Jharkhand. He said that this department would save the language and cultural identity of the region. He transformed his vision into practice through the Department of TRL and safeguarded the regional identity. This Department worked as an intellectual centre for a separate Jharkhand.

Anthropological Survey of India (ASI) undertook two projects on *Rama-Katha* and the *Mahabharata* in the tribal and folk traditions of India. The seminar on *Mahabharata* was held at the Indian Institute of Advanced Studies in collaboration with the ASI. A number of papers were presented by scholars, out of which 25 papers were selected and published in a book titled '*The Mahabharata in the Tribal and Folk Traditions of India*' (1993). It was edited by K.S. Singh in 1993. K.S. Singh presented an overview of the folk and tribal versions of the *Mahabharata* prevalent in different parts of the country. He also drew upon the experiences in Chotanagpur to present a selected Munda song on the *Mahabharata* and Lord Krishna.

A systematic study of the tribal customary law was undertaken by the ASI to generate uniform data on all aspects of the customary law among the tribes of India. About 70 tribes were studied under the project. K.S. Singh (1993) edited these studies into a book form titled '*Tribal Ethnography : Customary Law and Change*'. They discussed ways by which the tribal societies can maintain their solidarity and social order, and settle disputes. He was concerned with the tribal customary laws. The need for their codification was keenly felt at all levels both in administration and judiciary so that knowledge of the interesting body of traditional norms and law is made available to the authorities in deciding matters which affect the tribal people. Tribal customary laws have survived intact, even flourished. The tribal communities have shown extraordinary resilience and pragmatism in coping with challenges and have adapted to their institution and their laws.

K.S. Singh edited '*Economics of the Tribes and their Transformation*' (1982) and discussed the major process of transformation of the economy of the tribes within the context of the development of the national economy. The major thrust of change is from the food gathering to the food production stage or from tribe to peasant. The reasons for this are three: First, there is pressure of population on land as the carrying capacity of land diminishes. Second, there is deepening of culture contact situations in which the tribal adopt the cultivation techniques and practices of advanced non-tribal peasant communities. Third, reservation of forest for commercial exploitation not only restricts, but also erodes tribal customary rights in forest and restricts, and in many cases eliminates the possibilities of shifting cultivation so as to minimize incidence of degradation of soil, to promote terrace cultivation, to apply the new agricultural strategy to the tribal region and to accelerate the pace of the flow of capital in the tribal region.

People of India: A Unique Research Project

K.S. Singh will be remembered in academics for his conceptualization and successful completion of the People of India (POI) Project. The 43-volume work, which covers cultural, biological and linguistic dimensions, has been acclaimed as a landmark in the field of anthropology and academics. The POI project identified and enlisted 4,694 communities all over the country and documented each of them. The project highlighted the basic economy and salient cultural features of each community and took note of the occupational diversification in the era of 20th century. The data on 4694 communities were collected from as many as 4,513 villages and 941 towns and cities spread over 438 districts of India. Four hundred and seventy scholars participated in the survey including 245 from outside the ASI. About 120 workshops and rounds of discussion were held at different locations of India. Total 27 institutions including ASI were involved in this project (Singh, 2011). The output of the collected data was classified into all India and State Volumes apart from an informative Anthropological Atlas. This atlas is focused on the distribution of cultural, biological and linguistic traits. There is special independent volume on Scheduled Castes and Scheduled Tribes. The POI project updated the colonial ethnographic account and formulated a comprehensive list of all the communities, concentration and livelihood pattern of every community. About 21,362 photographs covering 2,548 communities were generated to build up the visual documentation of the People of India.

For the first time software was developed for ethnography studies in India by the National Informatics Centre (NIC), Government of India. The data of POI project was processed on this software. This project was entirely 'swadeshi'. K.S. Singh discussed the matters with the junior and senior members, accepted their opinions to handle the project operations and recognised the contribution of each. Every member of the POI project, therefore, had developed an emotional attachment to this work, and the project was completed successfully.

Under his dynamic leadership, ASI was taken to a new height. The best Industrial and Commercial Profile Award was given to the ASI in recognition of its overall excellence in the field of research and publication (1984-1991) by the Madrid based International Organization named EDICOIN in 1991 at Geneva.

Other Academic Contributions

K.S. Singh was the Founder Director of National Museum of Mankind (NMM), which he cherished for long as his own child. He was associated with the conceptualization, designing and establishment of the first National Museum of Mankind. This museum, known as Indira Gandhi Rashtriya Manav Sangrahalaya, is first of its kind and is situated in Bhopal. The idea of National Museum of Anthropology was discussed with Prof. M.N. Srinivasan in the mid-1970s (Singh, 2007). He kept in touch with Srinivasan during all the discussions on the structure of the museum. K.S. Singh pointed out that although designed originally to explore the anthropological-biological, linguistic and cultural dimensions of the people of India in a holistic manner, it was reduced to a tribal museum (Basu & Jayaprakashan, 2010 : 286).

The story of publications of 'Tribal Law and Justice' by W.G. Archer is very interesting. Singh was the Director of ASI and Archer was interested to publish this book with the permission of the Bihar Government. Archer worked as Dy. Commissioner of Santhal Parganas from December 1942 to June 1945. The 'Tribal Law and Justice: A Report on the Santal' was prepared by Archer as DC. The permission of publication was required from the government. Singh took up the matter with the Government of Bihar and got the required permission. When Singh took up the manuscript for examination, he found many chapters were missing. Singh got the missing chapters from the famous India Office Library, London. The introduction of the book was written by K.S. Singh himself (Archer, 1984) and published by Concept Publishing Company in 2014.

Fr. P. Ponnet, a Belgian Jesuit priest with expertise in Munda culture and a friend of K.S. Singh, requested the latter for the publication of 15 & 16 volumes of the 'Encyclopaedia of Mundarika. Singh wrote the foreworu and ensured the publication of the two volumes of Encyclopaedia of Mundarika, after a passage of 30 years of the publication of the preceding volumes.

Singh wrote the foreword in the reprint of the famous book titled '*Census of India 1931 with Complete Survey of Tribal Life & System*', written by J.H. Hutton. The reprint was published by Gian, New Delhi, in 1986. He introduced '*Santhal Dictionary*' by Rev. A.P. Bodding (Reprint) published by the Gian Publishing House, New Delhi, in 1992. He introduced many prestigious publications.

Singh was felicitated on 30 March, 1993, at Park Hotel, Kolkata. A festschrift entitled '*People of India: Bio-cultural Dimensions*' edited by S.B. Roy and Ashok K. Ghosh was presented to Singh. This K.S. Singh festschrift is a collection of 29 research papers contributed by the scholars and teachers in the field of anthropology, tribal study and sociology.

He authored, edited and introduced about 60 books, and wrote about 270 research papers, report, reviews, and so on. He delivered 10 prestigious lectures, visited 32 countries to attend conferences. He examined 40 M.Phil and Ph.D dissertations (Roy & Ghosh, 1993; Mishra & Jayaprakashan, 2011). He received three fellowships – the Indian Institute of Advanced Study, the Jawaharlal Nehru Fellowship, and the Post-doctoral Fellowship, for delivering lectures at universities of Heidelberg, Chicago, Virginia, and Harvard on tribal society, Agrarian system and tribal movements. He was a Senior Fellow at the Indian Council of Social Science Research (1981-82) as well (Walter Hauser in *Seminar*, 2006).

Singh read widely the contribution of British scholar Bernard S. Cohn and other scholars as a post-doctoral fellow at Chicago in 1972. Singh encountered Cohn for his intellectual grounding as a trained historian who imbibed deeply the insight and techniques of anthropology.

According to Mahasweta Devi (1993) a famous literary personality, "I wrote my novel '*Aranyer Adhikar*' based upon his book." Dr. K.S. Singh's book '*Birsa Munda and his Movement*' helped and encouraged her in finding the course of her life. But writing a novel was not enough. She started going to them and gradually over the decades, she tried to do whatever she could for the voiceless section of the Indian society.

Further, she commented that the above-mentioned book linked a tribal movement to the pre-independence Indian freedom struggle, traced the origin of Birsa's movement to other tribal agrarian movements. This movement was proved to be more effective than revolts and other tribal agrarian movements against the British and generated new consciousness as a cultural and religious movement.

Xavier Institute of Social Service (XISS), in collaboration with Ranchi Archdiocese, organised a Symposium on the occasion of Platinum Jubilee of Ranchi Archdiocese on 'The Catholic Church in Jharkhand: Challenges and Prospects of Development' at Ranchi during 7-9 November, 2002. Prof. H.K. Singh, was the Organising Secretary of the symposium and he invited Dr. K.S. Singh for the inaugural speech. K.S. Singh expressed his thought on the role of missionaries in the development of Jharkhand. The selected papers and the proceedings of the symposium were published by XISS in a book titled '*The Catholic Church in Jharkhand: A Mediator of Change*'.

The Management of XISS is grateful to Mrs. Bimleshwari Singh, the wife of Late Dr. K.S. Singh, for donating his personal library of about 4,000 books to the institute.

It was the wish of Dr. Singh that his last rites be performed as per Mundari rituals and ashes be immersed in Tajna river in Khunti. Dr. Singh started his carrier as an IAS from Khunti. This was the *Karmakshetra* of Dr. Singh. Where he immersed with Birsa Munda. His family members organised his last journey from Delhi to Khunti and his last rites were performed on the shores of Tajna river in the presence of his well-wishers, among whom the author of this article was also present.

Dr. Singh has made several significant departures from the conventional anthropological or politico-historical analysis of Tribal Movements in his studies. These studies are based on hard facts supported by various archival sources: land records, forest records, communication between different administration and between the participating tribal leaders, intensive field experiences and his academic interest. His penetrative anthropo-historical analysis of the tribal issues can be noticed in their discourses. Singh's experiment with methodological synthesis between history and anthropology has produced insightful papers (1980,1982,1983,1986,1991 & 2002). He was one of those intellectuals whom people will remember as an Indian scholar-Administrator.

Publications of K.S. Singh

Books authored

1966 : *The Dust-Storm and the Hanging Mist: A Study of Birsa Munda and His Movement in Chotanagpur 1874-1901*. Kolkata: Firma K.L. Mukhopadhyaya.

1972 : *The Indian Famine 1967: A Study in Crisis and Change*. New Delhi: People's Publishing House, p. 311.

1978 : *Colonial Transformation of the Tribal Society in Middle India*. New Delhi: Government of India, Ministry of Home Affairs, p. 28.

1979 : *Birsa Munda Aur Unka Andolan*. Classical Publication, p. 275 (Hindi).

1983 : *Birsa Munda and His Movement 1874-1901: A Study of Millenarian Movement in Chotanagpur*. Kolkata: Oxford University Press, p. 283.

1985 : *Tribal Society in India : Anthropo-Historical Perspective*, New Delhi: Manohar, p. 327.

1986 : *Place Names and Personal Names: An Anthropo-Historical Perspective*. Mysore: Place Names Society of India.

1993 : *Material traits survey additional data : Basketry in India*. Kolkata: ASI, p.84 (Jointly with B. Das Gupta, T. Bagchi & P. Chowdhury).

2001 : *Birsa Munda Aur Unka Andolan 1872-1901*. New Delhi: Vani Prakashan, p. 347 (Hindi).

2002 : *Birsa Munda and His Movement 1872-1901*, Centennial Edition. Kolkata: National Book Trust, p.127.

2011 : *Diversity, Identity and Linkage : Explorations in Historical Ethnography*. New Delhi: Oxford University Press, p.156.

People of India Series: Authored/Co-Authored

1992 : *People of India Vol. 1 : An Introduction*. Kolkata: Seagull Books.

1993 : *People of India Vol. 9 : Language and Scripts*. Delhi : Oxford University Press.

1993 : *People of India Vol. 11 : An Anthropological Atlas*. Delhi : Oxford University Press.

1994 : *People of India Vol. 10 : The Biological Variation in Indian Populations*. Delhi : Oxford University Press.

1996 : *People of India Vol. 7 : Identity, Ecology, Social Organisation, Economy Development Process and Linkages: A Quantitative Profile*. Delhi : Oxford University Press.

1996 : *People of India Vol. 8 : Communities, Segments, Synonyms, Surname and Titles*. Delhi : Oxford University Press.

1997 : *People of India Vol. 2 : The Scheduled Castes*. Delhi : Oxford University Press.

1997 : *People of India Vol. 3 : The Schedule Tribes*. Delhi: Oxford University Press.

1998 : *People of India Vol. 4 : The India's Communities (A-G)*. Delhi : Oxford University Press.

1998 : *People of India Vol. 5 : The India's Communities (H-M)*. Delhi : Oxford University Press.

1998 : *People of India Vol. 6 : The India's Communities (N-Z)*. Delhi : Oxford University Press.

2001 : *People of India Vol. 1 : An Introduction*. (rev. ed.). Kolkata: Anthropological Survey of India.

Edited Series People of India

1993 : *People of India Vol. 21 : Goa*, Mumbai : Popular Prakashan.

1993 : *People of India Vol. 28 : Lakshadweep (1-3 part)*. Chennai: Affiliated East-West Press.

1994 : *People of India Vol. 12 : Andaman Nicobar Islands*. Delhi: Affiliated East-West Press.

1994 : *People of India Vol. 18 : Dadar and Nagar Haveli*. Mumbai: Popular Prakashan.

1994 : *People of India Vol. 19 : Daman and Diu*. Mumbai: Popular Prakashan.

1994 : *People of India Vol. 23 : Haryana*, Delhi : Manohar.

1994 : *People of India Vol. 32 : Meghalaya*. Kolkata : Seagull Books.

1994 : *People of India Vol. 34 : Nagaland*. Kolkata : Seagull Books.

1994 : *People of India Vol. 35 : Orissa (1-3 part)*. Kolkata: ASI.

1994 : *People of India Vol. 36 : Pondicherry*. Chennai : Affiliated East-West Press.

1994 : *People of India Vol. 39 : Sikkim*. Kolkata : Seagull Books.

1994 : *People of India Vol. 41 : Tripura (1-3 part)*. Kolkata : Seagull Books.

1994 : *People of India Vol. 42 : Uttar Pradesh (1-3 part)*. Kolkata: Seagull Books.

1994 : *People of India Vol. 43 : West Bengal (1-2 part)*. Kolkata : Seagull Books.

1995 : *People of India Vol. 14 : Arunanchal Pradesh (1-3 parts)*. Kolkata : Seagull Books.

1995 : *People of India Vol. 33 : Mizoram*. Kolkata : Seagull Books.

1996 : *People of India Vol. 24 : Himachal Pradesh*. Delhi : Manohar.

1997 : *People of India Vol. 17 : Chandigarh*. Kolkata: Seagull Books.

1997 : *People of India Vol. 20 : Delhi* : Manohar.

1997 : *People of India Vol. 40 : Tamil Nadu*. Chennai: Affiliated East-West Press.

1998 : *People of India Vol. 31 : Manipur*. Kolkata : Seagull Books.

1998 : *People of India Vol. 38 : Rajasthan* (1-3 part). Mumbai: Popular Prakashan.

2002 : *People of India Vol. 15 : Assam (1-2 parts)*. Kolkata: Seagull Books.

2002 : *People of India Vol. 16 : Bihar (1-2 parts)*. Kolkata: Seagull Books.

2002 : *People of India Vol. 26 : Karnataka (1-2 part)*. Delhi : Affiliated East-West Press, 2002. *People of India Vol. 27: Kerala. (1-3 part)*. Chennai : Affiliated East-West Press.

2003 : *People of India Vol. 13 : Andhra Pradesh (1-3 parts)*. Delhi: Affiliated East-West Press.

2003 : *People of India Vol. 22 : Gujarat*, Mumbai : Popular Prakashan.

2003 : *People of India Vol. 25 : Jammu & Kashmir*. Delhi : Manohar.

2003 : *People of India Vol. 37 : Punjab*. Delhi: Manohar.

2004 : *People of India Vol. 30 : Maharashtra*. Mumbai : Popular Prakashan.

People of India Vol. 29 : Madhya Pradesh. Kolkata: ASI.

Articles in Edited Books

1969 : "Tribal Organizations in Chotanagpur and Its Development", in M.K. Choudhuri (Ed.) *Proceedings of the National Seminar on Trends of Socio-Economic Change in India 1871-1961*. Shimla: Indian Institute of Advanced Study, pp. 547-58.

1969 : "Pattern of Agricultural Changes in Tribal Chotanagpur", in M.K. Choudhuri (Ed.) *Proceedings of the National Seminar on Trends of Socio-Economic Change in India 1871-1961*. Shimla: Indian Institute of Advanced Study, pp. 652-61.

1969 : "Temples in Ranchi District", in Dr. Satkari Mookerji Felicitation Volume. Varanasi : Chowkhamba Publications, pp. 436-42.

1970 : "Mahatma Gandhi and Adivasis", in L.P. Vidyarthy (ed.) *Gandhi and Social Science*. Delhi : Bookhive, pp. 122-46.

1971 : "Munda Land System and Revenue Reforms in Chotanagpur during 1869-1908", in R.S. Sharma (Ed.) *Land Revenue in India : Historical Studies*, New Delhi : Motilal Banarasidas, pp. 80-107.

1971 : "State formation in tribal society : Some preliminary observation", in R.S. Sharma & V. Jha (Eds.) *Indian Society: Historical Probing in Memory of D.D. Kosambi*. Delhi : People's Publishing House, pp. 388-398.

1972 : "Agrarian Crisis in Chotanagpur", in K. Suresh Singh (Ed.) *Tribal Situation in India*. Shimla : Indian Institute of Advanced Study, pp. 374-87.

1972 : "Famine Scarcity and Economic Development," in K. Suresh Singh (Ed.) *Tribal Situation in India*. Shimla : Indian Institute of Advanced Study, pp. 388-95.

1977 : "From ethnicity to regionalism: A study in tribal politics and movement in Chotanagpur from 1900-1975", in S.C. Mulik (Ed.) *Dissent Protest and Reforms in Indian Civilization*. Shimla : Indian Institute of Advanced Study, pp. 317-42.

1978 : "The Munda Land System", in P. Ponett (Ed.), *The Munda World : Essays on Honour of J. Hoffman*. Ranchi: Catholic Press, pp. 29-35.

1979 : "Tribal ethnicity in multi-ethnic society: A study in the process of conflict and integration in post-colonial Chotanagpur", in K.S. Singh (Ed.) *Trends in ethnic group relations in Asia and Oceania : Race and society*. Perish: UNESCO, pp. 56-59.

1980 : "The freedom movement and tribal sub-nationalism, 1920-47", in B.R. Nanda (Ed.). *Essay in Modern History*. Delhi : Oxford University Press, pp. 154-66.

1981 : "Religion and Morality in Kautilya and Michiavelli", in *K.P. Jaiswal Commemoration Volume*. Patna: K.P. Jaiswal Research Institute, pp. 3347-3454.

1982 : "Tribal Movement in Tripura", in K.S. Singh (Ed.) *Tribal Movements in India*. Delhi : Manohar, Vol. 1, pp. 317-38 (Jt. Author Bhabanad Mukherjee).

1982 : "A forest satyagrah", in K.S. Singh (Ed.). *Tribal Movements in India* (Vol. 2). Delhi : Manohar, pp. 177-86.

1982 : "Tribal Autonomy Movement in Chotanagpur", in K.S. Singh (Ed.) *Tribal Movements in India*. Vol. 2. Delhi : Manohar, pp. 1-29.

1982 : "Mahato-Kurmi Mahasabha Movement in Chotanagpur", in K.S. Singh (Ed.) *Tribal Movements in India* (Vol. 2). Delhi: Manohar, pp. 109-17.

1982 : "The Gond Movements", in K.S. Singh (Ed.) *Tribal Movements in India* (Vol. 2). Delhi : Manohar, pp. 177- 85.

1985 : "Father Camil Bulcke", in Shankar Dayal Singh (Ed.). *Father Camil Bulcke Ek Sant Sahityakar*. Patna: Mukta Kantha, (Hindi).

1986 : "Agrarian dimensions of tribal movements", in A.R. Desai (Ed.). *Agrarian struggles in India after independence*. Delhi : Oxford University Press, pp. 145-67.

1986 : "Anthropology, Development and Culture", in K.S. Singh & A. Kalla (Eds.). *Anthropology Development and Nation Building*. Delhi : Concept, pp. 13-36.

1987 : "Chotanagpur Raj Mythology, Structure and Ramifications", in S.C. Sinha (Ed.). *Tribal politics and state system in precolonial eastern and north eastern India*. Kolkata: K.P. Bagchi & Co.

1987 : "Anthropological Survey of India and Visual Anthropology", in K.S. Singh (Ed.) *A Portrayal of people : Essays on visual anthropology*. New Delhi : ASI, and INTACH, pp. 20-29.

1987 : "Sri Babu as we know him", in *Bihar Kesari Dr. Sri Krishna Singh Smriti Kalash*. Patna : Sri Krishna Janma Satabdi Samaroh Samity, pp. 273-76.

1987 : "Poverty development and administration : A study in their interrelationship with reference to Bihar", in A.N. Sharma & Saibal Gupta (Eds.). *Bihar, Stagnation or Growth*. Delhi : Spectrum, pp. 47-52.

1988 : "Tribal women: An anthropological perspective", in J.P. Singh *et. al* (Eds.). *Tribal Women and Development*. Delhi : Rawat, pp. 3-10.

1988 : "Adivasis, Gondwana, Jharkhand, Munda, Santhal", in *Encyclopaedia of Indian History*. New York: The Asian Society, pp.14-15, 514, 217, 381-82.

1988 : "Regional development in tribal areas of India", in Moonis Raza (Ed.). *Regional Development and Planning in India and Soviet Union*.

1991 : "Relevance of Anthropology," in B.G. Halber & C.G.H. Khan (Eds.). *Relevance of Anthropology: The Indian Scenario*. Jaipur: Rawat, pp.181-86.

1992 : "Cultural policy, cultural pluralism and visual anthropology : An Indian Perspective", in R.S. Singh (Ed.). *Visual Anthropology and India*. Kolkata: ASI, pp. 5-19.

1992 : "The Anthropological Survey of India: Yesterday, Today and Tomorrow: A Personal Perspective", in K.S. Singh (Ed.). *The history of the ASI : Proceedings of a seminar*. Kolkata: ASI, pp. 5-19.

1992 : "Ethnography, caste and ethnicity in India", in K.S. Singh (Ed.). *Ethnicity, Caste and People: India and the Soviet Union*. Delhi : Manohar, pp.13-25.

1992 : "Haribaba and his movement in Chotanagpur", in Budhadev Chaudhuri (Ed.). *Tribal Transformation in India.* Vol. 3. Delhi: Inter-India,pp. 344-57.

1992 : "The Munda epic: An interpretation", in Geeti Sen (Ed.). Indigenous vision: *People of India attitude to the environment.* Delhi : Sage, pp. 75-90.

1992 : "Towards an ethnography of People of India", in *Ethnicity, caste and people, Proceedings of the Indian Soviet Seminar held in Kolkata and Leningrad.* Delhi: Manohar, pp. 13-25.

1993 : "Tribal perspectives 1969-1990", in Mrinal Miri (Ed.). *Continuity and Change.* Shimla: Indian Institute of Advanced Study.

1993 : "Material traits survey additional data: Basketry in India". Kolkata: ASI, p. 84 (Jointly with B. Das Gupta, T. Bagchi & P. Chowdhury).

1993 : "Tribal versions of Ram-katha: An anthropological appraisal", in K. Singh (Ed.). *Tribal folk tradition of India.* Kolkata: ASI, pp. 49-66.

1993 : "The Mahabharata: An anthropological perspective", in K. Singh (Ed.). *Tribal Folk Tradition of India.* Kolkata: ASI, pp. 1-16.

1993 : "The famine code: The context and continuity", in Jean Floud & Amrita Rangaswami (Eds.) *Famin and Society.* Delhi : The Indian Law Institute,pp. 139-61.

1993 : "A Memoir: Words from friends and colleagues for Prof. J.S. Garewal." Shimla: *Indian* Institute of Advanced Study. p. 31.

1995 : "Birsa Munda and his movement in Chotanagpur 1874-1901", in Ram Dayal Munda (Ed.). *We fought together for freedom.* Delhi: Oxford University Press, pp. 27-45.

1995 : "Inequality in the tribal society, emerging trends, contradictions", in Manorama Saviar & Indira Munshi (Eds.). Indian Society: *Essays in honour of Prof. A.R. Desai.* Jaipur: Rawat, pp. 71-84.

1995 : "Reflections on the current debate concerning the indigenous people", in Amar Kumar Singh & Mona K. Jabi

(Eds.). *Tribals in Indian development: Defamation and discontinue.* Delhi: Har-Anand.

1995 : "A contemporary Indian ethnography", in D. N. Jha (Ed.). *Society and ideology: Essay in honour of Prof. R.S. Sharma.* Delhi: Munshi Ram Manoharlal.

1996 : "G.S. Ghurye, Verrier Elvin and Indian Tribes", in A.R. Momin (Ed.). *The legacy of G.S. Ghurye: A centennial festschrift.* Mumbai: Popular Prakashan, pp. 39-46.

1996 : "Fifteen Munda Songs", in R.K. Bhattacharya & A.K. Ghosh (Eds.). *Sociology in the rubric of social science.* Kolkata : ASI, pp. 29-34.

1997 : "Tribe and caste: A colonial paradigm", in Dev Nathan (Ed.). *From tribe to caste.* Shimla: Indian Institute of Advanced Study, pp. 31-44.

1998 : "The People of India: Diversities and Linkages", in N. Appaji Rao (Ed.). *Indian human heritage,* Hyderabad: University Press, pp. 78-86.

1998 : "Political rights, devolution of powers, autonomy and participation: A parliamentary statement", in B.K. Roy Burman & B.G. Verghese (Eds.). *Tribal and Indigenous People.* Delhi: Konark, pp. 159-61.

1998 : "Diversity, heterogeneity, integration: An ideological perspective", in S. Setter & P.K.V. Kaemal (Eds.). *We lived together.* Delhi: Pragati Pub.,pp. 233-39.

1998 : "Meshing the past, the present and the future", in *Rajiv Gandhi's India : A golden jubilee retrospect (vol.4).* Delhi: UBS Publishers,pp. 22-23 & 130-35.

1998 : "Birsa Munda (1875-1900): Freedom fighter and leader of tribal resurgence." Souvenir. Rourkela: Birsa Munda Statue Committee.

1999 : "Tribes: Partition and Independence", in S. Setter & I.B. Gupta (Eds.). *Pangs of Partition.* Delhi: Manohar.

1999 : "Panel discussion", in Kailash Agarwal (Ed.). *Dynamics of identity and inter-group relations in North East India.* Kolkata: ASI, pp. 244-47.

2003 : "Gender roles in history: Women as hunters", in Govind Kelker, Dev Nathan & P. Walter (Eds.). *Gender relations in forest societies in Asia, Patriarchy at odds.* Delhi: Sage.

2004 : "Ecology, ethnicity, regionalism and state formation: An exploration of the Jharkhand movement", in Rajiv Balakrishnan (Ed.). *Jharkhand Matters: Essays on ethnicity regionalism and development.* Delhi: Konark.

2004 : "Jharkhand and Jharkhand movement: A personal perspective", in Rajiv Balakrishnan (Ed.). *Jharkhand Matters: Essays on ethnicity regionalism and development.* Delhi: Konark.

2004 : "Rethinking forest and forest dwellers and ecological history", in B.B. Chaudhury & A. Bandopadhyaya (Eds.). *Tribes, forest and social formation in Indian history.* Delhi: Manohar, pp. 39-50.

2005 : "Colonialism and tribal economy", in Vinay Bhushan Chaudhary (Ed.). *Economic history of India from eighteenth to twentieth century (vol. 3, part 3).* New Delhi : PHISPC, Centre for Studies in Civilization, pp. 41-56.

Articles in Journals

1957 : "Political philosophy of Vivekanand", *Journal of Indian School of Mines and Applied Geology*, 12-13,pp. 49-51.

1958 : "Role of mining and minerals in ancient India", *Journal of Indian School of Mines and Applied Geology*, Vol. 14, pp. 45-57.

1963 : "The Haribaba Movement in Chotanagpur 1931-32", *Journal of the Bihar Research Society*, XlLX, pp. 284-96.

1969 : "Development schemes as a factor of change in tribal areas", *Journal Social Research*, Vol.9, pp. 52-64.

1969 : "Integration of the tribes and development of tribal economy", *Tribe*,Vol. 6(3), pp. 42-46.

1970 : "Emergent scarcity relief: The new strategy", *Journal of the National Academy of Administration*, 16(4), pp. 45-47.

1971 : "State formation in tribal society: Some preliminary observation", *Journal of Anthropological Society*, l.6, pp. 161-81.

1973 : "Industrial development", *Commerce* 127 (3263), pp. 41-44.

1975 : "Chotanagpur: A centenary overview", *Bihar Herald*, pp. 94-97.

"Industries for the weaker section", *Kurukshetra*, 23(8), 16th January, pp. 6-7.

1976 : "The Chero: Anthropo-historical approach to their study", *Indian Museum Bulletin*, 11(1), pp. 55-56.

1978 : "Colonial transformation of tribal society in middle India", *Economic & Political Weekly*, 13(30), pp. 1221-32.

1978 : "Mia'djagar (Survey and settlement operation in Ranchi", *Adivasi*, 32(6), pp.16-17 (Mundari).

1978 : "Appeal to Horo Sena Samiti", *Adivasi,* 32(5), (Mundari).

1978 : "Appeal to Adivasi", *Adivasi*, 32(6).

1979 : "Lack coated urea: An experiment in the diversification of the uses of lac and transfer of technology from lab to farm phase 1," *Journal of Social and Economic Studies*, 7(11), pp. 219-27.

1979 : "Lack coated urea: An experiment in the diversification of the uses of lac and transfer of technology from lab to farm phase 1", *Journal of Social and Economic Studies*, 7(12), pp. 27-30.

1982 : "Transformation of tribal society: Integration vs. assimilation", *Economic & Political Weekly*, XXIV, 14-21 August 1982.

1982 : "Tribal identity movement: Based on script and language", *Man in India*, 62(3), pp. 234-45.

1984 : "Colonialism, anthropology and primitive society: The Indian scenario,1924-47", *Man In India*, 64, pp. 379-413.

1984 : "The literate administrator", *Administrator*, 29(3), pp. 201-06.

1985 : "Script reform and development: A study of two movements among the Ho tribe in Singhbhum. *South Asian Anthropologists*, 5(2), pp. 111-23.

1986 : "A day in the Dangs", *Human Science*, 35(1), pp. 71-73.

1986 : "Administrator as an anthropologist", *Journal of the Indian Anthropological Society*, 21(1), pp. 23-5.

1986 : "The Fathers", *Man in India*, 66(4) , pp. 305-12.

1986 : "People of India", *Man in India*, 67(3), pp. 232-39.

1987 : "Indian Anthropology 2000 AD: Problems and perspectives. *Human Science*, 36(3), pp. 217-29.

1987: "Man and environment: A perspective", *Human Science*, 36 (2), pp. 209-12.

1987 : "Jawahar Lal Nehru and the tribals and their transformation", *Human Science*, 37(1), pp. 1-9.

1988 : "Tribal peasantry, millenarianism, anarchism and nationalism: A case study of the Tana Bhagat in Chotanagpur", *Social Scientist*, 1(11), pp. 36-50.

1988 : "Indo-USSR: An academic exchange", *Human Science*, 37(4), pp. 428-30.

1988 : "Ethnography of Rajasthan", *Human Science*, 37(4), pp. 348-55.

1988 : "People of India : A national project", *Indian Association of Social Science, Quarterly Bulletin*, 7(2),pp. 112-123.

1988 : "Land rights of tribal women", H*uman Science*, 37(3), pp. 260-68.

1988 : "A temple in a tribal village", *Human Science*, 37(2), pp. 97-102.

1988 : "Ethnography of L.K. Anantha Krishna Iyer and its relevance", *Human Science*, 37, Special Number, pp.10-18.

1989 : "Ethnicity and polityformation in tribal India", *Human Science*, 38(4), pp. 267-73.

1989 : "Professor N.K. Bose and the Anthropological Survey of India", *Geographical Review of India*, 51(2), pp. 1-12.

1989 : "Human response to famine", *Human Science*, 38(4), pp. 267-273.

1989 : "Tribal unrest", *Human Science*, 38(3), pp. 165-67.

1990 : "Environment, culture and people's action: An anthropological appraisal", *Journal of Anthropological Survey of India*, 39(1), pp. 1-6.

1990 : "On self, forest and environment", *Journal of Anthropological Survey of India*, 39(4), pp. 231-35.

1990 : "Tribal violence", *Journal of Anthropological Survey of India*, 39(2&3), pp. 127-32.

1991 : "Environment, technology and management in tribal areas", *Man in India*, 71(4), pp. 545-70.

1991 : "Island Anthropology: Retrospect and Prospect", *Man in India*, 71(4), pp. 545-70.

1991 : "The People of India project: A preliminary report", *Indian Association of Social Science Quarterly Bulletin*, X (2), pp. 75-80.

1991 : "Ethnography, old and new", *Journal of Anthropological Survey of India*, 40(1&2), pp. 1-9.

1991 : "People of India", *Man in India*, 71(3), pp. 232-49.

1991 : "Quality of life: An anthropological perspective", *Journal of Anthropological Survey of India*, 40(3&4).

1992 : "The Munda Epic", *India International Centre Quarterly*, Summer, pp. 73-89.

1992 : "Solar tradition in tribal folk culture of India", *India International Centre Quarterly*, Winter, pp. 28-39.

1992 : "More on the ethnography of Rajasthan", *Journal of Anthropological Survey of India*, 42(1), pp. 8-17.

1992 : "People of India: The profile of a national project 1985-1992", *Current Science*, 64(1), pp. 5-10.

1993 : "Hinduism and tribal religion: An anthropological perspective", *Man in India*, 73(1), pp. 1-16.

1993: "The problems of marginalised tribes", *Seminar*, Issue 412. December.

1994 : "Environment issues: A Gandhian perspective", *Gandhians in Actions*, 1(1).

1993 : "The heritage we share: An anthropological dimension", *Social Science Probings 11*, March-December, pp. 91-97.

1995 : "A rejoinder: Short notes and communications", *Eastern Anthropologists*, 48(1).

1996 : "Ethnicity: Ethnic movement and ethnic conflict resolution: A personal perspective", *Social Science Probings*, 13, March-December, pp. 65-72.

1998 : "The tribes and the 1857 uprising", *Social Scientist*, 26 (1-4), pp. 76-85.

1990 : "Grassroots governance, perspective on Panchayati Raj", *Social Change*, 28(1), March 1990, pp.12-23.

2000 : "Whether the marginalised one", *Eminence*, 1(8), January 2000, pp. 62-63.

2000 : "A perspective on the Anthropological Survey of India", *Seminar*, Issue 495, November 2000, pp. 40-44.

2000 : "Tribal customary laws policy implication", *Yojana*, 44(8), April 2000, pp. 18-21.

2003 : "Science history and anthropology: A perspective on Prof. D.D. Kosambi and his impact", *Social Science Probings*, Winter 2003, pp. 64-85.

2003 : "Concept of tribes 'a note'", *The Eastern Anthropologist*, Vol. 56 (2-4) April & October, 2003, pp.105-200.

2005 : "Revisiting the Bihar Famine of 1967", *Social Science Probings*, 17(1), 2005.

Book Reviewed in Journals

1964 : S.P. Sinha, "Life and Times of Birsa Bhagwan", *Journal of the Bihar Research Society*, 1(1-4) : 130-37.

1966 : J.C. Jha, "Kol Insurrection in Chotanagpur", *Journal of Bihar Research Society*, 3(1-4) : 222-25.

K.M. Patra, "Orissa Under the East India Company", *The Indian Archives*, 20(1) : 117-18.

1971 : V. Virottam, "The Nagvanshi and the Chero", *The Indian Archives*. 22(1-2), January & June 1971, pp. 117-18.

1974 : Surajit Sinha (Ed.). "Aspects of Indian Culture and Society", *The Indian Historical Review*, 1(1), pp. 414-16.

1976 : W.G. Archer, "The hill of flutes, life love and poetry in Tribal India : A portrait of the Santhal", *The Indian Historical Review*, 2(2), pp. 494-97.

1976 : Andre Beteille, "Studies in agriculture and society", *The Indian Historical Review*, 2(2), pp. 494-97.

1976 : J.Troisi, "The Santals : A classified and annotated bibliography", *The Indian Historical Review*, 2(2), pp. 494-97.

1977 : N.K. Bose, "The Structure of Hindu Society", *The Indian Historical Review*, 3(2), pp. 573-74.

1977 : I.P. Desai & B. Chaudhury, "History of rural development in modern India", (Vol. 2). *The Sociological Bulletin*.

1977 : Fidelia De Sa, "Crisis in Chotanagpur with special reference to judicial conflict between Jesuit Missionaries and British government official", *The Indian Historical Review*, January, 4(2), pp. 294-95.

1978 : H. Mathur, "Anthropology in the development process", *Indian Book Chronicle, News and Reviews*, September 1978, pp. 306-08.

1979 : Amir Hassan, "Folklore of Buxar", *Indian Book Chronicle News Review*.

1979 : J.B. Bhattacharjee, "The Garus and the English", *The Indian Historical Review*, 5(1-2), pp. 294-95.

1979 : B.B. Sinha, "Socio-economic life in Chotanagpur", *Indian Quarterly*.

1980 : Bhupinder Singh (Ed.). "Transformation of Tribal World", *Journal of Social and Economic Studies*, 8(1), pp. 173-74.

1980-81 : G.S. Ghurye, "The burning caldron of North-East India", *The Indian Historical Review*, 8(1), pp. 365-66.

1992 : Adrian C. Mayer (Ed.). "Culture and morality: Essays in honour of Christopher von Furer Haimendorf," *The Indian Historical Review*, 7(1-2), pp. 344-345.

1981-82 : Charles Frenz, "Ideas and trends in world anthropology", *The Indian Historical Review*, 8(1-2), pp. 266-68.

1982-83 : B.B. Mishra, "District administration and rural development", *The Indian Historical Review*, 9(1-2), pp. 293-95.

1984 : E.F. Oaten, "My memoirs of India", *The Hindustan Times*. 20th May 1984.

1984 : Suchibrata Sen, "The Santhal of Jungle Mahals, an agrarian history, 1793-1861", *The Indian Archives*, 32(2), pp. 86-88.

1985-86 : J.C. Jha (Ed.). "Indian National Congress and the tribal," *The Indian Historical Review*, 12(1-2), pp. 432-33.

1985-86 : J.C. Jha, "Tribal revolt of Chotanagpur (1831-32)", *The Indian Historical Review*, 12(1-2), pp. 403-04.

1986 : S.K. Gupta, "The Scheduled Caste in modern Indian politics: Their emergence as a political power", *The Indian Archives*, 34(1), pp. 99-101.

1986-87 : Sitakant Mahapatra, "Modernization and social change in Santal society", *The Indian Historical Review*, 13(1-2), pp. 294-96.

1987 : G. Prakash Reddy, "Politics of tribal exploitation", *Human Science*, 37, pp. 37-38.

1987 : David Hardiman, "The coming of Devi : Adivasi assertion in Western India", *Contribution to Indian Sociology*, 22(1), pp.115-16.

1988 : Edward Dayken, "Tribal Guerrillas, the Santals of West Bengal and Naxalite Movement in India", *Contribution to Indian Sociology*, 22(1), pp. 115-16.

1988 : K.N. Sahay, "Changes in tribal identity of Chotanagpur: A study of conversion from one tribal group to another", *Journal of North East India Council for Social Science Research*, 12(2), pp. 50-51.

1988 : R.N. Thakur, "Himalayan Lepchas", *Contribution to Indian Sociology*, 23(1), pp.19-21.

1987-88 : R.S. Khare, "Culture and democracy : Anthropological reflections on modern India", *The Indian Historical Review*, 14(1&2), pp. 365-66.

1987-88 : A.R. Foning, "Lepcha my vanishing tribe", *Contribution to Indian Sociology*, 22(11), pp. 314-15.

1989 : Moonis Raza & Aiyazuddin Ahmad, "An atlas of tribal India", *Human Science*, 38(3), pp. 257-59.

1989 : Upendra Baxi (Ed.). "The right to be human", *Human Science*, 38(3), pp. 259-61.

1991 : Ananthi Jeba Singh, "Scripting integration, script for tribal languages for the promotion of literacy", *The Times of India*, 7 April, 1991.

1991 : Christopher Von Furer Haimendorf, "Life among Indian tribes: An autobiography of an Anthropologist", *The Indian Economic and Social History Review*, 28(2), pp. 209-11.

1992 : James Clifford & George E. Marcus, "The poetics and politics of Ethnography", *The Times of India*, 1st March, 1992.

1992 : Robert Perkin, "The Munda of Central India", *Down to Earth*.

1992 : Sushan B.C. Devalle, "Discourses of ethnicity : Culture and protest in Jharkhand", *The Times of India*, 23rd August, 1992.

1992 : Govind Kelkar & Dev Nathan, "Gender and the tribal women, land and forest in Jharkhand", *The Times of India*, 21 June, 1992.

1992 : G.M. Joshi, "Tribal Bastar and the British administration", *The Indian Archives*, 39(1), Jan-June 1992, pp. 72-74.

Books Edited

1972 : *Tribal Situation in India*. Shimla. Indian Institute of Advanced Study.

1982 : *Economics of the tribes and their transformation*. Delhi: Concept.

1982 & 1983 : *Tribal movement in India*. 2 Vols. Delhi : Manohar Pub.

1987 : *Anthropological development and nation building*. (with A.K. Kalla) Delhi: Concept.

1989 : *Hamari Adivasi Virasat—Our Tribal Heritage*. Kolkata: ASI.

1898 : *Jawahar Lal Nehru tribes and tribal policy*. Kolkata: ASI.

The ASI Andaman and Nicobar Island tribes Series: The Great Andamanese, the Onge, the Shompen, the Sentinels, the Jarwas, the Nicobarese. Kolkata: ASI (n.d.).

1991 : *The History of Anthropological Survey of India*. Kolkata: ASI and Seagull.

1991 : *Visual Anthropology and India*. Kolkata : ASI.

1991 : *Ethnicity, people and caste: Proceedings of the joint seminar held in Kolkata*. Kolkata : ASI & Seagull.

1993 : *Tribal Ethnography, Customary Law and Change*. Delhi : Concept.

1993 : *Rama-katha in tribal and folk traditions of India*. Kolkata : ASI & Seagull.

1993 : *The Mahabharata in the tribal and folk traditions of India*. Kolkata : ASI.

1998 : *Tribal movement: From antiquity to modernity in tribal India*. Delhi : Inter-India.

Awards & Distinction

1953 : Srimati Radhika Sinha Gold Medal for standing first in first class in History Hons., Patna University (PU).

1953-55 : Merit Scholarship, Patna University.

1955 : Jackson Memorial Prize for the best paper entitled "Role of India in League of Nations", P.U.

1955 : Gold Medal for standing first class in M.A. (History), Patna University.

1985 : Birsa Munda Award for outstanding service rendered to the tribal community.

1995 : G.S. Ghurye Award.

1993 : Twentieth Century Award, American Biographical Institute, USA.

1994 : Man of the Year Award, International Biographical Centre, Cambridge.

1995 : Limca Book of Records (1995) for the largest work of its kind (POI) in the world.

Conclusion

K.S. Singh was a versatile scholar from being an administrator to an ardent practitioner of historical ethnography. In course of long tenure on tribal matters, he penned many academic papers on tribal movement, agrarian relations, tribal customary law, tribal economy, tribal women, and so on. He adopted a combined methodology of historical research and anthropological fieldwork in his landmark study. To a social historian, he highlighted the need for the study of tribal society and culture in the perspective of time; to a social anthropologist, he conveyed the idea of studying the tribal society and culture. He believed that there could be no social anthropology without social history in India; also, there could be no meaningful social history without social anthropology. We are indeed grateful to Late Dr. K.S. Singh for his contribution to the academic world and especially for the development of Jharkhand.

References

Basu, K.K. & Jayaprakashan, G. (2010). "Indira Gandhi Rashtriya Manav Sangrahalaya : A museum of with a difference." In

K.K. Basa (Ed.), *Multiple heritage role of specialised museum in India*. New Delhi : Serials Publications.

Mahasweta, D. (1993). "A personal portrait." In S.B. Roy & Ashok K. Ghosh (Eds.), *People of India : Biocultural dimension* (K.S. Singh festschrift). New Delhi: Inter-India Publications.

Mishra, K.K. & Jayaprakasan, G. (Eds.), (2011). *Tribal movements in India : Vision of Dr. K.S. Singh*. New Delhi: Manohar.

Roy, S.B. & Ghosh, A.K. (Eds.). (1993). *People of India : Bio-cultural dimensions* (K.S. Singh festschrifts). New Delhi: Inter-India Publications.

Singh, K.S. (1995). "Birsa Munda and his movement in Chotanagpur 1874-1901." In Ravi Dayal (Ed.) *We fight together for freedom: Chapters from the Indian National Movement*. New Delhi: Oxford University Press, pp. 27-45.

Singh, K.S. (1975). *The Indian famine*, 1967. New Delhi : Peoples Publishing House.

Singh, K.S. (2002). *Birsa Munda and his movement 1872-1901: A study of a millenarian movement in Chotanagpur*. Kolkata: Seagull.

Singh, K.S. (Ed.). (1993). *The Mahabharata in the tribal and folk traditions of India*. Shimla : Indian Institute of Advanced Study & Anthropological Survey of India.

Singh, K.S. (2007). "Remembering M.N.Srinivasan." In P.K. Mishra (Ed.), M.N. Srinivasan : *Man and his work*. Jaipur : Rawat Publications.

Singh, K.S. (2011). *Diversity, identity and linkages: Explorations in historical ethnography*.New Delhi : Oxford University Press.

RANN SINGH MANN (1936-2013)

Prof. Rann Sing Mann was born on 15th November, 1936 in a village in Delhi. All his elementary education was in Delhi. At the under graduate level he chose to study in the physical science stream. All through this and also for a while at post graduate level, he played volley ball for the University of Delhi. Finally, he became the captain of the University team and represented Delhi University at several inter-University competitions.

Being sensitized in village life, Rann Singh Mann found it easy to shift to social anthropology for M.Sc., which he completed in 1960. Almost within years of passing M.Sc., Prof. Mann was appointed as an Instructor in the Tribal Organisation and Study Centre in Udaipur. Here he came in regular contact with tribal groups of Rajasthan and Gujarat. His romance with his roots, however, brought him back to his village in order to organize, plan and execute fieldwork for his Ph.D. thesis. In 1973 he was awarded Ph.D. on the topic *Social Structure and Social Change in a Delhi Village*, by University of Delhi.

Very soon he was selected for the post of superintending anthropologist at the Anthropological Survey of India (ASI). This again brought him back to Udaiur where ASI had a regional station. Thus, having seen the Bhil, Bhilala, Mina, Garasia and Saharia tribes through time gave him the necessary insights into issues of social change leading to the publication of many meaningful papers on the subject. In the subsequent years, social change became one of his favourite perspective for studying tribes and multi caste villages. He got posted in various regional centers of ASI and at almost each of these centres he brought out book volumes of great value.

Prof. Mann has published seven books. Most of his books till now taken as the only reliable accounts of the contemporary status of tribes in remote areas. Of these *the Ladakhi Nature-Man-Spirit-Complex* and *The Bay Islanders* are worth mentioning. His research papers deal with such diverse topics as tribal polyandry, awareness and attitude of Minas and social barriers to nutrition among Indian tribes. His complete involvement in and passion for the subject soon saw him elevated to the position of Director of ASI. This was at the time when the survey had undertaken a mammoth Project of bringing out a compendium of People of India in several volumes. Data were being collected by scholars from all corners of India and the head office had the almost impossible task of compiling them in a meaningful pattern.

It was shortly after this that he took a premature retirement from ASI and came to Delhi and joined his Alma Mater the Department of Anthropology, Delhi University as a Professor. His rich experience in field and his continuous involvement in publishing in the past made him a very successful teacher. He took up to teaching many challenging paper for the specializing batches. He also successfully guided a number of Ph.D. thesis during this short period of service in the Department of Anthropology at Delhi University before he retired in 2002. He remained academically active and addressed research seminars and also helped ASI in advisory capacity until the year of his death. On 1st September, 2013, he expired after a brief illness.

Prof. Mann was a fun loving person who otherwise very serious in his work. He was a voracious reader and an excellent speaker. With his demise, social anthropology in India has lost a very important scholar of all India experience.

Excerpts from:

Bhattacharya, D.K. 2013. 'Prof. Rann Singh Mann (1936-2013)'. *Indian Anthropologist* 43(2) : 101-102.

II

Foreign Builders of Indian Anthropology

SIR WILLIAM JONES

Sir William Jones was Chief Justice of Calcutta High Court. But he had deep interest in linguistics. The day of 15th June, 1774 was a memorable day in the history of Indian Anthropology. On this very day, Sir William Jones had established Royal Asiatic Society of Bengal at Kolkata. He had started publication of research Journal through this Society. The name of Journal was Journal of Royal Asiatic Society of Bengal. He was chief editor of this Journal. He was also chairman of Royal Asiatic Society of Bengal.

With his best effort, scholars began to study man, society and culture in India. In this way, he laid the foundation of Indian Anthropology. Since then Indian anthropology went on progressing continuously. With the help of Asiatic Society of Bengal, a museum was also started. In the beginning, Asiatic Society of Bengal worked much on Indian languages and literature. Later on, the society began to study antiquity of man in India, Indian tribes, castes, races, marriage, family, kinship. Articles, notes, papers and essays were published on man, society and culture of India.

JONES PRINCEP

In the year 1833, Sir Jones Princep was appointed as Secretary of Royal Asiatic Society. Now, Indian anthropology attained extra force to grow. He was a scientist and believed in scientific discovery, exploration, excavation, description, explanation and analysis. He studied Brahmi and Khorathi script. He proved that Ashoka and Priyadarshi were same. He was a great scholar of science of money and inscription. He had attracted the attention of scholars towards explorations and excavations of prehistoric archaeological sites.

Indian archaeology and Indian Prehistoric anthropology had great hope from his scholarly supervision. But he met untimely death. As a result Indian archaeology and Indian prehistoric Anthropology had to bear a great loss. His students, James Furgusson had presented pictorial history of Indian architecture.

ALEXANDER CUNNINGHAM

The Government of British India established the Department of Archaeology in the year 1861. The charge to run this newly established Department of Archaeology was assigned to Sir Alexander Cunningham. Being Head of Archaeological Survey of India, he had encouraged research works in the area of Indian archaeology with great interest. He had made an intensive survey of Land of Punjab, Uttar Pradesh, Rajasthan, Madhya Pradesh, Bihar and Bengal. Through the survey of lands of those states, he was able to furnish a description of immovable remains, buildings, and sites of historical importance. Survey made by Cunningham was of a great archaeological value in India. This survey opened the door of future researches in Indian archaeology.

The main purpose of Cunningham's archaeological survey was to discover the Buddhist sites as described by Chinese traveller Hiuen Tsang. The description of Chinese traveller had played significant role in Cunningham's archaeological survey of India.

He attempted to go to every place visited and described by Chinese traveller. This work was not so easy due to lack of communication facility. He travelled on foot, used horses and bullockarts to visit all Buddhist sites described by Chinese traveller. That is why he was regarded as father of India Archaeological Survey.

It was also true that he had destroyed a number of archaeological remains. But he was not only responsible for that. At that time, the scientific methodology of archaeology was not developed. Another thing was that he wanted to do more and more survey in less time.

When he retired from the post, Indian Archaeological Survey was reorganised. According to this reorganisation, the coordinational rights of Director General was abolished. The work of western India was given to Wargess. He was an architect by profession and interest both. He made survey of all sites of western India from the point of new of art and artistic behaviour. He also presented diagrams and paintings of sites surveyed. With his academic efforts, the artistic behaviours of dynasties of Satvahana, Chalukya, Rashtrakuta, Pallava and Hoysal were explored as cave painting, drawings and, temples erection.

The most famous book of Alexander Cunningham is "*Ancient Geography of India*".

SIR JOHN MARSHAL

The Indian Archaeological Survey was reorganised in 1900. Sir John Marshal was appointed as a Director General of Indian Archaeological Survey. He served on this post from 1904 to 1934. He had attained training in Archaeology from Creat, Greece and Turkey. In his able guidance, Indian Archaeological Survey had made considerable progress. During his 30 years of service, he enriched Indian archaeology by his new discoveries. He had established the branches of Archaeological Survey of India at Mysore, Travancore, Jaipur and Baroda. As he had received training in Archaeology from Greece, he attempted to establish link between Greece and Indian archaeology. He explored the glorious past of India through excavations and explorations. With his efforts, Indian Archaeology was divided into different Mandalas. The scholars incharge of each Mandala were made responsible for explorations and excavations of new sites, conservation of sites, buildings, temples and other archaeological materials already explored.

The year in between 1914 and 1920 was not good so far as achievement of archaeological survey in India was concerned. Due to the occurrence of First World War, Archaeological Survey in India did not get momentum. But even in this slow progress period, some sites were excavated and buildings were explored. Takshila and Nalanda sites were excavated and explored in this period. Sanchi, Sarnath, Bhita sites were also excavated in this period.

There was no doubt that Indian archaeology attained progress in the period of Marshal, but the early dark period remained untouched. Till date no researches were undertaken on the basis of which historical reconstruction of Indian subcontinent was not attempted systematically. It was not attempted to reconstruct the history of India from early stone age to the rise of civilisation. But for this, only Indian archaeology was not responsible. At that time, the main function of archaeology in the world was to collect ancient artistic and aesthetic materials for decorating the museum. The another matter was that in the mind of Western scholars there was a concept that the history of India was not too old. Besides Takshila, no other sites were excavated which could reveal the history of people of India of an age. There was general contention among Western scholars that in the religion based country like India; only the study of archaeological remains of religious sites and places would be useful. Therefore, religious places and their construction of buildings, images, shrines, and temples were the archaeological property in the mind of Western scholars. The Archaeological Survey of India considered its main responsibility to protect and conserve those monuments.

Marshal was well aware that real vestiges for the reconstruction of Indian history were not considered by the scholars. In his book,

"*Cambridge History of India*", he had written that the knowledge of dark early age of India could not be attained only by the study of shrines, temples, *Maths* and monuments. After 2 years of publication of this book, he discovered the well developed evidences of existence of civilisation in Indian subcontinent at Harappa and Mohenjodaro. It was a sensitive news for the work of history. After discovery of Harappa and Mohenjodaro, the two sites of Indus Valley Civilisation, historians of the world had to rethink over the antiquity of India. Mohenjodaro and Harappa were located at a distance of 700 kms from each other, but possessed similar traits of civilisation. This attracted the historians to study the origin, development and diffusion of Indian civilisation. This also brought a change in approaches of Archaeological Survey of India. Now Archaeological Survey of India could not remain only a department of collecting ancient materials and remains.

An important event occurred in the year 1935. In this very year under the auspices of Cambridge Yale Expedition, study related to Ice age culture began in Kashmir Valley and Punjab. Now, we had solid evidences of 3000 B.C. old civilisation. But man of India would not have entered in this stage suddenly. He would have entered in this stage after passing through different stages. In order to solve these questions, the knowledge of prehistoric culture of India was essential.

SIR MARTIMER WHEELER

Martimer Wheeler was Director General of Indian Archaeological Survey. He was supporter of scientific excavation. When he was appointed as Director General, he came to know that the balanced development of Indian archaeology had not taken place. Full attention was paid on Buddhist places of north India, but south India was completely untouched. Due to absence of remains with date and original materials, dating of South India was not definite till 4th-5th century. He solved this problem of history of South India. He did excavation in South India. On the basis of excavation, the attempt was made to decide the date. Thus, he provided full form of Indian archaeology.

He observed that megalithic burials were scattered here and there in South India. Megalithic was not found in any place in Indian history.

Observing the pottery of Roman period of Pondicherry, he did excavation at Arica Mendu. On the basis of this excavation, he found trade relation between India and Rome during 6th century A.D. He also did excavation of Brahmagiri and Chandravalli. In these excavations plenty of material remains were available on the basis of which cultural sequence of south-west and south-east India could be established.

He observed that the Archaeological Survey of India was lacking the trained archaeologists. Students of different universities were quite unaware of the excavational study of archaeological sites. He connected the students of universities with excavation work. He also took up excavation work along with students.

In the excavation of Arika Mendu, Brahmagiri and Chandravalli, he had requested the universities to allow and send students for training in excavation work. For this purpose, he had provided economic assistance to the students who had taken part in excavation work.

H.H. RISLEY

Risley was basically a scholar of Indian Civil Services. He had enriched Indian Physical Anthropology by his researches and writings. He was Commissioner, Census of India, 1901.

He had published for the first time his book, "*Tribes and Castes of Bengal*" (1890). In this book, he provided a brief description about tribes and castes of Bengal. According to him, it was very difficult to draw a dividing line between tribe and caste.

When he became Commissioner, Census of India (1901), he got attracted towards the presence of racial elements in Indian population. He divided the racial elements of Indian population in seven classes. He laid the foundation stone of racial study in India in his book, "*People of India*" (1915). According to him, seven racial elements present in Indian population were as follows:

- Turkey-Iranian
- Indo-Aryan
- Scytho-Dravidian
- Aryo-Dravidian
- Mongole-Dravidian
- Mongoloid
- Dravidian

Among these seven races, Dravidian, Aryan and Mongoloid were original. The other four races were result of admixture of above three original races.

He had not included the Negroid race in the racial classification of Indian population. According to him, Negroid race had not contributed any traits in Indian population. He treated Dravidian race as the earliest race of India. He did not accept any relation between Dravidian race of India and tribes of Australia. He also did not accept the relation between Negrito of Philippines island and the tribes of Andaman and Nicobar islands. He was quite convinced that Dravidian race was the earliest race of India.

J.H. HUTTON

After Risley, J.H. Hutton was appointed as a Commissioner, Census of India, 1931. Being Commissioner of Census of India, he was attracted towards racial elements in Indian population. He disapproved the racial classification of Indian population given by H.H. Risley. According to him, Risley like other scholars had also confused race with language. Dravidian and Aryan are languages spoken by the people of India. They are not racial groups. Hence, race and language should not be confused with each other. Race is based on physical traits of people, whereas language is a kind of dialect spoken by the people for the purpose of communication. He also rejected the view of Risley that Dravidians were the earliest racial groups of India. Risley had not considered those racial groups which had migrated to India in different periods and whose physical traits are found in the population of India till today.

According to Hutton, Negrito racial stock is the earliest inhabitants of India which were originated at Africa. They had migrated to India through sea coast of Arab, Baluchistan and Iran. Since this racial group was completely destroyed by racial groups who migrated India later on, therefore, no traits or Negrito racial stock are found in Indian population today.

After Negrito, another race who migrated to India was Proto-Australoid. The ancestors of this racial group were the inhabitants of Palestine. They had migrated to India from western side. It has two branches. One branch had knowledge of agricultural work and other group had knowledge of metal work. According to the people of Proto-Australoid racial group having the knowledge of metal work had developed the Indus Valley Civilisation.

After the arrival of Proto-Australoid racial group in India, the people of Mongoloid racial group came to India from eastern side and spread up to Indonesia through Bay of Bengal.

After Mongoloid racial group, the people of Alpine racial stock migrated to India.

At the end, Indo-Aryan racial group, migrated to India in Punjab.

He attempted to solve the conflict between tribe and caste. He took into consideration the religion as a hard norm. According to him, those groups which had adopted Hindu beliefs and rituals should be treated as caste. Contrary to this, the group which was animistic and naturalistic should be treated as tribe. He had placed other norms under secondary category. He had advocated for the rights of self-decision making and self-governance for the tribals.

Publications

1921 : *The Angami Naga,* London : McMillan & Company.

1921 : *The Sema Naga,* London : McMillan & Company.

1923 : *The Connections of Different Nagas of Assam,* Census of India, 1921, Section-III.

1931 : *Ethnographic Notes by Various Hands,* Census of India, Section-I, Part III, Government of India Press.

VERRIER ELWIN (1902-)

Verrier Elwin was a foreign anthropologist who enriched Indian anthropology by his field researches. He was born in England. His parents were Bishop of a Church. He received his early and higher education in England. After attaining higher education, he was appointed principal in a school. But his friends advised him to go to India to make study of Indian tribes. Following their advice, he came to India. In 1927, he came to India for the first time and began to live in Brista Seva Sangh. But he did not take any interest in propogation of religion of the Sangh. Being influenced by Mahatma Gandhi, he began to live in Sabarmati Seva Ashram. He met here with Thakkar Bapa. Being influenced by Thakkar Bapa, he began to work in Harijan Bastis. Thereafter, he came in contact with Sardar Ballabh Bhai Patel. Being influenced by Ballabh Bhai Patel, he joined freedom movement. He had written a book on Bardoli Movement of Patel. The title of the book was, "*The Disturbed Gujarat Village*". He had also written a book under the title, "*The Dawn on Indian Freedom*". When his parents were ill, he went back to England to meet his parents.

When he returned from England, he had to face problem because he had joined freedom movement of India. British Government of India had banned on his return passport. But, he became successful somehow to come back to India. This time, he turned his attention towards Indian tribes. He went to Betul of Madhya Pradesh for the study of tribals. Later on he went to Patangarh. He studied the tribals for 22 years under the supervision of A.C. Haddon. He began his career as an ethnographer. In series he made study of tribals of

Madhya Pradesh and published monograph. He did publications on monographic study of Baiga, Agaria, Maria and Muria tribes of Madhya Pradesh and brought to light the cultural heritage of Madhya Pradesh.

In his first book, "*The Baiga*", he postulated the 'National Park Theory' for the development and preservation of tribals. Due to his 'National Park Theory' he was criticised as an isolationist.

He did study of myths of central India and published a book. He had studied the arts and artistic behaviour of tribals of Madhya Pradesh and published book on them.

He was so closely and deeply associated with tribals of Madhya Pradesh that it was not possible for him to forget them. He lived in tribal village with tribals in tribal ways. In his life, the tribals of Madhya Pradesh had found emotional place. He turned his emotional relation into marital relation. He established marriage with two Gond girls Sita and Geeta and became Indian for ever. His life was very simple. He was interested in the development of tribals. He led a very simple life in his research camp. There was a cook and a typist along with him in research camp.

After studying tribes of Madhya Pradesh, he moved to Orissa to study the tribals. He also published monographs on tribes of Orissa.

He had advocated for planned acculturation. He advised for the proper conservation of tribals for their real life. The proper protection of tribals would definitely bring pleasant future in tribal life. They would not have to face the problem of loss of nerves by proper conservation.

After Orissa, he went to North-East to study tribals, of North-East regions. In 1952, he went to Assam on the invitation of Governor and studied tribes of NEFA (Manipur and Nagaland). He collected information on myths, religion and philosophy and published books on them.

For the development and welfare of tribals, Elwin had formulated the Panchsheel programme of Pt. Nehru, the then Prime Minister of India. He was tribal adviser to Pt. Nehru. He was chairman of Devar Commission set up for the development of tribals. That is why Devar Commission is also known as Elwin Commission. He was also adviser to the Government of India for tribal affairs.

Although he was criticised very much by other scholars for his 'National Park Theory'. He was also termed as isolationist, but he believed in unity and integrity of India. He had four sons and they had adopted Hindu, Islam, Sikh and Christian religion. He never created obstruction in adopting them four major religions of India. Although he was a foreigner by birth, but he had become Indian by his belief and work. He maintained Indianness throughout his life.

Publications

1939 : *The Baiga*. John Murray, London.

1942 : *The Agaria*. Cambridge : Oxford University Press.

1943 : *Maria Murder and Suicide.* Cambridge : Oxford University Press.

1943 : *The Aboriginals.* Cambridge : Oxford University Press.

1947 : *The Muria and their Gothul.* Cambridge : Oxford University Press.

1947 : *Myths of Middle India*. Cambridge : Oxford University Press.

1948 : "Notes on Juang". *Man In India,* Vol. 28.

1950 : *Bodo Highlanders.* Bombay : Oxford University Press.

1951 : *Tribal Arts of Middle India.* Cambridge : Oxford University Press.

1952 : *The Loss of Nerves.* Bombay : Oxford University Press.

1954 : *Tribal Myths of Orissa.* Bombay : Oxford University Press.

1955 : *The Religion of an Indian Tribe.* Bombay : Oxford University Press.

1958 : *The Myths of North-East Frontiers of India, NEFA, Shillong.* Kolkata : Oxford University Press.

1959 : *India's North-East Frontiers Agency in the Nineteenth Century.* Kolkata : Oxford University Press.

1960 : *The Philosophy of NEFA : Nagaland Advisors Secretariat,* Research Department, Shillong.

1962 : *The Art of NEFA,* Shillong.

C. VON FURER HAIMENDORF (1909-1995)

Christoff Von Furer Haimendorf was born in 1909 at Vienna. His father was a high official in Civil Service of Austria. He received degree in Anthropology from Vienna University in 1927. In 1931, he received D.Phil. degree from the same university. Being influenced by British anthropologist Malinowski, he came to India in 1936 for a year. In this period, he studied the Naga tribe of Assam. After making study of Naga tribe, he returned to his country. In 1939, he again came to India. But as Second World War had started and he belonged to enemy country, he was imprisoned. He was kept in Hyderabad Jail of Andhra Pradesh state. As he was anthropologist, he could not remain silent in jail. He applied his skill in the study of Chenchu, Reddy and Raj Gond tribes of Andhra Pradesh. He also worked among the tribes of Assam and Arunachal Pradesh.

When Second World War was over, he became adviser to Hyderabad Nizam. He established a number of institutions in Hyderabad for the development of India.

In 1949, he was appointed as Reader in Oriental and African Institute of London University. In 1951, he became Professor in the same university. He did everything for the development of this institute. In 1953, he came to Assam to study the tribals.

Publications

1939 : *The Naked Naga.*

1941 : "Seasonal Nomadism and Economics of the Chenchus of Hyderabad". *Journal of Royal Asiatic Society of Bengal,* Vol. 7, Letters.

1942-43 : "The Fortune of Primitive Tribes". *Indian Journal of Social Work,* Vol. 3.

1943 : *The Chenchus : Jungle Folk of Deccan.* London : Macmillan and Co.

1945 : *The Tribal Population of Hyderabad.* Hyderabad : Revenue Department (Census).

1945 : *The Reddis of Beson Hills : A Study in Acculturation* (with Elizabeth Von C. Furer Haimendorf), London : Macmillan and Co.

1946 : "A Note on Tribal Justice in Apatanis." *Man In India,* Vol. 26.

1946 : "The Agriculture and Land Tenure Among the Apatanis. *Man In India,* Vol. 26.

1947 : *Explorations in Eastern Himalayas.* Tour Diaries of Special Officer, Subansari Area.Shillong : Assam Government Press.

1948 : *The Raj Gond of Adilabad : A Peasant Culture of Deccan* (with Elizabeth C. Von Furer Haimendorf). London : Macmillan and Co.

1950-51 : "The Pradhan : The Bard of Raj Gond". *Eastern Anthropologist,* Vol. 4.

1955 : *The Himalayan Barbery.* London : John Murray, Albemark St. Co.

1962 : *The Apatanis and Their Neighbour : A Primitive Civilisation of Eastern Himalayas.* New York : Routledge and Kegan Paul.

A.C. MAYER

A.C. Mayer was Professor in London School of Economics. He came to India to make a study of Indian village and caste system. For this purpose he had chosen a village named Ramkheri in Madhya Pradesh state. The village Ramkheri was located at a distance of 12 km from Devas town of Malwa Plateau. Its distance from Ujjain was 48 km. He had made study of this village between 1954 and 1956. On the basis of researches in Ramkheri village, he had published his book, "*Caste and Kinship System in India*" (1960). The village had a population of 912 persons distributed in 27 castes at the time of study. This was a bigger village of the area. Mayer was influenced by S.F. Nadel and C. Von Furer Haimendorf. Under their influence, he conducted field researches in Ramkheri village.

In the tradition of British Social Anthropology, Mayer studied the social structure of the village in context with caste and kins link. Mayer distinguished three layers of membership in a caste. The lowest is that of an effective local sub-caste population which Mayer called the Kindered of Cooperation. This varied for each individual at any time. Around this is a group which was called as Kindered of recognition. Within which marriages were held and kin links could be traced through mutual kins. This group was rather large and amorphous and was much the same for sub-caste group of a single village. Beyond this, there were people who were recognised as a member of a sub-caste which was endogamous, named and separate from other sub-castes. It was usually spread over a wider area and therefore, not an effective group. In the light of study on caste and kinship, Mayer made an observation that it was the sub-caste which was really endogamous and the caste had no mechanism for settling disputes for adjusting the status of members. Here Mayer was in full agreement with Ghurye's statement that it was caste which was recognised by the society at large but it was the sub-caste which was regarded by the particular caste and the individual.

Another major significance of the book was the analysis of distinctions between internal and external aspects of a caste. The external relationship existed mostly whereas the external order of the caste group was based to a large extent on kinship relations within the population of adjacent village caste groupings. Here, Mayer seemed to be influenced by M.N. Srinivas's distinction between vertical ties within a settlement and horizontal links between villages. Mayer observed that caste ranking in Ramkheri was ritual criteria. Caste groups were at the same time status group. The clearest expression of ritual status was in terms of rules of commensality and concept of purity and pollution.

Mayer's study was of great significance from the point of view of methodology. Although he was concentrated on the study of a village, he reflected the need for understanding the village network. The studies of caste and kin links are spread over the region. Mayer had paid several visits to neighbouring villages with a view to understand the village in relation to the region. He also highlighted significantly the structural network of caste. His distinction between external and internal aspect of caste system, the difference in the roles of a villager in respect of the village, the sub-caste, and the ritual status of different castes were valuable contributions.

OSCAR LEWIS

Oscar Lewis was an anthropologist of Illinois University of America. He had come to India as a consultant anthropologist for Ford Foundation. He had conducted field research in a Rampur village in Delhi state. In the light of his field research in Mexico, Lewis got a chance to do field research in India. His field research at Rampur continued for over a period of eight months. The period of fieldwork was from October 1952 to June 1953. In the study of Rampur village, he had taken assistance of seven Indian students. In this collaborative research of a village Rampur, traditional anthropological techniques like observation, interview, schedule, case histories, village records and village census were applied. Rampur was a Jat village which had a population of 1052 distributed into 12 castes at the time of study.

Based on field date obtained from the village Rampur, Lewis published his two books, which were as follows:

- *Group Dynamics in a North Indian Village*, 1954.
- *Life in a North Indian Village.*

In his first volume submitted to the Planning Commission, Government of India, Lewis had dealt with locus of power and meaning of leadership in a Jat village. The nature, number, size, age composition, economic and social characteristics as well as internal factors of factions were described in detail. The process of leadership formation and its practical importance for community development programme were meaningfully examined. This work was of special significance because it was the first attempt to analyse systematically factions in Indian village. In this work, no attempt was made to analyse carefully the interfactional alliances, hostilities, tensions and discords as predominant quality of inter-factional relations.

The second book of the Lewis was a full length study which provided almost a complete coverage of important aspects of village. This village study was of a special significance firstly because it was only a full length publication about a village in cultural zone of Punjab. Secondly, the village was close to the Capital of India, Delhi. Being close to the capital of India, the village was reflecting some unique features. Thirdly, it was one of the first few village studies published by an American Anthropologist. Fourthly, this study was made by a scholar who had a first hand experience of village studies in America. Fifthly, the study was conducted by a team of researchers which was one of earliest efforts in group research.

The study brought out total pictures of the village Rampur. The villagers were presented as a people, rather than a mere figure in statistical tables. The Jajmani System and factions were analysed and discussed at a high level of abstraction and provided some generalisations on the basis of comparisons with some other similar studies. The festivals were also described and analysed elaborately. But kinship, family and caste did not find elaborate treatment.

The study of caste, locus of various activities in the village, was discussed only in relation to Jajmani system. The caste hierarchy, stereotype, intercaste relation, and rules of commensality were not considered. Lewis had proposed a functional definition of caste. To him, 'Caste was an endogamous social unit'. The membership of which was determined by birth, it was associated with some kind of particular occupation, and followed restrictions about acceptance of food and water from other caste groups. His analysis of small cohesive groups within the caste called Dhar was carefully identified and its functions were also well defined. These small cohesive groups in the village provided the locus of power and decision making process. They contributed the compartmentalised and segmented nature of village social organisation.

The book also provided a comparative analysis of Rampur with Tepoztlan, a Mexican village, in order to illustrate the variety of cultural forms in the peasant society and a need for a typology.

The similarities were greatest in the material culture, level of technology and economy and differences were the greatest in social organisation, value system and personality structure. In the light of such comparison, Lewis concluded that the concept of 'Peasant Society' was not sufficient for describing different cultural areas. He also suggested that separate institutions or aspects of culture developed at different historical circumstances. It is evident that Lewis was looking down upon the wider rural community rather than the village and showing its interrelationships with the national culture and civilisation.

Contribution on Culture of Poverty

Oscar Lewis had done a series of studies in Mexican villages. They were as follows:

1959 : *Five Families* : *Mexican Case Studies in Culture of Poverty,* New York.

1963 : *The Children of Sanchez* : *Autobiography of a Mexican Family,* New York.

1965 : *Lovida* : *A Patorical Family in Culture of Poverty,* New York.

1967 : *Pardomartins* : *A Mexico Peasant and his Family,* New York.

In the above Mexican studies, Lewis had attempted to show as to how poor economic conditions were responsible for birth of similar culture. The poor economic conditions give birth to similar aspiration and behaviour. Thus, poverty plays significant role in formation of culture. Poverty influenced the behaviour pattern of people. The poor of everywhere had similar cultural behaviours. In his Mexican study, he found that the Mexican having poor economic conditions showed similarity in fear and despair. They did not have any interest in modern games and sports. They did not participate in any modern games and plays. Their personality possessed traits like fearfulness, hopelessness and shyness. Thus, comparing the poor families of Mexico, Lewis propounded the concept of 'Culture of Poverty'.

Concept of Rural Cosmopolitanism

Based on his researches at Rampura village, Lewis propounded the Concept of Rural Cosmopolitanism in his book, "*Life in a North Indian Village*" (1958). He propounded this concept to show the reality of an Indian village. There was general notion that Indian village possessed closed economy and self-sufficiency. But he found that the root of unity in Indian villages was very deep. This unity was not limited only to person to person relation. But this type of feeling was also found with forest, trees, birds, animals, plants, river, mountains, lake, sea, tank, stream and others. In this way, all natural objects were related to the internal structure of the village. He observed that the Indian village showed extension in land relation, marital relation, religious relation, political relation, service relation and trade relation. He termed the extended system of relationship of an Indian village as 'Rural Cosmopolitanism'.

McKIM MARRIOTT

McKim Marriott was Professor of Anthropology at Chicago University of America He was a close associate of Robert Redfield. He came to India as a rural analyst to make study of Indian village. His visit to India was supported by An Area Research Training Fellowship granted by Social Science Research Council of America. He carried on rigorous fieldwork at a village named Kishangari from March 1951 to 1952. The village was located at a distance of 100 miles south-east of Delhi in Aligarh district. It was a Hindu village with 875 persons belonging to 24 castes. The Brahmins were most populous. This village was a research laboratory for McKim Marriott where he did many types of researches.

In the light of field materials, Marriott undertook to answer two questions raised by two American anthropologists—Robert Redfield and Milton Singer. These questions were as follows:

- Can such a village be satisfactorily comprehended and conceived as a whole in itself?

- Can understanding of one such village contribute to the understanding of culture and society at large?

Through these two questions, attempt of Marriott was to refine anthropological methods of holistic analysis when applied to the villages of Complex Indian Civilisation. Marriott in his paper, 'Little Communities in an Indigenous Civilisation' published in his edited book, "*Village India*" (1955), tackled these two questions in a systematic and analytic manner. He introduced the useful concepts like parochialisation and universalisation.

Concept of Universalisation and Parochialisation

In course of his analysis, Marriott applied Redfield's concept of little tradition and great tradition. He established that both little communities and great communities were mutually necessary condition for each other's existence in their present forms. He was of opinion that one must consider both thoroughly in order to understand either. Marriott also presented a penetrating analysis of festivals and proposed the concept of universalisation and parochialisation. Through these two concepts, he attempted to make great tradition and little tradition as a dynamic concepts.

According to Marriott, universalistion is a process through which traits of little communities reach in great traditional communities and become universalised. Parochialisation is an opposite concept through which traits of great traditional communities reach in little traditional communities and become parochialised little communities and great traditional communities are not in isolation. They are interdependent, interrelated and maintain mutual existence.

The concepts of great tradition and little tradition were criticised by Lucy Dumont and Pock. They had raised doubt as to whether there was a little tradition in the same sense as there was a great tradition and whether exactly the same relations existed between them and between the corresponding communities. They considered it possible to demonstrate the homogeneity of two levels and to extend to both the relations discovered on the popular level.

Contribution on Caste Ranking

McKim Marriott in his book, "*Caste Ranking and Community Structure in Five Regions of India and Pakistan*" (1960) undertook a comprehensive study of caste ranking in 1953. The result of comprehensive study was published in 1960 after certain revisions. He wanted to observe certain contextually determined regularities to varied horizontal and vertical aspects of caste. The study also reflected as to how difference in degree of elaboration of caste ranking in various regions in India and Pakistan might be affected by difference in certain other gross dimensions of community structure.

Marriott took into consideration four major and several minor determinants which gave rise to elaborate caste ranking in two villages—Kishangarhi and Ramnagala, both situated in Aligarh district of Uttar Pradesh state. Opinions about ranking of 36 castes available in these two neighbouring villages were sought from a sample of 14 males in Kishangarhi and 8 males in Ramnagla. The caste ranking of 36 castes were grouped as highest, high, lowest and low. The highest group was further divided as very high, merely high and not so high. Similarly, the lowest block was divided simply low, medium low and very low. It was found that castes were assigned to their minor sub-blocks with less agreement than to four major blocks.

In the light of empirical and statistical analysis of caste ranking in these two villages, Marriott concluded that caste ranking appeared to be shaped and determined by at least four general dimensions of community structure, which were as follows:

- The number of ethnic group within the community.
- The existence of correlative stratified interaction among the groups as a whole.
- The consistency of stratified interaction among individual members of different groups.

The degree to which community hierarchy is separated from possibly in consistent hierarchies elsewhere. These four determinants were shaped by such basic features of social structure as the size of local settlement, the degree of local centralisation in economic, political and religious organisations and the range and combination of extra local ties of marriage and descent.

Marriott further suggested that a knowledge of these four determinants could assist in exploring caste origin, in explaining differences and similarities among local system of ethnic ranking and in understanding current trends of social change in South Asia. Being impressed by his study of caste ranking Marriott continued his interest in field study. He utilised his methodology on a bigger sample to refine the concepts and knowledge of caste ranking more precise and certain.

DAVID C. MANDELBAUM

David C. Mandelbaum was Professor of Anthropology at California University of America. He had come to India to study Indian village and Indian tribe before our Independence. He had made study of Kota tribe of South India. He had published papers on the basis of study of Kota tribe. He had also contributed papers in the book "*Village India*" edited by McKim Marriott and "*India's Village*" edited by M.N. Srinivas.

His publications were as follows:

1938 : "Polyandry in Kota Society". *American Anthropologist*, Vol. 40.

1941 : "Culture Change among Nilgiri Tribes". *American Anthropologist*, New Series, Ralph Linton, Vol. 4.

1955 : "Technology Credit and Culture Change in Nilgiri Village". In M.N. Srinivas edited book, *India's Village*.

1955 : "The World and World View of Kota". In McKim Marriott edited book, *Village India*.

Mandelbaum had published books in two volumes dealing with analysis of Indian society. These volumes were as follows:

1972 : *Society in India : Continuity and Change.* Vol. I, Bombay : Popular Prakashan.

1972 : *Society in India : Change and Continuity.* Vol. II, Bombay: Popular Prakashan.

In these two volumes, Mandelbaum covered the interpretations and interactions of basic groups of Indian social system. They were : *Varna*, *Jati*, *Jati* clusters, family, kinship relations, village, region, civilisation and then continuity and change. He had used the term *Jati* in place of caste. The *Jati* had found discussion throughout the book. He had devoted the Part III and Part IV of the first volume of the book on *Jatis*. In the first part of the first volume, he studied the relations among people of different *Jatis*, while in the second part he analysed the relationship within the *Jatis* itself. His analysis of *Jati* relationship was based both on his rigorous reading and fieldwork. In this way, he presented a very comprehensive picture of the Indian society. From his analysis, it emerged prominently that hierarchical ranking was central to relations among people of different *Jatis*. It was further explained as to how hierarchy was significant within a *Jati* as well as among *Jatis*. The chapters on *Jati* organisation described as to how members of *Jati* maintained their group and suggested as to why opposition within a *Jati* was in existence. It was one of the most outstanding contributions in Indian anthropology because it presented a very insightful and comprehensive appraisal of society in India.

MORRIS E. OPLER

Opler was Professor of Anthropology at Cornell University in America. The vast rural track of Uttar Pradesh attracted Morris E. Opler to come in India as early as 1947 to conduct researches in Indian villages. Opler's repeated efforts and his continued training programme in Uttar Pradesh drew the attention of a number of graduate students from Cornell University. This had made Uttar Pradesh as a stronghold of village studies. Opler's collaboration with Lucknow University also provided incentive to a team of Indian scholars including D.N. Majumdar and S.C. Dube to undertake and encourage village studies in Uttar Pradesh in particular and in India in general. Opler's efforts in encouraging village studies in Uttar Pradesh also succeeded owing to his collaboration with R.D. Singh, a resident of a village in eastern Uttar Pradesh.

Along with R.D. Singh, Opler made study of U.P. Villages like Madhopur, Rampur and Senapur. Based on researches in these villages, Opler and R.D. Singh wrote some papers and got them published in research Journals. They were as follows:

1948 : "The Division of Labour in an Indian Village". In G. Coon edited book, *A Reader in Anthropology.*
1952 : "Economic, Political and Social Change in North Central India". *Human Organisation*, Vol. 2, No. 2.
1956 :"The Extension of an Indian Village". *Journal of Asian Studies,* Vol. 16.
1962 : "Two Villages of Eastern Uttar Pradesh". *Indian American Anthropologist,* Vol. 54.

In their first paper, "The Division of Labour in an Indian Village", they had described inter-caste relationship and Jajmani system. Inter-caste relationship and Jajmani system were based on division of labour in Indian village.

In their second paper, Opler and Singh presented a comparative picture of two villages—Madhopur and Rampur. This paper was based on fieldwork done in these two villages in 1949 with the support of Cornell University. The criteria for the selection were not mentioned. However, these two villages were of different sizes and were located in different socio-religious environments. The village Rampur was located near the shrine city, Allahabad was nearly twice in size of Madhopur. The organisation of castes in these two villages was also somewhat different. The village Madhopur had a population of 1852 distributed into 23 castes. Thakurs and Chamars were numerically dominant caste in this village. The high status of Thakur was reinforced by the ownership of 82 per cent of land. There were two families of Brahmins in the village but they were uninfluential because they were dependent on other castes of the village.

The village Rampur had a population of 3000 distributed into 24 castes along with 600 Muslims. Owing to the location of the village near the Shrine city on the bank of river Ganga, the maximum population in the village was of Mallahs (Boatman). Next to Mallahs, the population of Brahmins Pandas. The Ahirs of the village were powerful because of conspicuous absence of Thakurs in the village.

In another joint paper, the author had examined economic, political and social changes in Madhopur village. They found that modern forces had brought out the modern forces of changes in the village.

Among the papers written by Opler special mention must be made of one on the 'Extension of an Indian Village'. The paper was read at Symposium on "Village Study in India". In the light of data collected from the village Senapur, he attempted to analyse the network of the village in terms of its extensions and in context of larger units of Indian civilisation. He established the brides in the village were brought from the outside of the village, but from respective castes throughout the region. 15 per cent adult males were employed outside the village. Market towns and educational institutions attracted the villagers. The administrative towns and religious centres were influencing the villagers in many ways. Describing all these he concluded that the involvement of the village Senapur with organisations, places and events outside the village was considerable for a long time. Yet, it was not interfered with a separate identity and cohesiveness of the community.

In another supplementary paper, Opler's collaborator R.D. Singh brought out the unity of the village Senapur. In his paper, Singh attempted to answer two questions : How can we identify an Indian Village? and where should we look for its unity? On the basis of his observation he located the unity of the village in the oldest shrine. The oldest shrine of the village was uniting the villagers, the village Panchayat, the sentiments of villagers, inter-caste relationship of the village and other village institutions. He concluded that it would be fruitful to observe and analyse the behaviour of the people at the level of community specially in the context of new village institutions.

Methodologically, these two papers on 'Unity and Extension of the Village' had proved to be quite challenging and provocative. In addition to these joint papers, Opler had interests on the study of religion and politics. He had contributed papers on religions and political life, too.

Under the guidance of Opler, J.M. Planant, a scholar of Cornell University did research exclusively on 'Religious Life and Values' for his Doctoral Dissertation of Cornell University. J.M. Planant in his doctoral dissertation presented a full length description of religious life in an Indian village Senapur.

Barnerd Cohn, an another scholar of Cornell University made detailed and special study of cultural process on the Chamar of Madhopur for his doctoral dissertation.

Under the auspices of Cornell India Research Project another predoctoral Scholar of Cornell University, W.A. Rowe did field research in Senapur between August 1955 and July 1958. He wrote a doctoral dissertation on social and economic mobility in a low caste north Indian community. The thesis was submitted to Cornell University in 1960. Though his thesis had remained unpublished but his findings were available in two of his papers—

- "The Marriage Network and Structural Change in a North Indian Community". *South-West Journal of Anthropology,* Vol. 16, No. 2, 1960.
- "Social and Economic Mobility in a Low Caste North Indian Village", 1964.

In his first paper Rowe dealt with the exogenous nature of Indian Village and marriage network which grew up on account of it. The changes going on in the social structure of the village had found special treatment in this paper.

In his second paper, Rowe described the contemporary functioning of the Jajmani system in Senapur village. He dealt with exchange of services and emphasised upon the economic activities of the Noniyas. Rowe did not consider the strains and stresses within the system leading to its decay nor did he consider the norms and the sanction of Jajmani system.

Under the direction of Morris E. Opler, another scholar M.S. Luschinsky studied the Senapur village (1954-57) and wrote an article on, "Problems of Culture Change in Indian Village" published in *Human Organisation,* Vol. 22 (1963). In this paper, Luchinsky described the innovations in the field of public health, education, land reform and village Government. The spread of innovation in the village was determined by nature of message source, if human has its position in social hierarchy, the nucleus or nuclei through which it was channelled into the village and its relative status in hierarchy and the number of intergroup friendship ties and mediation nuclei.

Under the guidance of Morris E. Opler, John T. Hitchcock of Cornell University studied a village named Khalapur in western Uttar Pradesh. The village was located in Saharanpur district of Uttar Pradesh. Hitchcock was Station Director of Cornell India Research Programme Station in the village. Fieldwork in this village was carried out from October 1953 to July 1955 with the financial assistance of Ford Foundation and the Board of Overseas Training and Research. He was assisted by an interpreter who had helped him in establishing rapport and data collection. The result of fieldwork was submitted in the shape of a doctoral dissertation on the topic of 'Rajput of Khalapur : A Study of Kinship, Social Stratification and Politics' (1956). He also wrote papers on 'The Idea of Martial Rajput's' and 'Leadership in a North Indian Village'. In his first paper, he presented the ideal behaviour of martial Rajputs which in actual practice was weakened. The two thousand Rajputs of Khalapur traced their descent from illustrious ancestors. They believed in their innate capacity as warriors and rulers. He also quoted the local folk tales and drew upon epics—the *Ramayana* and *Mahabharata* to establish the martial character of Rajputs. He had given a new slant on the study of a dominant caste in an Indian village. Although he had worked under Opler, but he was influenced by the concepts of traditions propounded by Robert Redfield and Milton Singer.

In his second paper on leadership, Hitchcock contrasted the two types of leaders of an Indian village : Traditional and Non-traditional. The traditional leaders held the Government instituted office of Mukhia or headman and the non-traditional leader was the principal of a newly established intermediate college. Both the leaders belonged to Rajput caste. Both leaders drew power from the affiliation with outside agencies. He made comparison between status and roles of traditional and non-traditional leaders of the village Khalapur. He also showed transformation of leadership due to outside urban influence, education, politics and changing connections with wider political system of the nation and the administration.

The same village Khalapur was studied by P.M. Mahar and J.J. Gumperz during the same period.

Mahar who had strong background of sociology carried out extensive research in intergroup relationship with special reference to the position of Harijan. She brought out the dominant nature of Rajput castes and pointed out changes in caste relationship due to internal strains and stresses and external modern factors like education, election, political parties, Government institutions and others.

In an another paper based on fieldwork during the same period at Khalapur (1954-56), she attempted to rank Hindu and Muslim castes of the village. As she was interested mainly in formulation of a technique of ranking castes in the village, she did not provide any material on the village.

An another scholar of Cornell University, John J. Gumperz made study of the same village Khalapur in the same period and wrote a number of papers on socio-linguistics of the village. He identified social stratification in terms of linguistic differentiation. The title of research paper was, 'Dialect Differentiation and Social

Stratification in a North Indian Village' published in *American Anthropologist,* Vol. 60, No. 4 (1958).

In his another paper, he had devoted his attention on mass communication and media of cultural transformation. He also dealt with religious performances of Khalapur and attempted to analyse their social function in respect of local communicational network. The main contribution of this article was the analysis of the methods of transmission in the religious sphere of rural life. But he did not give any analysis of an actual process by which a great traditional element was accepted by the villagers and incorporated in their rites and festivals or how a little traditional element was universalised. He was also not concerned with the psychological aspects of this process. His main concern was with the media of communication.

An another scholar of Cornell University P.M. Kolenda had worked as a post-doctoral fellow in this Cornell-Lucknow Research Project. She studied the same village Khalapur in the same period. In the light of her field inquiry, she attempted to answer the questions like, Do ordinary people of India adapt themselves to Hindu theory of *Karma* and *Punarjanma*? Concentrating on the fieldwork among untouchable sweeper caste, it was established that the great traditional religious ideas were not practised by untouchable sweeper caste. They observed a simpler, localised and parochialised form of religion. The Hindu concept of *Karma* postulated that one's fate was the direct result of one's conduct in previous life. However, the villagers were always trying to raise their status. The sweepers of Khalapur interpreted the doctrine to suit their own requirements for preventing or relieving misfortune in the world, rather than attaining salvation. The sweepers believed that God and fate were not absolute. The events and supernatural elements existed independent of them.

Ralph H. Retztaff, an another scholar of Cornell University, conducted fieldwork in Khalapur village on Village Government in the same period. He was also associated with 'Cornell-India Research Programme'. He conducted field enquiry on Village Government. He published a book, "*Village Government of India*"

(1962). In this book, he attempted to explore the functioning of Village Government in historical perspectives. He described the traditional Panchayat of the village of various types and traced their evolution around village Khalapur. He also examined the functioning of official Gram Panchayat which came into existence in July 1949. He observed that the official Gram Panchayat failed due to weak leadership of Pradhan. It was chiefly used by the dominant caste Rajput of the village as a Judicial body. The Panchayat's elections always created tensions, group rivalries and reinforced the village factionalism.

HERALD A. GOULD

Herald A. Gould was an American scholar. He had come to make village study in India as post-doctoral fellow from National Science Foundation and Fellow of National Institute of Science. He had chosen a village Sherapur from the district of Faizabad of Uttar Pradesh State. He carried out field researches in this village in 1959-60 and again in 1960-62. In the light of his field enquiry in Sherapur, Gould had written several research papers on Jajmani system, characteristics of peasantry, village exogamy and others. They were as follows:

1958 : "The Village Jajmani System". *South-Western Journal of Anthropology,* Vol. 14, No. 4.

1959 : "The Peasant Village : Centrifugal or Centripetal". *Eastern Anthropologist,* Vol. 13, No. 1.

1961 : "A Further Note on Village Exogamy in North India". *South-Western Journal of Anthropology,* Vol. 17.

1964 : "Jajmani System of North India : Its Structure, Magnitude and Meaning". In *Ethnology,* Vol. 3, No. 1.

The first research paper of Gould reported about the functioning of Jajmani System in Sherapur village which had 12 castes and 21 families. The families maintained service type of relations with their clients in washing clothes, carpentry and barbery. Gould also reported about the system of payments of grains bi-annually to these service castes. He also brought out the fact that landowning castes dominate the landless and the menial. In his interpretation, Gould was influenced by W.H. Wiser's work on Jajmani System.

In his second paper, Gould suggested that Indian village was both centripetal and centrifugal. Peasantry was self-contained and autonomous. He also observed the village dependent on urban centres and on the numerous processes of national culture. He termed the first set of characteristics as centripetal and the second set of characteristics as centrifugal. In his penetrating analysis, he identified three sets of experiences, which were as follows:

- Locals reinforcing experiences.
- Tradition reinforcing experiences.
- Modern reinforcing experiences.

Exemplifying these experiences, he suggested that marriage represented the local reinforcing experiences of the village and symbolised the relative power of centripetal tendencies in the peasant community; while pilgrimages represented the traditional reinforcing experiences which again symbolised the relative power of non-industrial civilisation. Educational institutions, modern towns and modern markets were example of modern reinforcing experiences. Thus, Gould made a fascinating and refreshing analysis of the interactional pattern in Sherapur village. The interactional pattern was both centripetal and centrifugal. Gould introduced the term Proletarianisation. Through the process of proletarianisation lower castes and classes had become defunctionalised in rural areas and were forced to migrate in urban areas for doing work as labourers in industrial complexes. In Sherapur, the upper castes were also proletarianised because they were also migrating to urban areas for business and works.

In his third paper, Gould discussed the rules of village exogamy as observed in Sherapur. Since it was only a note, it tells us little about village life in India.

Gould wrote a very comprehensive paper on structure, magnitude and meaning of Jajmani system in Sherapur. Based on his repeated fieldwork, he presented in detail substantive data on economic interactions. He attempted to examine three issues:

(i) The types of relationship and reimbursement which Jajmani system involved;
(ii) The kind of ecological units that was appropriate for study of economic interaction in rural India; and
(iii) The relative magnitude of traditional economic interaction.

He had considered these three issues on the basis of his own substantive data as well as in the light of other similar studies. According to Gould, the relevant unit of Jajmani system was a network of economic relationships whose spatial dimensions were defined not by corporate boundaries, but by the location of households of specialists and their clients. He suggested that traditional economic interaction persisted in spite of economic and political upheaval because it was of fundamental importance for the maintenance of social status and organisation. It depended upon the social organisation of Hinduism which was still strong today.

Gould's main contribution to the general model of Jajmani system was his recognition that it integrated the belief about pollution. But he had ignored the caste differences in the capacity to pollute.

The views expressed by Herald A. Gould related to Jajmani system was criticised by P.M. Kolenda, a scholar of Cornell University in her paper, 'Towards a Model of Hindu Jajmani System' published in *Human Organisation,* Vol. 22, No. 1. Special issues : Contours of Culture Change. The relation between Jajman and Kamin was not based on fictitious kinship as reported by Gould. Their relationship was based on different types of customs, rites and rituals.

MILTON SINGER

Milton Singer was Professor of Anthropology at Chicago University, USA. He was a close assistant of Robert Redfield. That is why he was known as Redfieldian. He came in India in 1954. He made study of cultural role of Madras city in 1955-56. Thereafter, he studied traditions of civilisation, structure and change of traditional India, and modernisation of great tradition. His main publications were as follows:

1956 : "Cultural Role of City" (with Robert Redfield). *Man In India,* Vol. 36, No. 3.
1958 : "The Great Tradition in Metropolitan Centre of Madras". In *American Folklore,* Vol. 71, No. 28.
1958 : (ed.) "Traditional India : Structure and Change." *Journal of American Folklore,* Vol. 78, No. 28.
1972 : "When a Great Tradition Modernises : An Anthropological Approach to Indian Civilisation".
1975 : "Structure and Change in Indian Society."

Contribution on Cultural Role of City

He along with Robert Redfield made study of cultural role of Madras city and published a research paper, 'Cultural Role of a Metropolitan City, Madras', which was published in *Man In India,* Vol. 36, No. 3 (1956). According to them, traditional towns were centres of civilisations in India since ancient period. Their tradition was of great tradition. They had an influence area. Village had the tradition termed as little tradition characterised by illiteracy and magic. The towns had great traditions characterised by literacy, religion, art and aesthetic behaviour. The people of great tradition and little tradition were bound by religion morally. That is both traditions had interactions, interdependence and co-existence. In the maintenance and transmission of cultural traits to villages, the great traditional cities played significant role. From the point of view of urbanisation, the great traditional cities represented the example of primary urbanisation. The towns which developed due to mining and industries, represented secondary urbanisation. The towns of secondary urbanisation had secular characteristics, whereas towns of primary urbanisation had religious characteristics. Thus, they attempted to know the cultural role of cities through primary urbanisation process, not through secondary urbanisation process.

Contribution on the Study of Madras City

In his paper, 'The Great Traditions in Metropolitan Centre of Madras' (1958), he has talked about three methods by which great traditions of Metropolitan Madras was parochialised. They were as follows:

- By the study of Religious Geography.
- By the study of Cultural Representatives and their organisation.
- By the study of Cultural Performances.

In this way, Singer attempted to study the great traditional Metropolitan Madras on the basis of religious geography, religious specialists and religious performances. In this way, he had developed a methodology to make study of a great traditional city in India. For this purpose, he had postulated the concept of religious geography, religious specialists and religious performances. With certain modifications Professor Vidyarthi had propounded the concept of Sacred Complex to study great traditional city Gaya. He had propounded the concept of Sacred geography, Sacred specialists and Sacred performances to study the Sacred complex of great traditional city in India in his book, "*Sacred Complex in Hindu Gaya*" (1961).

Contribution on Traditional India : Structure and Changes

In his edited work, "*Traditional India : Structure and Change*" (1958), he had attempted to present papers contributed by different scholars on structure and change in traditional India. This volume included papers dealing with textual and contextual analysis of oral and recorded traditions. Although the theme of the book was to understand the image of new India in the light of her deep-rooted rich heritage, almost all papers had some bearing on religious traditions, which obviously had been the common idioms of Indian history. The paper dealt with the various dimensions of Indian civilisation and analysed some aspects of cultural media and cultural performances including the religious ones. A few of these papers dealt with some aspects of religion of a specific community. For example McCormack's paper dealt with media of communication found among the Lingayat sect and Raghavan's paper dealt with methods of religious instruction in south India. There were also papers which dealt with religious aspects of specific communities like Anavils of Gujarat by Nayak, the Chamar of Senapur by B.S. Cohn and the Nayar by Kathaleen Gough.

Contribution on Modernisation of Great Tradition

In his book, "*When a Great Tradition Modernise : An Anthropological Approach to Civilisation*" (1972), he attempted to show that the great tradition was also influenced by the process of modernisation. Adaptation of great tradition had taken place with modernisation process. As a result, new traits were adopted in great traditional centres. Material of worship, method of worship, decoration of Sacred centres, method of performances, Bhajans, Kirtans, prayers like cultural media were influenced by the modern traits. Thus, modern traits had got entry into great traditional centres.

A.R. BEALS

Beals was an American anthropologist who came to India to make study of Indian villages for his doctoral dissertation. At first instance he worked in a village Namhali located near Bangalore city. The investigation was carried out in 1952-53, for 15 months with a view to describe the history of external factors which had changed the social structure of the village since 1800. As a result of his research in Namhali, Beals presented a doctoral dissertation on cultural change and social conflict in a south Indian village at the University of California, USA in 1954. Although his thesis was not published in the form of a book, but he wrote a long paper entitled, 'Interplay among Factors of Change in a Mysore Village' published in McKim Marriott's edited book, *Village India*. In this paper, he brought out six factors which were responsible for the growth of the village. They were as follows:

- Trade and Commerce
- Communication and Manufacture
- Statewide Government
- Increasing Population
- Education
- Money Economy

These factors combined vigorously at different times to produce veritable changes in the village. In this paper, Beals described only one fact of a multifaceted village society. Only changes brought about through the external factors were examined. Changes were seen as a whole without considering the variations in different strata of village society. It was obvious that the internal factors of change were equally important as the different sections of the people were not uniformly affected.

In his second paper entitled, 'Change in Leadership in a Mysore Village' (1955), published in M.N. Srinivas' book *India's Village*, Beals had analysed the impact of increasing urbanisation on village leadership. The traditional pattern of leadership was in the process of disintegration, while new factions, cliques and mutual discrimination were started dominating the village leadership.

Beals did second fieldwork in a village named Gopalpur in Yadgiri Tehsil of Mysore state which was located at a distance of 15 miles from Bangalore. A.R. Beals had made study of this village in 1959-60 along with his wife. Based on fieldwork in the village Gopalpur, Beals had published a booklet "*Gopalpur : A South Indian Village*" (1962). In this book, he attempted to describe the insider's view of the villagers. Castes in the village were ranked hierarchically according to their ritualistic criteria specially food consumption and traditional occupation whch were placed along a scale of purity and pollution. He also noted a correlation between caste and class. The position of Brahmin was quite high because they worshipped a hierarchy of God. The high God Shiva and Basava were worshipped by high caste people and the vegetarian Brahmin priest. Hanumanta was unsophiticated and warrior God. He was a lower God. Hanumanta was worshipped by almost all villagers during community based festivals. There were non-vegetarian Gods and Goddesses associated with low castes. They were concerned with the practical need of the villagers. The village life was marked by several fairs and festivals and almost after every 28 days a villagewide ceremony was performed. In the performance of these ceremonies, representative of every caste performed a special role and all villagers used to participate.

Based on same field materials supplemented by short visits, Beals had made a valuable contribution to the study of South Indian villages. His book, "*Village Life in South India*" (1974), is based on field material collected from three Mysore villages namely Elephant, Namhalli and Gopalpur located in different parts of Mysore state. Beals went on to emphasise the relationship between villages and their surroundings. Following up an ecological approach, he described the ecosystem of the village as an integration between cultural tradition of a set of people and their environment.

In a series of ten chapters, Beals described in an analytical manner the ecological basis of economy, technology, the network of intra- and inter-village relationship. In this way, he presented a fresh model to understand village life in South India.

The frequent use of South Indian civilisation by Beals was not only weak but also misleading. Several publications of Milton Singer, Raghavan and others had established as to how South Indian villages were part of a greater network of Indian civilisation and channels of communication both in past and present.

W. McCORMACK

Cormack was an another American scholar. He came to India to make village study. He selected two villages named Morsavalli and Huillipanhalli near Bangalore in Mysore state. Morsavalli had a population of 504 persons and Huillipanhalli had a population of 252 persons. Based on his fieldwork, he had written two research papers which were as follows:

1958 : "Sister's Daughter's Marriage". *Man In India*, Vol. 38, No. 2, Ranchi.

1960 ; "Factionalism in a Mysore Village". In *Leadership and Political Institutions in India* (ed.) by Park and Tinker.

In his first paper, he attempted to explore the implications of sister's daughter's marriage on the basis of kinship terminology. In his second paper, Cormack brought out the fact that the power of traditional leadership was declining in the village for three reasons:

- Secularisation.
- Doubt about neutrality and good character of some village elders.
- Personal interest of leaders in village disputes.

He also observed increase in factional leadership due to the operation of several external factors.

E.B. HARPER

E.B. Harper was an another American scholar who had come to India to make study of Indian villages. He selected a village named Totagadal in Maland of Mysore state. He along with his wife stayed in this village from November 1954 to February 1956. He studied the pattern of Jajmani system prevalent in the village Totagadal. He discovered two types of economic transaction in the village which were as follows:

- Jajmani System
- Malnad System

The Jajmani system and Malnad system were occurring between Jajmans and artisan community of the village. In Jajmani system, Jajmans and artisans were bound by patron-client relationship and payment was made twice in a year in kind, besides some gifts on festive and ceremonial occasions. Malnad system was payment to artisans in cash. It was concerned with cash transaction, whereas Jajmani system was concerned with payment in kind periodically. Harper observed that Jajmani system was disintegrating into Malnad system in Indian villages. He asserted that Malnad system was also traditional, but he did not present the historical data. He had dealt with Jajmani and Malnad system in his paper, 'Two Systems of Economic Exchange', published in *American Anthropologist*, Vol. 61, No. 5, Chicago (1959).

In his second paper entitled, 'Political Organisation and Leadership in a Karnataka Village', published in *Leadership and Political Institutions in India* (ed.) by Park and Tinker (1959), Harper had examined the position and role of dominant caste, namely Hawik Brahmin of the same village. He further examined the dynamics of village leadership, feuds, factions, and the role of parties in decision making. He concluded that the village retained its tradition in the form of leadership and process of decision making. He observed that since individual Hawik Brahmins were major leaders determined by political dynamics of feuds, faction and party, they could strengthen and weaken the position of a non-Brahmin leader.

T. SCARLETT EPSTEIN

Epstein was a British scholar who had come to India to make study of Indian village. She had come to India in 1954. She had selected two villages namely Wangala and Danela for field enquiry. She did fieldwork in the period between 1954-56 for two years in Wangala and Danela villages of Mysore region. Wangala was a wet (irrigated) village and Danela was a dry (unirrigated) village. The village Wangala was located at a distance of five miles from Mandala. It was a multi-caste irrigated village of 192 households at the time of study. On the basis of field enquiry, Epstein had made publication of papers and books which were as follows:

1959 : "A Sociological Analysis of Witch Beliefs in a Mysore Village". In *Eastern Anthropologist,* Vol. 12, No. 4.

1960 :"Economic Development and Peasant Marriage in South India". In *Man In India,* Vol. 40, No. 3, Ranchi.

1962 : *Economic Development and Social Change in South India,* Manchester University Press.

In first paper, Epstein had described the persistence of belief in witchcraft in South Indian villages. Witches were believed as possessed by spirit and they caused harm to their enemies. The villagers were very much afraid of witches and they did not allow children, pregnant and lactating women to come before witches. They did not allow milk cattle and pregnant cattle to appear before them.

In her second paper, 'Economic Development and Peasant Marriage in South India', Epstein had dealt with impact of peasant economy on marriage system. She was of opinion that economic development had increased marriage expenses of peasant communities. In marriages modern traits were being used.

The book, "*Economic Development and Social Change in South India*", written by Epstein was the first full length village study in Mysore region. She was such a scholar who combined in herself the competence of both an economist and social anthropologist. In this book, Epstein had made an attempt to bring out the impact of irrigation on economic and social organisation of the village within regional economy. In the analysis of elements of structural change, the author established a positive correlation between economic organisational and ritual change. The economic change, however, was the determining variable. The persistence of economic and social values had made a delay in social change. The study was comparative and synchronic study of two varieties of development within a quarter of a century. The vigorous and controlled way of comparisons had made the book significant. It was not a case of cultural change as cultural development in Wangala in comparison to Danela.

GEITAL P. STEED

Steed was an anthropologist of Columbia University. Steed had come to India in 1949 and selected the village Kasandra located in Sanad Taluka of Ahmedabad district in Gujarat. The village Kasandra was located at a distance of 35 miles from Ahmedabad city in Gujarat state. Steed had made study of this village in the period between November 1949 and January 1951. The fieldwork was carried out with the help of three Indians and four American collaborators. The village had population of 850 persons at the time of study. The fieldwork was done with a view to study aspects of personality formation in three villages of north India, the other two being a Hindu Halmet in Rajasthan and a Muslim village in U.P.

In a long paper, personality formation in Hindu village in Gujarat, Steed attempted to formulate an approach to the study of personality formation in an Indian village. In the first instance approach was stated theoretically and then documented with evidence accumulated at two levels of field enquiry—sociological and ontogenetic. The discussion of social structure and the portrait of single informant was aimed principally to delineate sociological horizons in personality formation.

In the light of socio-psychological data about the village and stage of adjustment of 26 years old Indra Singh, the ideal virtues and value orientation of Rajputs were discussed at the axis of self. This community was examined from the viewpoint of good life and changes in personality structures in the context of changing social norms in the village.

E. KATHLEEN GOUGH

Gough was a lady anthropologist who had come to India to make study on Indian village. Gough made study of three villages located in Kerala state during the period 1947-1949. On the basis of field researches, she published few papers on village life in Kerala.

Along with the study of three villages of Malabar coast, Kathleen Gough later worked in two villages of Tanjor in Tamil Nadu. She had done fieldwork in a Brahmin village Kumbapetai located at a distance of 8 miles north of Tanjor town during October 1951-52. The village had 16 castes and one Muslim family. Her publications were as follows:

1955 : "Social Structure of a Tanjor Village". In M.N. Srinivas edited book, *India's Village*.

1958 : "Cult of Dead Among Nayars". In Milton Singer edited book, *Traditional India : Structure and Change.*

1959 : "Criteria of Caste Ranking". In *Man In India*, Vol. 39, No. 2.

1960 : "Caste in a Tanjor Village". In E.R. Leach edited book, *Aspects of Castes in South India, Ceylon and North West Pakistan.*

In series of papers, Kathleen Gough wrote about the social structure, kinship system, caste organisation and caste ranking in Tanjor village. She noted considerable change in the traditional social structure of the village. The village which was relatively an isolated, closed, stationary system with traditional economic intercaste relationship had moved half way in transition from this relatively static feudal sub-system economy to a much wider expanding capitalist economy. The breakdown of feudal economic system, the emergence of lower caste groups in economic rivalry rather than cooperation and widening range of social relation outside the village had endangered the power of Brahmins and unity of the village. The kinship ties within and between villages were gradually weakened by increasing heterogeneity of wealth, education and occupation.

Gough had also described the roles of various caste specialists in context of traditional and modern economy in Tanjor village. She also established the role of dominant caste, the Brahmins as the administrators of the village who traditionally judged five types of cases:

- Disputes between persons of the same lower castes who failed to reach settlement through their own assembly.
- Disputes between members of different lower castes.
- Offences by a person of lower castes against a person of another village.
- Attack of lower caste persons by the high castes or the dignities of Brahmins themselves.
- The general breaches of the normal laws of the village which threatened to disturb the public unity.

She observed that at all events Brahmins still attempted to prevent criminal cases from passing into the hands of police or at worst to mitigate the official sentence in accordance with the laws of caste.

Gough showed that during the past 30 years, the intercaste tensions and competition had witnessed polarisation. The decline of caste restrictions was accompanied by a new ideology which had released a new spirit of competition and challenges to the existing caste order. In Tanjor village in 1952, one major conflict that overrode all others was between the landed and landless. Such a situation had come due to acute agricultural overpopulation; concentration of landownership within a small fraction of the population; and failure to develop industrial employment for surplus villagers. In the light of these trends, it seemed logical for her to conclude that such economic and class conflict would increasingly weaken the identity of castes.

F.G. BAILEY

F.G. Bailey was a noted British Social Anthropologist. He came to India to make village study in 1952. He studied a non-tribal village named Bisipara. The village Bisipara was located at a distance of eight miles from the administrative centre of Koldman of Fulbani district. The village was surrounded by dense forest and had population of 700 persons distributed in 180 families. The field researches were carried out in 1952-54 under the guidance of H.M. Glackman. The preliminary results were published in a couple of papers published in *Economic Weekly* and later compiled in Srinivas' volume *India's Village* (1955). His publications were as follows:

1955 : "An Oriya Village". In M.N. Srinivas edited book *India's Village*.

1958 : "Caste and Economic Frontiers". Oxford University Press, Bombay.

1960 : "Tribe, Caste and Nation". Oxford University Press, Bombay.

1963 : "Politics and Social Change : Orissa". University of California Press, Berkeley.

The full length book on Bisipara was published in 1958 under the title, "*Caste and Economic Frontiers*". This book aimed at analysing the changes which had occurred in internal organisation of an Oriya village as a result of the extensions of its economic and administrative frontiers. It was a study of change in a peasant economy which had come into prolonged contact with traders, frontiers and which was caused by caste system, government policies, and other external contacts. Although the author was mainly concerned with synchronize appraisal of the situation, the changes in the internal organisation had been reviewed diachronically since mid-19th century. Bailey also examined the political implications of these developments in the village and pointed out the modifications in traditional political structure resulting from contact between a relatively simplest peasant economy and modern world.

Taken on the whole, the study of an Oriya village presented an excellent cross-section of the interrelationship of economic, social and political forces in an Indian village. The study confirmed the result of other anthropologists that in studying the microcosm they were also studying the macrocosm. By describing the changes with a short range history, the book provided a historical perspective to the village study. Taken on the whole, the book was a theoretically sophisticated village study which examined important problems facing Indian villages. The author also examined the economic and political implications of Sanskritisation in the context of the village as well as wider economy of the state. Although the book could not present a total picture of Bisipara, but it made a departure from the other village studies by emphasising the interrelation of various aspects of the village life.

In his next book, "*Tribe, Caste and Nation*" published in 1960, Bailey made study of political activities and political changes in highland Orissa. The book based on field researches in Bisipara between 1952-54 was supplemented by an another spell of field researches in the village Bedari in 1953. Although the material for analysis were drawn from two villages—Bisipara and Bedari, the book presented the study of political organisation of tribal system interacting with non-tribal counterparts of the region. The analysis was presented in a manner which brought out the social organisation of the tribes in relation to the region and for that matter the nation. Bailey pointed out as there were no accepted criteria for distinguishing a tribe from caste, a continuum between the two was more a reality. He suggested two ways by which a tribe might become a caste. But in modern caste which was politically active, both the tribes and the traditional castes were being merged.

Bailey had published another book, "*Political and Social Change : Orissa*" in 1959. The book was published in 1963. The book was based on materials collected from a village Mohanpur which was in close contacts with an urban centre in comparison to villages Bisipara and Bedari. The village was located near Cuttack and could be reached in ten minutes by bus and within an hour on foot. The village had a population of 1300 persons divided into 20 castes. The village was greatly exposed to external influences and the local of power resided outside the village. In spite of such a situation, the village had a unity of its own with the traditional village council, schools, common village festivals and common observance of rituals and ceremonies.

Bailey had distinguished three levels of political activities in Orissa—the state, the constituencies, and the villages. He attempted to examine their relationships. He tried to find out conceptual framework into which both the specialised roles of representative constituencies and the undifferentiated roles of traditional society would fit. He suggested that it was 'arena' rather than group which was the key concept. On the whole, the book conveyed an impression that Bailey was concerned with conflict, social change and process in general rather than with structure which formed an equilibrium. He demonstrated rightly a consistent awareness that political actions could be understood by placing them in social matrix. But he could not analyse it properly and adequately.

The book was divided into three parts, but could not appear to be integrated into a satisfactory way. First part of the book dealt with comparison and description of two villages. It appeared like social anthropology. Second part was concerned with political forces and appeared like political sciences. Third part of the book appeared like history with social incidence. The two villages—Mohanpur and Bisipara were not really comparable because their history and surrounding were quite different.

Although Bailey conducted field researches in Orissan villages for a long time, but he could not create an atmosphere of village studies in Orissa. The reason behind this was absence of the Department of Anthropology in Orissa state. The Department of Anthropolgy was started in the state of Orissa in 1960, but no research project on village study was encouraged.

W.H. WISER

W.H. Wiser was an American Missionary. He had come to India to make study of Indian village institutions. He was stationed at a village named Karimpur near Lucknow along with his wife Charlotte V. Wiser. He had conducted field enquiry at Karimpur village and submitted a doctoral dissertation at Cornell University, USA in 1933 on "Social Institutions of a Hindu Village in North India". He had also wrote books which were as follows:

1930 : *Behind the Mud Wall.* In collaboration with his wife Charlotte V. Wiser.
1936 : *Hindu Jajmani System.*

Methodologically, these books were based on intensive fieldwork of Wisers, who lived in the village consecutively for five years for undertaking the surveys as well as for improving the standard of living of the low castes in general and Christians in particular. Since the village Karimpur was in direct influence of Brahmins, it furnished an excellent model for the study of long established Hindu village communities. Both husband and wife Wisers had learnt Hindi and worked through Hindi medium. They were also assisted by two Hindu youth who helped Wisers as interpreters. Wisers were able to establish rapport with villagers through their medical aids which justified their stay in village society.

In the view of the intensive field enquiry, application of participant observation techniques, and continuous team work by Wisers and their two young sons, the insiders' views of the villagers could be gathered. The two books: *Behind the Mud Walls* and *Hindu Jajmani System* written by Wisers could be considered as first set of social anthropological studies in India. The book, "*Behind the Mud Walls*" (1930) was a true life account of the villagers, though it was heavily impressionistic and mingled with experiences of authors' in the village. Leadership and agents of authority were discussed at length, though separately. The intercaste relations had found some treatment, though their interrelationships were not discussed systematically. As Jajmani system formed the theme of a separate book, hence no mention about this system was made in the book, *Behind the Mud Walls.* There were causal references about the festivals. The impact of caste system on entire life of individuals living in the village were brought out. Although there were certain minor shortcomings, but Wiser's book, *Behind the Mud Walls,* presented the first-hand account of life in a north Indian village.

In his another book, "*The Hindu Jajmani System*" (1936), the service relations of many castes with others which each in turn was master and servant were discussed. This system of interrelatedness in service within the Hindu community was conceptualised as Jajmani System. Wiser described at length the Jajmani relationships among 24 different castes including three castes of Muslims and Christians whose traditional occupation corresponding to *Varna* were brought out. He pointed out that Jajmani system was promoting inequality rather that equality. Although he attempted to present hierarchy of castes, but failed to discuss the basis of ranking or procedure of determining the place of a caste in hierarchy. He also pointed out changes which were occurring in Jajmani system due to modern education, manufacturing of goods, urban courts of British administration and political movements.

The study of Jajmani system by Wiser was of special significance. He made intensive fieldwork in the village Karimpur and took up the problem of Jajmani system for his enquiry. His approach to relate all Muslims and Christians deserved special attention. He justified it by remarking that in terms of education and in village parlance these groups were referred to as caste. In this stratification he failed to understand that occupation and the use of the term *Jati* for them was not enough. It would also be considered that Hindu Jajmani system of the Bhangi, Christians and Muslims perhaps got sanction from the local tradition, but Wiser had left these questions unanswered. Throughout his work, he emphasised that Jajmani system was based on ancient Hindu law.

In the analysis of Wiser's Jajmani system, the concept of purity and pollution did not figure at all. In the later analysis Jajmani system was considered by many anthropologists in terms of pollution and purity concept which pervaded the Hindu way of life. This explanation was more plausible than Wiser's who had traced the origin of the system exclusively from scriptures. The absence of purity-pollution concept in Wiser's analysis was a big void which was indicated by many scholars later. But in spite of these and several other gaps, Wiser's work was the first detailed analysis of complex change of goods and services of castes involved in Jajmani system. In this respect, it was a pioneer work. It is important also because it was first systematic village study in anthropological tradition. It was also analytical and not mere ethnographic description of a village.

G.M. CARSTAIRS

Carstairs had come to India in 1951 with financial support from Rockfeller Foundation of America to make study of Indian village. Carstairs had chosen Deoli in Rajasthan state. This village was situated in the foothills of Aravali range near Udaipur. He had undertaken the fieldwork of this village in 1951-52. The study was undertaken in collaboration of Getal P. Steed. The study aimed to test certain theories of personality development to account for the causes of character formation in a non-western society where the process of socialisation was different. At the time of study, the village had a total population of 2417 persons distributed in 594 households and 36 communities including Sikhs, Muslims, Bhils and others. In course of fieldwork, he had used certain psychological experiments like Raven's professive matrices tests and Rorschah test. In addition to indepth interviews, 45 case histories from 13 Rajputs, 11 Brahmins, 12 Banias, and 9 Muslims were collected.

On the basis of field enquiry and application of psychological texts, Carstairs made generalised statement regarding the basic personality structure of high caste Hindus of Deoli. According to him, Rajput being the martial community emphasised authority and wider personal fortitude, pride and self-assertions. In the light of these they were supposed to enjoy the right to take life, keep concubines, drink alcohol and eat meat.

The Banias subscribed to the values of Brahmins but emphasized wealth above everything. The great majority was of Banias in the village. The great majority of Banias of the village tempered their materialism with philanthropic and religious needs.

Carstairs had considered the influence of socialisation on the formation of cultural traits found among the High Caste Hindus. According to him, development of personality stemmed from two sources—one being the individual biological inheritance and other their learning experiences deliberately or involuntarily. He analysed the environment to indicate its influence on the personality formation starting from the experience occurring latest in adult career and retressing the consecutive type of learning backwards to childhood.

In discussing the unconscious process in understanding the high caste Hindu national character, the author assumed the events which had occurred in the early stages of human psychological maturation had an enduring influence on personality formation, the characteristic of national character. He had dealt with basic facts which had influence on Hindu personality formation. High caste Hindu personality structure emerged as paranoidic suspiciousness, egocentricity and reluctance to make other than superficial and transient relationship and ever shifting uncertainty together with a longing for stability and assurances. In contrast, they had the greatest self-assurance in formal etiquette as well as when relationships concerned formal groups. Further, the people displayed an apparent lack of sympathy with regard to each other's sexual appetite which was depicted and suppressed as much as possible. The villages showed goodwill and tolerance. Within these general personality traits, Carstairs found certain differences among the three castes—Brahmin, Rajput and Bania.

In general, the study of Carstairs was unique, inspiring and opened up new areas of research. In the words of Margaret Mead, this study should not only enrich our materials on national character and caste character in India, but enrich our sense of the strongly contrasting phase, human culture offers to human beings. This book led to a better understanding of people's way of life and general respect for them by other cultures as Carstairs hoped. Carstairs had made provocative and penetrating analysis of the personality structure of high caste Hindus of Deoli in his book, "*The Twice-Born : A Study of High Caste Hindus*" (1957). His microcosmic approach to the understanding of national character of three high castes who were recognised as Twice-born was subjected to criticism as they constituted a minority in village population. The twice born possessed only 726 persons out of a total population of 2417 people. The majority of population not covered under this study formed very important part in village social structure and for that matter of Rajasthan or of India as a whole. In this situation, the claim of author to present the national character seemed to be partial and needed to be supplemented with similar several studies in different parts of India.

The study of Carstairs also backed adequate socio-cultural material about the village. Economic relations were obviously important for personality formation, but they were largely ignored. The social interrelationships of different castes and communities in the village were not described even though it was obvious that they confirmed or supported the basic personality structure of high castes. In conclusion, Carstairs handling of a delicate topic was perceptive, stimulating and valuable. His conclusions seemed to be valid to a large extent, but they obviously might undergo modifications by further researches of this kind in other villages of the region.

In addition to this major work, "*The Twice-Born : A Study of High Caste Hindus*" (1957), Carstairs had made study of three villages of Rajasthan and wrote a long paper on, "Patterns of Religious Observance in Three Villages of Rajasthan", published in *Journal of Social Research,* Vol. IV, No. 1-2 (1961), Ranchi. In this paper, Carstairs examined the continuum from the Bhil tribes at one end and peasant culture with many Sanskritic elements of the other in the sphere of religion. In showing the similarity and differences among the three representative villages, Carstairs indicated the gradual process of Sanskritisation and Hinduisation not in temporal but in spatial perspective. He brought out the presence of both great and little traditions in village religion, but he did not consider the process of interaction as Marriott had done in terms of universalisation and parochialisation.

HENRY ORENSTEIN

Henry Orenstein came to India in 1954 to make study of Indian village. He had chosen a village name Gaon in Poona district of

Maharashtra state. The village was located at a distance of one mile from the market town of Mot. The village was inhabited by 14 castes in which the dominant caste was Dhangar. They were traditionally shephards but now they had attained the status of Rajputs. In the light of these field data Orenstein had written two research papers, which were as follows:

1959 : 'Leadership and Castes in Bombay Village', in *Leadership and Political Institutions in India* edited by R.L. Park and I. Tinker.

1963 : 'Village, Caste and Welfare State', in *Human Organisation,* Vol. 22.

In his first paper, he attempted to show leadership practiced by the castes of the village Gaon. Each caste had its own caste leaders, but the role of dominant caste was of great importance in solving the village level disputes, intervillage level disputes, caste level conflicts, intercaste level conflicts and also in maintaining the unity in the village.

In his second paper, Orenstein had discussed the functioning of castes, village social structure and the role of Welfare State for the welfare and development of villagers.

Orenstein had also published a full length book, "*Gaon : Conflict and Cohesion*" (1963). In general he had tried to establish that the nature of caste system was undergoing change in India. The individual castes and their customs were changing due to the process of Sanskritisation, Westernisation and Secularisation.

LOUIS DUMONT

Louis Dumont was a French scholar. He was a keen student of caste system. He had several publications to his credit on this social institution of caste in India. In his writing, he was greatly influenced by Bougle and Hocart, both French scholars and sociologists. His most famous publication was, "*Homohierarchicus*", The Caste

System and Its Implications (1970). This book presented his views and findings of the caste system.

The French sociological tradition led Dumont to trace the role of ideology in moulding human behaviour. He wanted to bring sociology and Indology together. Following Bough, he chose the Hindu notion of fundamental opposition between pure and impure as his starting point for an understanding of caste system. In the light of purity-impurity concept, Dumont maintained the concept of opposition and went on to conclude that the opposition underlied hierarchy. The opposition revealed the superiority of pure over impure. It indicated that pure and impure be kept separate because it underlied separation. It also underlied the division of labour and the pure and impure occupations to be kept separate. The whole caste system was founded on the necessary and hierarchical co-existence of two opposites—pure and impure.

Dumont defined the hierarchy as the superiority of pure over impure. This constituted the keystone in Dumont's model of caste system.

In addition to understanding the definition of caste system, Dumont's concern in present work was to study the traditional social organisation of India from the point of view of theoretical comparisons. He attempted to construct a model of traditional caste system of an ideal type and did not involve himself in reconstructing the history of the caste system.

In spite of this concern with ideology that was with a system of ideas and values, he did not ignore ethnographical material. Dumont used ethnographic data elucidate, elaborate or qualify the various aspects of his thesis.

Dumont's book, "*Homohierarchicus*" (1970) was divided into 11 chapters in addition to several informative appendices. The book dealt with materials to establish hierarchy as indispensible element of social life anywhere in India.

Chapters 1 and 2 of the book dealt with concepts employed in the work and outlined the ideology of caste. The hierarchy and theory of *Varna*, which constituted the most crucial discussion, covered in chapters 3 and 4 of the book showed that the traditional division of labour was based on religious value rather than on economic value. Chapter 5 described the regulation of marriage in terms of concept of hierarchy, while chapter 6 explored rules concerning contact, untouchability, food and vegetarianism. In chapters 7 and 8, Dumont dealt with power within territory, justice and authority. Chapter 9 highlighted renunciation and sect. In the last two chapters 11 and 12, Dumont moved towards the problem of comparison. The comparisons of castes among non-Hindus and then outside India. In the light of these analyses, Dumont concluded that the hierarchy was a universal necessity recognised in a society. It might assert into a pathological form.

Dumont and Pock in their research paper 'Contribution to Indian Society', Vol. 3 (1959), criticised the concept of great tradition and little tradition. According to them, great tradition and little tradition were mental construct and a mental construct was an ideal type. The ideal type construct always differed from real type. Therefore, they doubted whether there was a little tradition in the same sense as there was a great tradition and whether the same relations were held between them and between the corresponding great community and little community. For Dumont and Pock, it was possible to demonstrate the homogeneity at two levels and to extend to both or a part of relations discovered at popular level.

PAUL G. HERBERT

Herbert was a foreign scholar who had come to India to make a study of Indian village. He had chosen a large village Knoduru located in Nallamallac hills south-west of the city of the Hyderabad. Based on field researches at Konduru for three years, he wrote a full length book under the title, "Konduru : Structure and Integration in a South Indian Village" (1971). In this book, Herbert had described the social and political organisation of an Andhra village. He had presented a wholistic picture of the quality of life in Konduru and made this monograph an excellent introduction to the social and political organisation of an Indian village and the region. He referred to leather workers and Panchalas as left hand castes.

DeTerra and T.D. Patterson

DeTerra was chairman of Yale-Cambridge Expedition for Exploration of Relationships between pluvial and interpluvial periods of South India with glacial and interglacial period of North India. T.D. Patterson and Tilhard de Chardin were member of Cambridge-Yale expedition team. In 1932, DeTerra had obtained stone tools from Himalayan region. He had also examined the collection of Todd and Wadia. After examining every fact, he had expressed opinion that the pluvials and interpluvial periods of South India and glacial and interglacial period were correlated. DeTerra, Patterson and Chardin had made a survey of Kashmir Valley and Punchha to Salt Lake located between Kashmir and Middle of Jhelam. This survey was of great value from the point of view of Indian Prehistoric archaeological anthropology. He had established the glacial and interglacial periods in Punjab and Kashmir and had established a correlation with pluvial and interpluvial periods of South India and Narmada Valley was in between the two.

JOAN MENCHER

Joan Mencher was an anthropologist. She had come to India to make study of an Indian village. She had chosen a village Angadi in Ernad Taluka of Calicut district of Kerala. It was a South Malabar village. The fieldwork was done in the period between 1956-1958. She had gathered data on social values and process of socialisation in Kerala village. The village had a population of 10,960 at the time of study. She had written a paper entitled, 'Growing up in South Malabar' published in *Human Organisation,* Vol. 22. In this paper, she suggested a correlation between form of family organisation, ideals of proper behaviour for men, women and children and some of the methods in calculating social values. The discussion covered various materilineal castes including Nayars, Pumkilas living in the village.

DAGFINN SILVERT SEN

Silvert Sen was a scholar of Oslo University. He had come to India to make study of an Indian village. He had chosen a village named Thyaga Samuthiram. The village was situated at a distance of six miles from Kumbakonam, the biggest town in Tanjor district of Madras state. The village was located on the bank of river Kaveri and had a population of 786 persons distributed in ten castes. The Brahmins had numerical dominance in the village. Silvert Sen had conducted fieldwork from January 1957 to January 1958. He had attempted to answer E.K. Leach's querry about disintegration of caste. If a caste turned itself into a political faction dit it cease to be a caste. In other words, tension and conflict which were related to existing economic and political order were the main focus of attention. The interrelations of various sets of social and economic relationships and not the village as such was the unit and object of study.

In course of his analysis of caste system, the ritual order, intercaste services, economy, system of cultivation, organisation of labour, temple assemblage, village council and modern political movement, he brought out the fact of weakening of power and domination of the traditionally privileged castes as well as the economic and political advancement of subordinate castes. He emphasized upon the importance of economy in the process of decay of traditional types and advancement of lower castes.

Describing the changes in temple organisation, he highlighted the temple assemblage of each caste with elected headman or leaders as important agents of political control whose loyalties were being claimed by new associations to secure a more enduring basis for their influence. In this way, he emphasised that economic system was more primary determinant of the fall of castes and the rise of new political organisation. In the dynamics of caste system, the conflict between high caste and low castes were purposively highlighted.

ANDRE BETEILLE

Andre Beteille had made study of a Tanjor village named Shripuram. It was a multicaste village located in the district of Tanjor of Tamil Nadu state. The village situated on the bank of river Kaveri had 92 Brahmins, 118 non-Brahmins and 89 Adi Dravid householders living in separate residential areas. Based on his field researches, he had paper and books which were as follows:

1964 : "A Note on Pongal Festival in a Tanjor Village". In *Man,* No. 89.

1966 : *Caste, Class and Power* : *Changing Pattern of Stratification in a Tanjor Village.* Bombay : Oxford University Press.

1969 : *Caste Old and New* : *Essay in Social Structure and Social Organisation.* New York : Asia Publishing House.

"Agrarian Relation in Tanjor District, South India". *Sociological Bulletin,* Vol. 1, No. 21, pp. 122-151.

Beteille had made a meticulous analysis of caste dynamics specially in relation to power structure in Tanjor villages of Tamil Nadu in both his excellent books mentioned above. Beteille attempted to understand the socio-political and economic movements in south India in terms of three-fold divisions of Hindu society into Brahmins, non-Brahmins and Harijans. He went on to establish that this division of society provided the basic framework for the analysis of problems of both distribution and process. In the light of evidence from Tamil Nadu, he termed this as 'Communal Politics', not as 'Caste Politics' as envisaged by M.N. Srinivas.

In the analysis of the politics in Tamil Nadu at the caste and faction level, he found the concept of dominant caste inadequate and out of date. He observed two major phenomena in Tamil Nadu which he had considered to be equally true for other parts of India.

First, the caste politics changed from one dominant caste to another and second, locus of power shifted from the caste system itself to differentiated structure of power. In the light of rich materials and critical analysis, Beteille made some general observations regarding the nature of castes in Indian politics. It needed to be quoted here at length.

Today the political system was becoming increasingly differentiated. This did not mean that it was unrelated to caste and class or it would be so in near future. But as the political system became more differentiated, new loci of power developed and these tended to acquire a weight of their own. In the past, dominant caste and faction were the only significant loci of power and the faction itself was largely structured by caste. With the development of Panchayati Raj, political parties and machines of various kind, this was no longer the case. Today it was possible for a man to acquire certain measure of power by virtue of this position in the party hierarchy, irrespective of his caste or class. No doubt, the membership of dominant caste helped a great deal, but other factors were also becoming important for a fuller understanding of the changing relations between caste, class and parties in addition to other major source of power.

Beteille's analysis of transfer of power and political conflict had found substantive illustrations from the study of village Shripuram. In Shripuram, the transfer of power from Brahmin to non-Brahmin was symbolised by the shift of Panchayat office from Agraharam to non-Brahmin quarters. This was associated with the replacement by a non-Brahmin of a Brahmin Panchayat president in the mid-forties. He made a historical appraisal of the situation and pointed out that one of the most important political phenomena of the past three decades in Shripuram as well as in Tamil Nadu as a whole. It was a shift of power from Brahmin to non-Brahmin. This was not necessarily or always meant to a shift from landowner to tenant cultivators.

In the light of this analysis, he observed that the political conflicts seemed to have followed more closely the cleavages of castes than those of class. The divisions of society into Brahmins, non-Brahmins and Adi-Dravida had been of more immediate relevance in mobilising political support than its division into landowners, tenants and agricultural labourers.

Thus, Beteille went on to provide an analytical scheme for the study of social change in South India in general and India in particular in the context of three orders of caste, class and power. Caste being the fundamental institution of traditional India continued to influence the process of modernisation and more so in the field of power and politics.

The two studies were supplementary to each other. They opened up new perspectives for the analysis of dynamics of caste analysis. Beteille had made an objective appraisal of situation in Tanjor villages and had indicated several refreshing and penetrating concepts for understanding the complexities of changing scenes in South India. The conclusions of these two studies though of great theoretical and methodological significance, remained confined to the understanding of situations only in areas where the sharp conflict between Brahmins, non-Brahmins and the Harijans existed. In case of North India, the situation was somewhat different and applicabilities of these conclusions were of limited nature.

In his paper, 'Agrarian Unrest in Tanjor, South India' Beteille established that the caste was a fundamental principle of social organisation in India, but it did not provide an exhaustive framework for understanding all aspects of social inequidity in the country. For example agrarian class structure was not merely an aspect of caste system. While examining the complexity of agrarian structure in Tanjor, Beteille came to the conclusion that the relationship between landowners and landless was the core of the problem which erupted into violent conflict.

BRENDA F. BECK

Brenda F. Beck had carried out 18 months fieldwork in the Konku region of Coimbatore district in Tamil Nadu. Her work presented indubitably new information about the kinship, political organisation, religious organisation of right and left sub-castes inhabiting that area. Her work provided a detailed case study of Konku, one of five traditional regions in Tamil Nadu, in terms of five levels of caste, sub-caste, clan, lineage and family. Her study focused on five territorially based units which nestled within each other in Konku region, sub-region, village revenue region, hamlet and household. At the category of sub-caste which were popularly levelled as right hand and left hand. The right division had an extensive political and territorial organisation heading by four titled families and had traditional right over most of farm land. *Jatis* of left division lived by their traditional skills and moved about the region where their services were needed. The right division had conquered the region or territory, whereas left division had come into Konku as persecuted refugees. In kinship, too, divisions were at variance The right group had an extensive clan and lineage organisation with close ties to the regional structure, whereas left hand group had no descent based organisation except for the vague category termed as *Gotra.* Further, because of their secure footing, the learned members of right division evinced much less interest in education and new urban jobs, whereas these features offered bright future to upper ranking sub-caste of the left division. Finally, Beck pointed out the contrast in marriage preference, kinship terminology, residence pattern and dowry between the two divisions. She observed the disjunction between those groups which held direct rights or claimed them indrectly through services provided for landowners and which were, thus immobile, and those groups such as weavers and other artisans and merchants whose profession accorded monetary wealth, mobility and certain independence.

CELESTIN BOUGLE

Bougle was a French sociologist. He had attempted to understand the origin, development and effect of caste system in India. Bougle had written a book, "*Essais Sur Le Regime des lasts* (Bibliotheque de Philosophe Contemporains)" in French in 1935. This book was translated into English by D.I. Pocock in 1971. This book provided materials on caste system and social stratification in India. The writing of Bougle, Essais on the caste system, was made available to English world. This book was a source of inspiration for A.M. Hocart and Luis Dumont to work on caste system in India.

In the introduction of the book, Bougle identified three features essential to the notion of caste. They were hereditary specialisation, hierarchy and mutual repulsion. He was of the opinion that the spirit of castes united these three tendencies and all three must be borne in mind if one wished to give a complete definition of caste system. To Bougle, concept of repulsion encompassed all those features by which each caste attempted to maintain its distinctiveness and separation from the other castes including commensal and connubial restrictions.

The book of Bougle was divided into three parts. The first part dealt with the root of caste system. The second part provided the vitality of the system. The effects of caste system were discussed in third part of the book. In course of his analysis about caste, Bougle did not make any attempt to show the origin of caste from a single determinant, descendants of fossilised occupational group or from the ancient *Varna* system. He emphasied upon systematic characteristics of caste and factors responsible for interrelationships among them. For him, it was unthinkable to define the caste in isolation from the other castes. Thus, Bougle's analysis of caste system was an inversion of the myth of caste system perpetrated by European predecessors.

THOMAS O. BEIDELMEN

Beidelmen had written a full length book on the comparative analysis of the Jajmani system under the title, "*A Comparative Analysis of the Jajmani System*" (1957). He had worked on this topic for his master degree. The thesis was submitted to Illinois University for Master degree under the guidance of Oscar

Lewis. In the background of a short account of previous works, Beidlemen offered an analytical and comparative appraisal of the Jajmani system in the light of recent researches. He also attempted to determine the locus of power within this system and threw light on the controversial questions as to whether or not it was an exploitative system. In analysing the Jajman-Kamin relationship, he took into account such factors as caste, rituals, kinship, occupation, land tenure, caste population, size and attempted to determine the nature of power enjoyed by each groups. Actual cases of disputes were presented and solutions were analysed.

Bibliography

Aiyappan, A. 1965 : *Social Revolution in Kerala Village.* Bombay : Asia Publishing House.

Atal, Yogesh. 1961 : "The Cult of Bheru in Mewar Village". Ranchi : *Journal of Social Research,* Vol. 4.

Atal, Yogesh. 1965 : *Adivasi Bharat.* New Delhi : Rajkamal Prakashan.

Atal, Yogesh. 1968 : *The Changing Frontiers of Caste.* Delhi : National Publication.

Bailey, F.G. : 1958 : *Caste and Economic Frontiers.* Bombay : Oxford University Press.

Bailey, F.G. 1960 : *Tribe Caste Nation.* Bombay : Oxford University Press.

Bailey, F.G. 1963 : *Political and Social Change : Orissa.* Bombay : Oxford University Press.

Balaratnam, L.K. 1958 : *Society in India.* Madras : Social Science Association.

Balaratnam, L.K. 1963 : *Anthropology on March.* Madras : The Book Centre, 1/155, Mount Road.

Beals, A.R. 1955 : "Change in Leadership of a Mysore Village". In M.N. Srinivas edited book *India's Village.*

Beals, A.R. 1955 : "Interplay among Factors of Social Change". In *Village India* edited by Marriott.

Beals, A.R. 1959 : "Leadership in a Mysore Village". in Park and Tinker edited book *Leadership and Political Institutions in India.*

Beals, A.R. 1962 : *Gopalpur : A South Indian Village*. Bombay : Asia Publishing House.

Beck, Brenda F. 1972 : *Peasant Society in Konku : A Study of Right and Left Sub-caste in South India*. Vancouver : University of British Columbia Press.

Berreman, G.D. 1963 : *The Hindus of Himalayas*. Berkeley : California University Press.

Berreman, G.D. 1963 : "Brahmanism and Shamanism in Rahar Village". In the book, *Religion of South Asia* edited by E.B. Harper.

Berreman, G.D 1969 : "Urgent Anthropology in India". In *Urgent Researches in Social Anthropology*. Indian Institute of Advance Study, Shimla.

Beteille, Andre. 1966 : *Caste Class and Power : Changing Pattern of Stratification in a Tanjor Village*. Bombay : Oxford University Press.

Beteille, Andre : 1969 : *Caste Old and New : Essay in Social Structure and Social Organisation in India*. Bombay : Oxford University Press.

Beidlemen, Thomas O. 1957 : *A Comparative Study of the Jajmani System*. New York, J.K. Augustin, Locust Valley, Association for Asian Studies.

Bose, N.K. 1929 : *Cultural Anthropology*. Bombay : Asia Publishing House.

Bose, N.K. 1932 : *Cannons of Orissan Architecture*. Kolkata : Ramchandra Chatterjee.

Bose, N.K. 1949 : *Structure of Hindu Society*. Kolkata : Vishwabharti Granthalaya.

Bose, N.K. 1967 : *Culture and Society in India*. Bombay : Asia Publishing House.

Bose, N.K. 1968 : *Kolkata : A Social Survey*. Bombay : Lalvani Press.

Bose, N.K. 1968 : *Fifty Years of Science in India*. Kolkata : Indian Science Congress Association.

Bougle, C. 1977 : *Essays on Caste System in India*. London : Cambridge University Press.

Carstairs, G.M. : *The Twice-Born : A Study of Community of High Castes*. London : Hogenth Press.

Chattopadhyay, K.P. 1952 : *Socio-economic Survey of Jute Labourers*. Kolkata : Calcutta University Press.

Chattopadhyay, K.P. 1957 : *Study of Change in Traditional Culture*. Kolkata : Calcutta University Press.

Chattopadhyay, K.P. 1965 : *Ancient Indian Culture : Concepts and Migration*. Kolkata : WBC Press.

Chattopadhyay, K.P. 1965 : *Santhal Way of Life*. Kolkata : Calcutta University Press.

Chauhan, B.R. 1970 : *The Towns in Tribal Setting*. Delhi : National Publishing House.

Cohn, B.S. 1955 : "Changing Status of Depressed Castes". In *Village India* edited by McKim Marriott.

Cohn, B.S. 1958 : "Changing Tradition of Low Castes". In *Traditional India : Structure and Change* edited by Milton Singer.

Dhillon, H.S. 1955 : *Leadership and Groups in South Indian Village*. Delhi : Planning Commission.

Dube, S.C. 1954 : *The Kamar*. Lucknow : Universal Publisher.

Dube, S.C. 1955 : *Indian Village*. London : Cornell University Press.

Dube, S.C. 1958 : *India's Changing Villages : Human Factors in Community Development*. London : Cornell University Press.

Dube, SC. 1962 : *Bhartiya Samaj Parichaymala*. Delhi : Rajkamal Prakashan.

Dube, S.C. (ed.) 1971 : *Essays on Modernisation*. Delhi : Vikas Publishing House.

Dube, S.C. 1973 : *Contemporary India and Its Modernisation*. Delhi : Vikas Publishing House.

Dube, S.C. (ed.) 1973 : *Tribal Heritage of India*. Delhi : Vikas Publishing House.

Dube, S.C. 1958 : *Power and Conflict in Village India*. London : Cornell University Press.

Dube, S.C. 1968 : *Institution Building for Community Development*. Hawaii : East-West Centre Press.

Dube, S.C. 1990 : *Tradition and Development.* Delhi :Vikas Publishing House.

Dube, S.C. 1992 : *Understanding Change : Perspective from Anthropology and Sociology.* Delhi : Vikas Publishing House.

Dumont, Luis. 1970 : *Homohierarchicus : An Essay in Caste System.* Chicago : Chicago University Press.

Elwin, Verrier. 1939 : *The Baiga.* London : J. Murray.

Elwin, Verrier. 1942 : *The Agaria.* London : Oxford University Press.

Elwin, Verrier. 1943 : *Maria Murder and Suicide.* Bombay : Oxford University Press.

Elwin, Verrier. 1947 : *The Maria and Their Gothul.* Geoffery Cambridge : Oxford University Press.

Elwin, Verrier. 1950 : *Bodo Highlanders.* Bombay : Oxford University Press.

Elwin, Verrier. 1951 : *Tribal Arts of Middle India.* Bombay : Asia Publishing House.

Elwin, Verrier. 1952 : *The Loss of Nerve : A Comparative Study Contact of People in Aboriginal Area of Bastar. Central Province of India.* Bombay : Asia Publishing House.

Elwin, Verrier. 1954 : *The Tribal Myths of Orissa.* Bombay : Oxford University Press.

Elwin, Verrier. 1955 : *The Religion of an Indian Tribe.* Geoffery Cambridge, Oxford University Press.

Elwin, Verrier. 1958 : *Myths of North-East Frontiers of India,* NEFA, Shillong.

Elwin, Verrier. 1959 : *India's North-East Frontier's Agency in Nineteenth Century.* Kolkata : Oxford University Press.

Elwin, Verrier. 1960 : *Philosophy of NEFA.* Shillong : Advertisers to Government of Assam.

Elwin, Verrier. 1960 : *Nagaland.* Shillong : Research Department.

Elwin, Verrier. 1962 : *Arts of NEFA.* Shillong : Advertisers to Government of Assam.

Epstein, T. Scarlett. 1959 : "A Sociological Analysis of Witch Belief in a Mysore Village". Lucknow : *Eastern Anthropologist,* Vol. 12, No. 4.

Epstein, T. Scarlett.1960 : "Economic Development and Peasant Marriage in South India". *Man In India,* Vol. 40, No. 3.

Epstein, T. Scarlett. 1962 : *Economic Development and Social Change in South India.* Manchester : Manchester University Press.

Ghurye, G.S. 1932 : *Castes and Races in India.* London : Kegan Paul.

Ghurye, G.S. 1938 : *Sex Habit of Middle Caste People.* Poona : Gokhale Institute of Politics and Economics.

Ghurye, G.S. 1943 : *Aboriginal So Called and Their Future.* Poona : Gokhale Institute of Politics and Economics.

Ghurye, G.S. 1945 : *Culture and Society.* Bombay : Popular Book Depot.

Ghurye, G.S. 1957 : *The Mahadeo Kolis.* Bombay : Popular Book Depot.

Ghurye, G.S. 1959 : *The Scheduled Tribes.* Bombay : Popular Prakashan.

Ghurye, G.S. 1960 : *After a Century and Quarter.* Bombay : Popular Prakashan.

Ghurye, G.S. 1961 : *Caste Class and Occupation.* Bombay : Popular Prakashan.

Ghurye, G.S. 1962 : *Family and Kinship in Indo-European Family.* Bombay : Popular Prakashan.

Ghurye, G.S. 1964 : *Indian Sadhu.* Bombay : Popular Prakashan.

Ghurye, G.S. 1968 : *Religious Consciousness.* Bombay : Popular Prakashan.

Ghurye, G.S. 1968 : *Social Tension in India.* Bombay : Popular Prakashan.

Ghurye, G.S. 1973 : *I and Other Explorations.* Bombay : Popular Prakashan.

Ghurye, G.S. 1974 : *Wither India.* Bombay : Popular Prakashan.

Ghurye, G.S. 1978 : *India Creates Democracy.* Bombay : Popular Prakashan.

Ghurye, G.S. 1979 : *Vedic India.* Bombay : Popular Prakashan.

Ghurye, G.S. 1980 : *The Burning Kaldram of North-East.* Bombay : Popular Prakashan.

Gough, E. Kathleen. 1955 : "Social Structure of a Tanjor Village". In M.N. Srinivas (ed.) book, *India's Village.*

Gough, E. Kathleen. 1958 : "Cult of Dead Among Nayars". In Milton Singer (ed.) book, *Traditional India : Structure and Change.*

Gough, E. Kathleen. 1960 : "Criteria of Caste Ranking". In *Man In India,* Vol. 39, No. 2.

Gough, E. Kathleen. 1960 : *Economic Development and Peasant Marriage in South India. Man In India.* Vol. 40, No. 3.

Gough, E. Kathleen. 1962 : "Caste in Tanjor Village". In E.R Leach (ed.) book, Aspects of *Castes in South India, Ceylon and North-Western Pakistan,* Cambridge.

Gough, E. Kathleen. 1962 : *Economic Development and Social Change in South India.* Manchester : Manchester University Press.

Gould, Herald A. 1958 : "The Village Jajmani System". *South-Western Journal of Anthropology,* Vol. 14, No. 4.

Gould, Herald A. 1959 : "The Peasant Village : Centripetal and Centrifugal". *Eastern Anthropologist,* Vol. 13, No. 1.

Gould, Herald A. 1961 : "A Further Note on Village Exogamy in North India". *South-Western Journal of Anthropology,* Vol. 17.

Gould, Herald A. 1964 : "Jajmani System of North India : Its Structures, Magnitude and Meaning". In *Ethnology,* Vol. 3, No. 1.

Guha, B.S. 1935 : "The Racial Affinity of People of India". Vol. 1, Part-III, 13, Shimla.

Guha, B.S. 1944 : *Racial Elements in Indian Population.* Bombay : Oxford University Press.

Guha, B.S. (ed.) 1951 : *The Tribes of India.* Two Volumes, New Delhi : Adimjati Sevak Sangh.

Guha, B.S. 1953 : "The Abor Mosup as a Training Centre for Youth". *Vanya Jati,* Vol. 1.

Gumperz, J.J. 1958 : "Dialect Difference and Social Stratification in North Indian Village". *American Anthropologist,* Vol. 60, No. 4.

Harper, E.B. 1959 : "Two Systems of Economic Exchange in Village India". In *American Anthropologist,* Vol. 61, No. 5, Chicago.

Harper, E.B. 1959 : "Political Organisation and Leadership in Karnataka Village". In *Leadership and Political Institutions in India* (ed.) by Park and Tinker.

Haimendorf, C. Von Furer. 1941 : "Seasonal Nomadism and Economics of Chenchus of Hyderabad". *Journal of Asiatic Society of Bengal,* Vol. 1.

Haimendorf, C. Von Furer. 1942 : "Fortunes of Primitive Tribes". *Indian Journal of Social Work,* Vol. 1.

Haimendorf, C. Von Furer. 1943 : *Chenchus : The Jungle Folk of Deccan.* London : MacMillan and Company.

Haimendorf, C. Von Furer. 1945 : "The Tribal Population of Hyderabad". *Journal of Social Work,* Vol. 3.

Haimendorf, C. Von Furer. 1945 : *The Redis of Bison Hills : A Study in Acculturation.* London : MacMillan and Company.

Haimendorf, C. Von Furer. 1946 : "The Agriculture and Land Tenure Among Apatanis". *Man In India,* Vol. 26.

Haimendorf, C. Von Furer. 1946 : "A Note on Tribal Justice Among Apatanis". *Man In India,* Vol. 26.

Haimendorf, C. Von Furer. 1947 : *Explorations in Himalayas.* Shillong : Assam Government Press.

Haimendorf, C. Von Furer. 1948 : *The Raj Gond of Adilabad : A Peasant Culture of Deccan.* (with Elizabeth Von C. Fürer Haimendorf). London : MacMillan and Company.

Haimendorf, C. Von Furer. 1950-51 : "The Pradhans : The Bards of Raj Gond". *Eastern Anthropologist,* Vol. 4.

Haimendorf, C. Von Furer. 1955 : *Himalayan Barbery.* London : John Murray, Albemark St. W.

Haimendorf, C. Von Furer. 1962 : *The Apatanis and Their Neighbours : A Primitive Civilisation of Eastern Himalayas.* New York : Routledge and Company.

Haimendorf, C. Von Furer. 1964 : *The Sherpas of Nepal.* London : John Murray.

Haimendorf, C. Von Furer. 1967 : *Morals and Merits.* London : John Murray.

Haimendorf, C. Von Furer. 1969 : *The Koniac Naga.* London : John Murray.

Haimendorf, C. Von Furer. 1979 : *The Gonds of Andhra Pradesh.* London : John Murray.

Hitchcock, T.J. 1958 : "The Idea of Martial Rajput". In Milton Singer edited book, *Traditional India : Structure and Change.*

Hitchcock, T.J. 1959 : "Leadership in North Indian Village." In Park and Tinker edited book *Leadership and Political Institutions in India.*

Herbert, Paul G. 1971 : *Konduru : Structure and Integration in a South Indian Village.* Minneapolis : University of Minnesota Press.

Hutton, J.H. 1921 : *The Angami Naga.* London : MacMillan and Company.

Hutton, J.H. 1921 : The Sema Naga. London : MacMillan and Company.

Hutton, J.H. 1923 : *Connections of Different Nagas and Other Tribes in Assam.* Shillong : Census of India, 1921, Vol. 3.

Hutton, J.H. 1931 : *Ethnographic Notes by Various Hands.* Census of India, 1931, Shillong : Government Press.

Ishwaran, K. 1964 : "Customary Law in Village India". *International Journal of Comparative Study,* Vol. 5, No. 2.

Ishwaran, K. 1966 : *Tradition and Economy in Village India.* London : Routledge and Kegan Paul.

Ishwaran, K. 1968 : *Shivapura : A South Indian Village.* London : Routledge and Kegan Paul.

Ishwaran, K. 1968 : *Caste in South Indian Village and Other Essays.* Bombay : Asia Publishing House.

Iyer, L.A. Krishna. 1924 : "Marriage Customs Among the Muthuvans of Travancore". *Man In India,* Vol. 4.

Iyer, L.A. Krishna. 1934 : "The Religion of Primitive Tribes of Travancore". *Quarterly Journal of Mystic Society,* Vol. 24, No. 3, Bangalore.

Iyer, L.A. Krishna. 1937 : *The Travancore Tribes and Castes.* Vol. I, Trivandrum Government Press.

Iyer, L.A. Krishna. 1939 : *The Travancore Tribes and Castes.* Vol. II, Trivandrum Government Press.

Iyer, L.A. Krishna. 1941 : *The Travancore Tribes and Castes.* Vol. III, Trivandrum Government Press.

Iyer, L.A. Krishna. 1944 : "Matriarchy in Kerala". *Man In India,* Vol. 24, No. 1.

Iyer, L.A. Krishna. 1948 : *The Coorg Tribes and Castes.* (with L.K. Balaratnam). Trivandrum Government Press.

Iyer, L.A. Krishna. 1961 : *Kerala and Her People.* Palaghat : Educational Supplied Depot.

Iyer, L.A. Krishna. 1961 : "Taboo Among Primitive Tribes of Travancore". *Quarterly Journal of Asiatic Society of Bengal,* Silver Jubliee No.Vol. 28.

Iyer, L.K. Ananta. 1908 : *The Cochin Tribes and Castes.* Vol. 1, Government of Cochin, London : Higgin Botham.

Iyer, L.K. Ananta. 1912 : *The Cochin Tribes and Castes,* Vol. 2, London : Higgin Botham and Co.

Iyer, L.K. Ananta. 1930 : *The Mysore Tribes and Castes.* Vol. 3, Mysore, Mysore University.

Iyer, L.K. Ananta. 1931 : *The Mysore Tribes and Castes.* Vol. 4, Mysore, Mysore University.

Iyer, L.K. Ananta. 1935 : *The Mysore Tribes and Castes.* Vol. 1, Mysore : Mysore University.

Karve, Iravati. 1968 : *Kinship Organisation in India.* Kolkata : Asia Publishing House.

Karve, Iravati. 1968 : *Hindu Society : An Interpretation.* Poona : Deshmukh Prakashan.

Khare, R.S. 1962 : "Ritual Purity and Pollution in Relation to Democratic Sanitation". *Eastern Anthropologist,* Vol. 15, No. 2.

Khare, R.S. 1963 : "Folk Medicine in North Indian Village". In *Human Organisation,* Vol. 22.

Kolenda, P.M. 1959 : "Towards a Model of Hindu Jajmani System". *Human Organisation,* Vol. 22, No. 1.

Lakshmana Rao, R.V. 1972 : *Communication and Development : A Study of Two Indian Villages.* Minneapolis : University of Minnesota Press.

Lewis, Oscar. 1954 : *Group Dynamics in a North Indian Village.* New Delhi : Planning Commission.

Lewis, Oscar. 1958 : *Life in a North Indian Village.* Illinois : Illinois University Press.

Luschinsky, M.S. 1963 : "Problems of Culture Change in Indian Village". In *Human Organisation,* Vol. 2.

Majumdar, D.N. 1937 : *A Tribe in Transition : A Study in Culture Pattern.* London : Longmans Green and Company.

Majumdar, D.N. 1944 : *The Fortune of Primitive Tribe.* Lucknow : Universal Publisher.

Majumdar, D.N. 1944 : *Races and Culture of India.* Allahabad : Kitab Mahal.

Majumdar, D.N. 1950 : *The Affairs of a Tribe : A Study in Tribal Dynamics.* Lucknow : Universal Publisher.

Majumdar, D.N. 1958 : *Caste and Communication in Indian Village.* Bombay : Asia Publishing House.

Majumdar, D.N. 196C : *Chor Ka Ek Gaon.* Bombay : Asia Publishing House.

Majumdar, D.N. 1962 : *Himalayan Polyandry.* Bombay : Asia Publishing House.

Majumdar, D.N. and T.N. Madan, 1956 : *An Introduction to Social Anthropology.* Bombay : Asia Publishing House.

Mancher, Joan. 1958 : "Growing UP in South Malabar". *Human Organisation,* Vol. 22. pp. 54-64.

Mandelbaum, David G. 1938 : "Polyandry in Kota Society". *American Anthropologist.* New Series, Ralph Linton, Vol. 4.

Madelbaum, David G. 1955 : "Technology Credit and Culture Change in Nilgiri Village". In M.N. Srinivas edited book, *India's Village.*

Mandelbaum, David G. 1955 : "The World and World View of Kota". In McKim Marriott edited book *Village India.*

Mandelbaum, David G. 1972 : *Society in India : Continuity and Change.* Bombay : Popular Prakashan.

Marriott, McKim. 1949 : "Interactional and Attributional Theory of Caste Ranking". *Man In India,* Vol. 39, No. 20.

Marriott, McKim. 1955 : "Village India". Chicago : *American Anthropologist.*

Marriott, McKim. 1960 : *Caste Ranking and Community Structure in Five Regions of India and Pakistan*. Poona : Deccan College.

Mathur, K.S. : *Caste and Ritual in Malwa Village*. Bombay : Asia Publishing House.

Mayer, A.C. 1952 : *Land and Society in Malabar*. Bombay : Asia Publishing House.

Mayer, A.C. 1960 : *Caste and Kinship in Central India*. London : Routledge and Kegan Paul.

McCormack, W. 1958 : "Sister's Daughter's Marriage in Mysore Village". *Man In India,* Vol. 38, No. 1.

McCormack, W. 1959 : "Factionalism in a Mysore Village". In *Leadership and Political Institutions in India* edited by Park and Tinker.

Mukherjee, R.K. 1967 : *Social Profile of a Metropolitan City,* Lucknow. Delhi : Asia Publishing House.

Opler, Morris E. 1956 : "Extension of an Indian Village". *Journal of Asian Study,* Vol. 16.

Orenstein, Henry. 1959 : "Leadership and Caste in a Bombay Village". In Park and Tinker edited book, *Leadership and Political Institutions in India.*

Orenstein, Henry. 1963 : "Village Caste and Welfare State". *Human Organisation,* Vol. 22.

Orenstein, Henry. 1965: *Gaon* : *Conflict and Cohesion.* Princeton : University Press.

Prasad, N. 1957 : *The Myths of Caste System.* Patna : Samjana Prakashan.

Prasad, N. 1964 : *Land and People of Tribal Bihar.* Ranchi : Tribal Welfare Research Institute.

Risley, H.H. 1895 : *Tribes and Castes of Bengal.* Kolkata : Secretariat Press.

Risley, H.H. 1905 : *The People of India.* Kolkata : Secretariat Press.

Roy Burman, B.K. 1961 : *Varmaung* : *An Ao Naga Village.* Monograph Series, Census of India, 1961, Part VI, Ministry of Home Affairs.

Roy Burman, B.K. 1966 : "Structure of Bridge and Buffer Communities in Border Areas". *Man In India,* Vol. 46, No. 2.

Roy Burman, B.K. 1969 : "Tribal Demography in India : A Preliminary Appraisal". In *Tribal Situation in India* edited by K. Suresh Singh, Indian Institute of Advanced Study, Shimla.

Roy Burman, B.K. 1970 : "Modernisation Process in Hills of North-East India". *Journal of Institute of Defence Study.*

Roy Burman, B.K. 1970 : *Demographic and Socio-economic Profiles of North-East India.* New Delhi, Office of Registrar General, Ministry of Home Affairs.

Roy Burman, B.K. 1973 : *Chetlat : A Village Monograph.* Census of India, New Delhi : Manager Publication.

Roy Burman, B.K. and H.L. Harit.1971 : *A Preliminary Appraisal of Scheduled Tribes in India.* New Delhi : Office of Registrar General of India.

Roy, S.C. 1912 : *The Munda and Their Country.* Kolkata : City Bar Library.

Roy, S.C. 1915 : *The Oraon of Chotanagpur.* Ranchi Bar Library.

Roy, S.C. 1925 : "The Birhor : Little Known Tribe of Chotanagpur." Ranchi : Man In India Office.

Roy, S.C 1928 : *The Oraon Religion and Custom*. Ranchi. Man In India Office.

Roy, S.C. 1935 : *The Hill Bhuiya of Orissa*. Ranchi : Man In India Office.

Roy. S.C. 1937 : The Kharia (Two Volumes). Ranchi : Man In India Office.

Sachchidananda.1964 : *Culture Change in Tribal Bihar.* Kolkata : Bookland Private Limited.

Sachchidananda.1968 : *Tribal Village in Bihar : A Study in Unity and Extension.* New Delhi : Munshi Ram Manohar Lal.

Sachchidananda.1972 : *Social Dimensions of Agricultural Development.* New Delhi : Munshi Ram Manohar Lal.

Sachchidananda.1976 : *Tribal Voters in Bihar.* Kolkata : Punthi Pustak.

Sachchidananda.1977 : *Sarvodaya and Development.* Kolkata : Punthi Pustak.

Sachchidananda.1977 : *Harijan Elite*. Delhi : Concept Publishing Company.

Sachchidananda.1980 : *Changing Munda.* New Delhi : Concept Publishing Company.

Sachchidananda.1984 : *Aspects of Women in India.* New Delhi : Concept Publishing Company.

Sachchidananda.1986 : *The Scheduled Castes.* New Delhi : Concept Publishing Company.

Sachchidananda.1987 : *Industrialisation and Social Disorganisation*. New Delhi : Concept Publishing Company.

Sachchidananda.1987 : *Shifting Cultivation in India.* New Delhi : Concept Publishing Company.

Sachchidananda. 1997 : *Tribal Study Series.* New Delhi : Serial Publications.

Sachchidananda. 2001 : *Dalit Women on Road.* New Delhi : Serial Publications.

Sachchidananda. 2005 : *Water Supply Management in Bihar.* New Delhi : Serial Publications.

Sankalia, H.D. 1956 : "Animals Fossils and Palaeolithic Industries from the Pravara Basin and Nevasa". *A.E.,* No. 12.

Sankalia, H.D. 1962 : *Indian Archaeology Today.* Poona : Deccan College.

Sankalia, H.D. 1964 : *Stone Age Tools.* Poona : Deccan College.

Sankalia, H.D. 1971 : "New Evidences for Early Man in Kashmir". *Current Anthropology,* Vol. No. 4-5.

Sankalia, H.D. 1974 : *Prehistory and Protohistory of India and Pakistan.* Poona : Deccan College Postgraduate Institute.

Steed, Geitel P. 1955 : "Personality Formation in a Hindu Village in Gujarat". In McKim Marriott edited book *Village India, American Anthropologist,* Vol. 57.

Silvertsen, Dagfinn. 1964 : "When the Caste Barriers Fall : A Study of Social and Economic Change in South Indian Village". Norway : Universities for Larger, George Allen and Unwin Ltd.

Singer, Milton (ed.). 1958 : "The Great Tradition in Metropolitan Madras". *American Folklore,* Vol. 71, No. 26.

Singer, Milton. 1958 : "Traditional India : Structure and Change". *American Folklore,* Vol. 78, No. 281.

Singer, Milton. 1972 : *When a Great Tradition Modernises : An Anthropological Approach to Civilisation.*

Singer, Milton (ed.). 1973 : *Entrepreneurship and Modernisation of Occupation of Occupational Culture in South Asia.* Duke University Monograph No. 12.

Singer, Milton and Robert Redfield.1954 : "Cultural Role of City". *Man In India,* Vol. 36, No. 3.

Singh, R.D. 1956 : "Extension of An Indian Village". *Journal of Asian Studies,* Vol. 16, No. 5.

Sinha, Surjit Ch. 1957 : "Tribal Culture of Peninsular India : *Dimensions of Little Tradition in the Study of Indian Civilisation". Man In India,* Vol. 37.

Sinha, Surjit Ch. 1957 : "The Media and Nature of Hindu-Bhumij Interactions". *Journal of the Asiatic Society, Letters and Science,* Vol. 23, No. 1.

Sinha, Surjit Ch. 1958 : "Change in Cycle of Festivals in Bhumij Village". Ranchi : *Journal of Social Research,* Vol. 1, No. 1.

Sinha, Surjit Ch. 1959 : "Bhumij Kshatriya Movement in South Manbhum". *Bulletin of Anthropological Survey of India,* Vol. 8, No. 2.

Sinha, Surjit Ch. 1961 : "Agriculture, Craft and Weekly Market in South Manbhum". *Journal of Anthropological Survey of India,* Vol. 10, No. 1.

Sinha, Surjit Ch. 1962 : "State Formation and Rajput Myth in Central India". *Man In India,* Vol. 42, No. 2.

Sinha, Surjit Ch. 1968 : 'Is there an Indian Tradition in Social Cultural Anthropology : Retrospect and Prospect'. Paper presented at New York Conference on 'On Nature and Function of Tradition' organised by Wenner Green Foundation.

Sinha, Surjit Ch. 1965 : "Tribe Caste and Tribe Peasant Continuum in Central India". *Man In India,* Vol. 45, No. 1.

Srinivas, M.N. 1942 : *Marriage and Family in Mysore.* Bombay : New Book Company.

Srinivas, M.N. 1952 : *Religion and Society Among Coorgs of South India.* Oxford : Claredon Press.

Srinivas, M.N. 1955 : *India's Village*. Kolkata : West Bengal Government Press.

Srinivas, M.N. 1959 : "Caste : A Trend Report and Bibliography". *Current Sociology*, Vol. 8, No. 2

Srinivas, M.N. 1962 : *Caste in Modern India*. Berkeley : University of California.

Srinivas, M.N. 1962 : *Caste in Modern India and Other Essays*. Bombay : Asia Publishing House.

Srinivas, M.N. 1966 : *Social Change in Modern India*. California : University of California Press.

Srinivas, M.N. (ed.). 1969 : *India's Social Structure*. Delhi : Allied Publisher.

Srinivas, M.N. 1976 : *The Remembered Village*. Berkeley : University of California Press.

Srinivas, M.N. 1976 : *Nation Building in Independent India*. Delhi : Oxford University Press.

Srinivas, M.N. (ed.). 1977 : *Dimensions of Social Change in India*. Delhi : Allied Publisher.

Srinivas, M.N. 1986 : *Dominant Caste and Other Essays*. Delhi : Oxford University Press.

Srinivas, M.N. 1989 : *The Cohesive Role of Sanskritisation*. Delhi : Oxford University Press.

Srinivas, M.N. 1992 : *On Living in a Revolution*. Delhi : Oxford University Press.

Srinivas, M.N. 1996 : *Village, Caste, Gender and Method*. Delhi : Oxford University Press.

Srinivas, M.N. 1997 : *Caste and Its Twentieth Century Avatar*. Delhi : Oxford University Press.

Vidyarthi, L.P. (ed.). 1960 : *Anthropology and Tribal Welfare in India*. Ranchi : Council of Social and Cultural Research, Bihar.

Vidyarthi, L.P. 1960 : *Indian Anthropology in Action*. Ranchi : Council of Social Cultural Research, Bihar.

Vidyarthi, L.P. (ed.). 1961 : *Bihar Ke Adivasi*. Patna : College Centre.

Vidyarthi, L.P. (ed.). 1961 : *Aspects of Religion in Indian Society*. Meerut : Ram Nath Kedar Nath.

Vidyarthi, L.P. 1978 : *Sacred Complex in Hindu Gaya.* New Delhi : Concept Publishing Company.

Vidyarthi, L.P. 1963 : *Maler : Nature-Man-Spirit Complex in a Hill Tribe of Bihar.* Bookland Pvt. Ltd.

Vidyarthi, L.P. 1964 : *Cultural Contours of Tribal Bihar.* Kolkata : Punthi Pustak.

Vidyarthi, L.P. 1966 : *Ghaghara : A Village in Chotanagpur.* New Delhi : Ministry of Home Affairs.

Vidyarthi, L.P. 1966 : *Bhartiyanagar.* New Delhi : Rajmahal Prakashan.

Vidyarthi, L.P. (ed.). 1968 : *Applied Anthropology in India.* Allahabad : Kitab Mahal.

Vidyarthi, L.P. (ed.). 1968 : *Tribal Labour : Agricultural and Industrial.* New Delhi : Manager of Publication.

Vidyarthi, L.P. 1969 : *Cultural Configuration of Ranchi.* New Delhi : Planning Commission.

Vidyarthi, L.P. 1970 : *Socio-Cultural Implications of Indus-Trialisation in India : A Case Study of Tribal Bihar.* New Delhi : Planning Commission.

Vidyarthi, L.P. 1973 : *Essays in Indian Folklore.* Kolkata : Indian Publication.

Vidyarthi, L.P. 1977 : *Student Unrest in Chotanagpur.* Kolkata : Punthi Pustak.

Vidyarthi, L.P. 1977 : *Peasant Organisation in India.* Council of Social-Cultural Research.

Vidyarthi, L.P. 1977 : *Rise of Anthropology in India : A Social Science Orientation in Two Volumes.* New Delhi : Concept Publishing Company.

Vidyarthi, L.P. (ed.). 1978 : *Growth and Development of Anthropology in Bihar.* New Delhi : Concept Publishing Company.

Vidyarthi, L.P. 1980 : *Trends in World Anthropology.* New Delhi : Concept Publishing Company.

Vidyarthi, L.P. 1980 : *Rise of World Anthropology.* New Delhi : Concept Publishing Company.

Vidyarthi, L.P., K.S. Mathur and I.P. Singh.1963 : *Manavshastra Ki Ruparekha*. Meerut: Kedar Nath Ram Nath.

Vidyarthi, L.P., B.N. Sahay and B.K. Srivastava.1970 : *Gandhi and Social Science in India*. New Delhi : Book Hive.

Vidyarthi, L.P. and G. Choube.1971 : *Bihar in Folklore Study*. Kolkata : Indian Publication.

Vidyarthi, L.P. and B.C. Agrawal.1973 : *Researches in Complex Society in India*. New Delhi : Indian Academy of Social Science.

Vidyarthi, L.P. and B.K. Rai.1976 : *Tribal Culture of India*. New Delhi : Concept Publishing Company.

Vidyarthi, L.P. and Narayan Mishra.1977 : *Harijan Today*. New Delhi : Classical Publisher.

Vidyarthi, L.P., B.N. Sarasvati and Makhan Jha.1978 : *Sacred Complex in Kashi*. New Delhi : Concept Publishing Company.

Vidyarthi, L.P., B.B. Lal and I.P. Singh.1978 : *Researches in Prehistory and Physical Anthropology in India*. New Delhi : Concept Publishing Company.

Vidyarthi, L.P. and V.S. Upadhyay.1979 : *Kharia : Then and Now*. New Delhi : Concept Publishing Company.

Vidyarthi, L.P. and B.N. Sahay.1979 : *Applied Anthropology and Development in India*. New Delhi : Concept Publishing Company.

Vidyarthi, L.P. and R.K. Prasad.1982 : *Dietary Pattern and Habit*. New Delhi : Concept Publishing Company.

Wiser, W.H. 1936 : *Hindu Jajmani System*. Lucknow : Lucknow Publishing House.

Index

Agricultural Anthropology, 111
Aiyappan, A., 78
  books, 79
  papers, 80
All India Oriental Congress, 9
American Anthropology, 42
American School of Diffusionism, 51
Annual Conference of Association for Asian Studies, 40
Anthony-Mikins Scholarship, 32
Anthropological Survey of India, 28, 29, 40, 46
Anthropology and Folklore Section, 8
Anti-Drink Society, 8
Asiatic Society of Bengal, 53, 192
Atal, Yogesh, 155

Bailey, F. G., 233
  publications, 234
Bardoli Movement, 200
Beals, A.R., 225
Beck, Brenda F., 249
Beidelmen, Thomas O., 251-252
Beteille, Andre, 247
  publications, 247
Bihar Legislative Council, 25
Bihar Tribal Welfare Research Institute, 28, 29
Bose, N. K., 39
  books in Bengali language, 41
Bose as a social worker, 44
  contribution on Caste Study, 46
  contribution on Civilisation at a Phase of Confidence, 49
  contribution on Gandhism, 50
  contribution on Prehistoric Archaeology, 51
  contribution on Problem of National Integration and modernization, 50
  contribution on Research Methodology, 51
  impact of diffusionism, 42
  impact of Franz Boas, 42
  impact of Silpis (Architect) of Orissa,.45
  influence of A.L. Kroeker, 42
  influence of Karl Marx, 43
  influence of Malinowski, 43
  influence of Sigmund Freud, 43
  publications, 41
  role as Director in Anthropological Survey of India,.46
  study of culture zones and pattern of unity, 48
Bougle, Celestin, 250
Brahmacharya Sangh, 8
Brahminical model of lifestyle, 87
'Bridge and buffer' concept, 150

Carstairs, G.M., 239
Caste system, 22
Chattopadhyay, Gauranga, 152
Chattopadhyay, K.P., 31
  books, 38
  publications, 34
Chauhan, B.R., 154
Civil Disobedience Campaigns, 94
Comprehensive Racial Survey of India, 29
Cornell-Lucknow Research Project, 68
Cunningham, Alexander, 193

Desanskritisation, 89
DeTerra and T.D. Patterson, 245
Devar Commission, 201
Dhillon, H. S., 157

Dikshit, K. N., 159
Dominant caste, concept of, 95
Dravidian language family, 26
Dube, S. C., 100
 contribution in Political Anthropology, 106
 contribution on Family Planning, 106
 contribution on Modernisation, 107
 contribution on Tribal Study, 103
 contribution on Village Study, 104
 contributions to Books and Journals,102
 publication of Books, 101
Dumont, Louis, 242

East India Company, 92
Elwin, Verrier, 200
 publications of,202
Epstein, T. Scarlett, 229
 publications, 229
Ethnographic and Folk Culture Society, 53

First World War, 195
Folkloric tradition, 136
Ford Foundation Fellowship, 114

Ghurye, G.S. 143
 contribution on Caste Study, 146
 contribution on Scheduled Tribes, 144
 contribution on Village Study, 145
 publications, 143
Gokhale Institute of Economics and Politics, 34
Gough, E. Kathleen, 231
 publications, 232
Gould, Herald A., 220
 publications,.220
Great tradition, 225
Guha, B.S., 26
 publications, 30

Haimendorf, C. Von Furer, 203
 publications, 203
Harijan Community, 112
Harijan Sevak Samiti, 8
Harper, E.B., 228
Herbert, Paul G., 244
Hindu society, 89, 90
Hutton, J.H., 198
 publications of, 200

Indian Anthropological Institute, 27
Indian anthropology,
 foreign builders of, 192-
 Indian builders of, 1-191
Indian Archaeological Survey, 194
Indian Institute of Advanced Study, 50
Indian Sociological Society, 82
International Congress of Anthropological and Ethnological Sciences, 3
Ishwaran, K.158
Iyer, L. A. Krishna, 4
 contribution of L.A. Krishna Iyer, 5
 contribution of L.K. Balaratna,.6
Iyer, L.A. Ananta Krishna, 1
 books, 3
 papers, 4

Jajmani system, 221, 228, 229
Jajmani, 47
Jhum cultivation, 123
Jones, William (Sir), 92
Journal of American Anthropologist, 42, 95

Karve, Iravati, 72
 books,78
 publications of Research Papers, 73
Khare, R.S., 151

Lakshmana Rao, Y.V., 156

Lewis, Oscar, 206
  concept of rural cosmopolitanism, 209
  contribution on Culture of Poverty, 208

Mahabharata, 21
Majumdar, D.N., 52
  books, 65
  contribution in applied and Action Anthropology, 69
  contribution in Cultural Anthropology, 65
  contribution on City Study, 69
  contribution on Physical Anthropology, 71
  contribution on Village Study, 67
  contribution through Research Papers, 54
Man In India, 10
Mandelbaum, David C., 212
  publications, 212
Man-Habitat interaction, 122
Mann, Rann Singh, 189-191
Marriott, McKim, 209
  concept of universalisation and parochialisation, 210
  contribution on Caste Ranking, 211
Marshal, John (Sir), 194
Mathur, K. S. 153
Mayer, A.C., 204
McCormack, W., 227
  publications, 228
Mencher, Joan, 245
Modernisation, 93
Mukherjee, R. K., 139
  publications, 139
Munda Raj, 24

Nature, 9
Non-Cooperation Movement, 50

Opler, Morris E. 213
  reserach journals, 214
Oraon-Munda Shiskha Sabha, 8
Orenstein, Henry, 241
  research papers, 242

Panchayati Raj Institution, 96
Panel on Backward Classes, 116
Permanent Council of International Congress of Anthropology, 33
Physical Anthropology, 17
Prasad, Narmadeshwar, 160
  contributions,160
Princep, Jones, 193
Puranic literature, 21

Ramayana, 21
Rationalism, 95
Risley, H.H., 197
Roy Burman, B.K., 148
  concept of Bridge and Buffer, 150
  contribution on Cultural Classification of Tribes, 149
  contribution on Geographical Distribution of Tribes, 149
  publications,148
Roy, S.C., 6
  books, 10
  contribution on Anthropology of Castes, 21
  contribution on Applied Anthropology and Tribal Policy, 24
  contribution on the Study of Folklore, 22
  contribution on the Study of Physical Anthropology, 17
  contribution on the Study of Prehistoric Archaeology, 18
  contribution on Tribal Studies, 14

major contributions in
Anthropology, 13
papers, 11
Royal Anthropological Institute of
Great Britain and Ireland, 53
Royal Asiatic Society of Bengal, 28

Sachchidananda, 108
contribution on Agricultural
Anthropology, 111
contribution on Industrialisation
and Social Disorganisation, 113
contribution on Political
Anthropology, 112
contribution on Scheduled Castes
Study, 112
contribution on Tribal Studies,110
contribution on Village Study,111
contribution on Women Study,113
publications,109
Sankalia, H. D., 160
Sanskritisation, 90, 91
Brahminical model of, 87
concept of, 86
Kshatriya model of, 88
Vaishya model of, 89
Secularisation, 94, 95
Sen, Dagfinn Silvert, 246
Simon Commission, 8
Singer, Milton, 222
contribution on Cultural Role of
City, 223
contribution on Modernisation of
Great Tradition, 225
contribution on the Study of
Madras City, 224
contribution on Traditional India:
structure and changes, 224
publications, 223
Singh, Kumar Suresh, 162
academic Contribution, 163
articles in Edited Books, 175
articles in Journals, 180
awards & Distinction, 188
book Reviewed in Journals, 184
books authored, 172
books Edited, 187
edited Series People of India, 173
other Academic Contributions, 168
People of India Series: Authored/
Co-Authored, 172
People of India: A Unique Research
Project, 167
Singh, R.D., 150
Sinha, Surjit Chandra, 147
publications, 148
Smithonian Institution, Washington
DC, 28
Social Anthropology, 21
Spread of Hinduism, 97
Srinivas, M. N., 81
Brahminical Model of
Sanskritisation, 87
concept of Dominant Caste, 95
concept of Sanskritisation, 86
concept of Spread, 97
concept of Vertical and Horizontal
Caste Solidarity, 98
contribution on Village study, 99
desanskritisation, 89
Kshatriya Model of Sanskritisation,
88
publication of Books, 85
publication of Papers, 83
secularisation, 94
Vaishya Model of Sanskritisation,
89
Steed, Geital P., 231

Tribal study, 103
Tribal Welfare Research Institute, 28

UNESCO, 101
University Grants Commission, 114
Upward social mobility, 90

Vertical and horizontal caste solidarity, concept of, 98
Vidyarthi, Lalita Prasad, 113
contribution of Folklore, 136
contribution on Applied and Action Anthropology, 137
contribution on Nature-Man-Spirit Complex, 122
contribution on Political Anthropology, 135
contribution on Psychological Anthropology, 135
contribution on Restudy, 138
contribution on Sacred Complex Study, 118
contribution on Scheduled Caste Study, 137
contribution on the Phases of Growth of Indian Anthropology, 128
contribution on Tribal Studies, 127
contribution on Urban and Anthropological Researches,132
edited Books, 117
publication of Books,116
Village study, 104

Westernisation, 90, 91
and modernization, 93
urbanisation and industrialisation, 92
Wheeler, Martimer (Sir), 196
Wiser, W.H., 236
publications, 237
Women study, 113
World Congress of Anthropological and Ethnological Sciences, 101

Zoological Survey of India, 27, 28